T0330047

# Economics, Culture and Social Theory

NEW HORIZONS IN INSTITUTIONAL AND EVOLUTIONARY
ECONOMICS

**Series Editor:** Geoffrey M. Hodgson
Research Professor, University of Hertfordshire Business School, UK

Economics today is at a crossroads. New ideas and approaches are challenging
the largely static and equilibrium-oriented models that used to dominate
mainstream economics. The study of economic institutions – long neglected in the
economics textbooks – has returned to the forefront of theoretical and empirical
investigation.

This challenging and interdisciplinary series publishes leading works at the
forefront of institutional and evolutionary theory and focuses on cutting-edge
analyses of modern socio-economic systems. The aim is to understand both the
institutional structures of modern economies and the processes of economic
evolution and development. Contributions will be from all forms of evolutionary
and institutional economics, as well as from Post-Keynesian, Austrian and other
schools. The overriding aim is to understand the processes of institutional
transformation and economic change.

Titles in the series include:

Institutions, Money and Entrepreneurship
Hayek's Theory of Cultural Evolution
*Edited by Jürgen G. Backhaus*

Productivity, Competitiveness and Incomes in Asia
An Evolutionary Theory of International Trade
*Hans-Peter Brunner and Peter M. Allen*

The Hardship of Nations
Exploring the Paths of Modern Capitalism
*Edited by Benjamin Coriat, Pascal Petit and Geneviève Schméder*

An Economic Analysis of Innovation
Extending the Concept of National Innovation Systems
*Markus Balzat*

Evolutionary Economics and Environmental Policy
Survival of the Greenest
*Jeroen C.J.M. van den Bergh, Albert Faber, Annemarth M. Idenburg and
Frans H. Oosterhuis*

Property Rights, Consumption and the Market Process
*David Emanuel Andersson*

The Evolution of Path Dependence
*Edited by Lars Magnusson and Jan Ottosson*

Economics, Culture and Social Theory
*William A. Jackson*

# Economics, Culture and Social Theory

William A. Jackson

*Lecturer in Economics, University of York, UK*

NEW HORIZONS IN INSTITUTIONAL AND EVOLUTIONARY ECONOMICS

**Edward Elgar**

Cheltenham, UK • Northampton, MA, USA

Published by
Edward Elgar Publishing Limited
The Lypiatts
15 Lansdown Road
Cheltenham
Glos GL50 2JA
UK

Edward Elgar Publishing, Inc.
William Pratt House
9 Dewey Court
Northampton
Massachusetts 01060
USA

A catalogue record for this book
is available from the British Library

Library of Congress Control Number: 2009933360

**Mixed Sources**
Product group from well-managed
forests and other controlled sources
www.fsc.org Cert no. SA-COC-1565
© 1996 Forest Stewardship Council

FSC

ISBN 978 1 84542 710 8

Printed and bound by MPG Books Group, UK

*To my parents*

# Contents

# Figures and tables

## FIGURES

## TABLES

# Preface

The late twentieth century saw a 'cultural turn' in academic work, evident in critiques of positivism and in the emergence of the New Left, postmodernism and cultural studies. Orthodox economics has played no part in this and appears oblivious to wider intellectual trends: its core principles are ahistorical and bereft of culture. The cultural turn has opened up space for a broader, cultural approach to economics, yet economic orthodoxy has been reluctant to acknowledge or respond to the challenge. Few mainstream economists read academic literature beyond their own specialised field. Heterodox economics is more receptive to cultural ideas, but even here the tendency is to keep to standard disciplinary boundaries. As a result, the implications for economics of recent cultural thought have not been fully explored.

An economics/culture divide is nothing new and goes back over two hundred years to the beginnings of modern economic theory. Culture as a formal concept stemmed from disquiet about how Enlightenment science had addressed society. Cultural thinkers objected to rationalism and empiricism being transferred crudely to social studies; instead, they advocated historical specificity, cultural awareness and interpretative methods. The earliest modern economists, in their wish to emulate natural sciences, provoked cultural criticism that started with literary counterblasts against classical economics in the early nineteenth century and has carried on ever since. Neglect of culture in present-day economics is merely the latest manifestation of an eternal stand-off between economics and cultural thought.

The current book has two aims:

1. To trace the history of the cultural critique of economics and show how, through academic specialisation, it has been diverted outside academia or into 'non-economic' disciplines such as anthropology, sociology and cultural studies;
2. To argue for the continued relevance of the cultural critique, discuss what it means for economic theory, and consider the prospects for a culturally informed economics.

A proper acknowledgement of the cultural critique would not yield a 'cultural economics' as a subset of neoclassical orthodoxy; on the contrary, it would recast economic method and theory across the whole discipline. Far from applying neoclassical theory to culture, it would apply cultural thought to economics.

Cultural thought embraces all the humanities and social sciences. To do it justice, one must breach disciplinary borders and delve into academic and non-academic literatures seldom noticed by economists. This is risky, of course, and tests an author's competence: there are obvious dangers of sketchiness, omission and error. Losses in detail or precision are, one hopes, offset by gains in breadth, depth and comparative insight. Writers in the cultural tradition have distrusted academic specialisation and disliked the artificial demarcation between social sciences. For them, culture pertains to any human behaviour, at both individual and social levels, and cannot be linked with some disciplines but not others. In the same spirit, an attempt to discuss and appraise culture should be interdisciplinary. What really matters here is the landscape of cultural thought, which is omitted from orthodox economics and often obscured in heterodox economics as well. Only by venturing outside the normal boundaries of economics can one appreciate the nature and value of cultural criticism.

I am grateful to Geoffrey Hodgson for his support and to Matthew Pitman and the staff at Edward Elgar for their work on the commissioning and production of the book.

William A. Jackson

# PART I

# Introduction

# 1. Cultural thought and its origins

Ever since the dawn of man, people have been born into a pre-existing society, however primitive, and raised according to its customs. Each generation has learnt the prevailing way of life and then, in turn, passed this on to the next generation. Culture can be traced back over hundreds of thousands of years, a period much greater than recorded history: human societies already had elaborate cultures long before farming, towns, markets and organised economies first appeared. An established culture has been fundamental to all economic activity, and major cultural changes have accompanied each stage of economic development.

Culture as an academic concept is far more recent. Ideas related to culture occurred in ancient and medieval philosophy but were never brought together into a coherent tradition of cultural thought, which emerged only in response to the Enlightenment. During the eighteenth century, after triumphs in the natural sciences, Enlightenment philosophers attempted to investigate society by similar rationalist and empiricist methods. Detailed study of this kind would, they believed, uncover the principles behind social behaviour. Sceptics about the Enlightenment were unhappy with its methods when applied to the social sphere. Sensitive to human diversity and complexity, they felt that such a mechanical, ahistorical stance was inappropriate for social studies. The concept of culture derived from a desire to break away from the methods of the Enlightenment (if not from its aims) and find alternative methods better suited to the humanities.

Modern economic thought was also a product of the Enlightenment but had fewer methodological scruples: the classical economists identified unconditionally with Enlightenment methods and were keen to use them. The wish to emulate natural sciences has been ever present in orthodox economics, from classical to neoclassical to current mainstream theory. Increased reliance on mathematics and econometrics during the late twentieth century merely confirmed the ambition to attain scientific rigour and keep a distance from the 'unscientific' humanities. Cultural thought, overtly critical of natural-science emulation, was never likely to appeal to orthodox economists – the subsequent course of the economics discipline has amply demonstrated this.

   In orthodox, neoclassical economics the word 'culture' seldom comes
to the fore, and cultural ideas are missing. Rational agents have fixed,
exogenous preferences whose cultural basis goes unexplained, while
the individualistic method plays down social structure and institutions.
Historically unspecific theory seems universal, as if the same models and
theories pertain everywhere, and historical or cultural differences are overlooked. Priority lies with the generic 'economic' behaviour of the instrumentally rational individual. The notion that all economics is cultural
and requires cultural thought is alien to orthodox economics, which views
culture as being somehow separable from economics and beyond the remit
of economists. By default, cultural approaches to economics are left to
heterodox economists or to authors in other disciplines such as anthropology, sociology or history.
   Economists' neglect of culture led to cultural criticism of economics
from outside the discipline. Few orthodox economists have heeded it;
most have ignored it. Modern mainstream economists show little interest
even in the history of economic thought, let alone in the broader expanses
of cultural thought. Although heterodox economists have been aware
of culture and sought to take account of it, their views have had limited
effect on the economic mainstream. The scope for a culturally informed
economics remains extensive, as this book will argue.
   Part I (Chapters 1 and 2) sets the scene by examining the origins of
cultural thought and how the various definitions of culture have changed.
Part II (Chapters 3 to 6) considers the cultural critique of economics,
from the classical age to the age of modern mainstream theory. Part
III (Chapters 7 to 11) looks at the implications of the cultural critique,
placing particular emphasis on relativism, idealism, structure and agency,
interpretative methods and social evolution. Finally, Part IV (Chapter 12)
evaluates the prospects for introducing cultural ideas into economic theorising and moving towards a culturally informed economics.

## 1.1   CRITICAL RESPONSES TO THE ENLIGHTENMENT

The Enlightenment of the seventeenth and eighteenth centuries saw the
birth of formal scientific methods and laid the foundations for academic
work in natural and social sciences (Hampson, 1968; Outram, 1995). Its
values of rationality and pursuit of objective, disinterested knowledge are
at the heart of academic study and normally presupposed without explicit
statement. Anyone employed as an academic and involved in teaching
or research is partaking in the Enlightenment project and at least tacitly

endorsing its aims. The authors of the Enlightenment went beyond a statement of aims, however, and advocated supposedly universal methods founded on rationalism and empiricism. Attempts to use the same methods everywhere led to a critical reaction from those who felt that other methods were needed when studying human societies. Criticism was directed not at the ends of the Enlightenment but at the chosen means of achieving them.

Having begun in the natural sciences, the Enlightenment has always been associated with naturalism: it aspired to replace religion with nature and appeal to natural rather than supernatural causes. Reason became paramount, and non-rational and transcendental sources of knowledge were rejected. Metaphysics, being inaccessible to reason or observation, were abandoned in favour of the study of material nature. The recommended methods started with a combination of rationalism in the Cartesian mode and inductive empiricism based on writers like Francis Bacon, but observation was later accepted as the ultimate fount of knowledge. Newtonian mechanics exemplified a successful theory, as it was rationalist, universal and backed by empirical evidence. The Newtonian system that dominated physics became a template for other sciences.

Studying human societies was not seen as being different from studying material nature. If everything obeyed a single set of natural laws, then human behaviour must follow the same laws as any other object of study and be open to the same methods. The outlook was naturalistic, proclaiming the unity of the sciences and denying any special quality to the humanities. All people were regarded as possessing a common human nature, in so far that they had the same physical make-up, material needs, ends in life and fundamental values. This human nature might not yet be understood, but it was subject to real and knowable laws that scientific research could unveil. The drive for omniscience was spearheaded by the French Enlightenment and the Encyclopaedists, whose declared aim was to produce an all-embracing compendium of knowledge. Naturalistic materialism reached an extreme in La Mettrie, who compared men with machines and argued that all psychic functioning is reducible to a material level, and Holbach, who incorporated human activity into a materialist natural system. The zeal of Enlightenment thinkers provoked a reaction against their disposal of psychic, social or spiritual phenomena – this critical response has been termed the Counter-Enlightenment (Berlin, 1979; Garrard, 2006). Among its innovations was the modern notion of culture.

The first formal cultural methods are often credited to the Italian philosopher Giambattista Vico, who worked obscurely in Naples during the early eighteenth century (Berlin, 1976b; Burke, 1985). Although committed to Enlightenment ideals, Vico was disturbed by the way that the Enlightenment had ridiculed historical study and replaced it with rationalism and empiricism. For Vico, ahistorical methods could never be a reliable source of knowledge in the humanities. His major work was the *New Science*, in which he sought to introduce methods relevant to the study of human societies but distinct from existing Enlightenment methods (Vico, 1744 [1999]). A desire for a scientific approach is evident in the title, yet Vico's perspective contrasts with the natural sciences and comes closer to the humanities. Three main novelties stand out.

First, Vico revived the old maxim that human beings can understand only that which they have created. In medieval times this had reinforced Christian humility by reminding us of our inability to comprehend the God-created universe. Vico deployed it positively by arguing that we can understand human societies because we created them and reproduce them in our everyday lives. The natural world, which was not created by human beings, is not susceptible to the same level of knowledge. According to Vico, we should distinguish between the human sciences and the natural sciences, and only the former can yield full understanding. His anti-naturalism implies a dichotomy between the subject matter and methods of the natural and social sciences; it differs from the supernaturalism of medieval philosophy and the naturalism of the Enlightenment.

Vico's second new argument was for the interpretative character of social studies: the reason why we can understand human societies is our capacity to interpret human behaviour. In the study of present-day socie-ties this capacity stems from direct personal experience or from empathy with the motives and experiences of others; in the study of past societies it stems from imaginative reconstruction of the values, attitudes and social context of earlier periods. The method rests not on external observation but on internal understanding or interpretation. For Vico, rational-ism could shed no light on human behaviour or social relations and did little more than build logical theories or systems. Empiricism could only describe the surface of observed events without penetrating down to a deeper understanding. The standard Enlightenment techniques were flawed in their application to human societies and should, Vico argued, be replaced by interpretative methods.

The third novelty of Vico was his case for historical specificity. If social sciences are to be interpretative, then researchers must understand the ideas, goals and social relations of past societies. Since behaviour and institutions vary over time, explanations for one period differ from those for other periods; interpretative methods are historically specific and tailored to the particular era under investigation. The contrast with the Enlightenment yearning for universal principles is stark. Many Enlightenment writers had dismissed historical studies as outmoded and irrelevant, whereas Vico lifted them to the summit of his methodology. His ideas, too radical to have much effect in his lifetime, were later rediscovered and appreciated as a forerunner of cultural thought. Though Vico's historical studies are now obsolete, his arguments about method retain much value and underlie subsequent work in the humanities and social sciences.

Ideas resembling Vico's became widespread and influential only towards the end of the eighteenth century, chiefly through the German reaction against the French Enlightenment. Philosophers of the French Enlightenment had mocked German society as being tainted with medievalism and inferior to the civilised heights of Classical Greece, Renaissance Italy or contemporary France. This provoked a defensive reaction from German scholars and a resolve to forge an alternative world view. The literary *Sturm und Drang* movement, associated with writers such as Goethe and Schiller, resisted ahistorical and mechanical views of human nature: its attitudes fed into the Romantic Movement and called forth a tradition of German cultural discourse. The clearest account of the cultural perspective can be found in the literary historian and philosopher Johann Gottfried Herder, who sought a coherent critical response to the French Enlightenment (Herder, 1784–91 [1968]; Barnard, 1965; Berlin, 1976a). Together with Vico, he is frequently identified as having inspired later cultural thinkers.

Herder rejected the belief that all societies can be judged by common criteria. Since each national or regional culture is unique, any attempt to assess them by a single yardstick would be inappropriate, illiberal and misleading. For Herder, the contempt shown by Enlightenment writers towards non-European societies or medieval Europe was the result of prejudice and narrow-minded commitment to present and localised ideals. A better understanding of other cultures and times could be obtained by engaging imaginatively with other beliefs and values. Despite their high-minded claims, Enlightenment philosophers were blinkered in their determination to impose their own values in all cases, without making any effort to investigate alternatives. Ranking societies by degree of civilisation had no significance other than exhibiting one's personal opinions or biases. Likewise, any assumptions that later societies are superior to earlier ones, as if part of some grand evolutionary design, were erroneous and damaging. Studies in the humanities should avoid applying current values to cases where they are inapplicable.

The uniqueness of each society is, in Herder's view, enshrined in its language, beliefs, values, traditions and history. Collective experiences accumulated over many generations are passed on to succeeding generations through culture, which shapes and moulds the behaviour of each member of society. All individuals belong to a society and depend on it for their identity and personal capabilities; transferred to a different society, they would be unable to function in the same way. Understanding individual behaviour requires recognising the cultural background and social environment. Within a given culture, people are free to exercise their creative potential and benefit from their inherited cultural resources. The artistic and linguistic content of a culture results from countless creative acts by individuals whose abilities rely on their social context. As each society develops and evolves, it follows a path distinct from other societies – there are no grounds to assume that societies will converge and arrive at the same destination.

Herder argued for pluralism, as against universalism, and ascribed to each culture an intrinsic worth. To judge one society by the values of another would be impossible, and attempts to do so would be misguided and perilous if acted upon. Enlightenment philosophy represented one style of thinking, in a specific time and place, but had no warrant as a yardstick for all human societies. Enlightenment thinkers were guilty of imposing their beliefs and values on societies where these were unsuitable. Pursuit of uniformity would destroy valuable cultures and close down avenues of human self-expression – the boundless variety of cultures observed in human history would be flattened into a staid monotony. Each culture, according to Herder, should be allowed to grow and develop without interference from others; the temptation to merge cultures or impose one on another should be resisted. Multiple cultures should be left to develop in parallel, not competing with each other but cooperating.

Herder's pluralism did not imply a wholesale relativism that would prevent mutual understanding between cultures. Beneath the many cultural differences was a common humanity rooted in human biology and the capacity for critical reflection. Even if the values of two societies were incompatible, it was still possible for a member of one society to enter imaginatively into the life of a member of another. Differences of culture, religion, language, lifestyle, climate and physical constitution could all be overcome by interpretative understanding. Every person might have been born in another time and place and, if so, would have been raised in a different physical and social context and by different values – our common humanity should permit us to consider how we might feel and act under varied social circumstances. As with Vico, Herder's approved method for social study was to seek an interpretative understanding of those living in different surroundings. Only in this way could the diversity and complexity of human social behaviour be grasped.

Vico and Herder distilled the essence of a cultural approach, offering an alternative to the culturally frigid methods of the French Enlightenment. As the eighteenth century progressed, cultural thought became more vociferous and attacked exaggerated claims of universality. The Counter-Enlightenment did not negate Enlightenment philosophy, but it propagated methods other than rationalism and empiricism, especially in the humanities. The contrasts between Enlightenment and Counter-Enlightenment underlie much later criticism of economic theory, and it is worth discussing them at greater length.

## 1.2 THE COUNTER-ENLIGHTENMENT

Unlike the Enlightenment, the Counter-Enlightenment was never organised as a movement with an intellectual programme and axiomatic beliefs. It emerged through disparate individual reactions to the Enlightenment and bloomed as the common elements in these reactions became apparent. The writings of Vico and Rousseau were important early influences, but much of the impetus came from German thinkers such as Hamann, Herder, Goethe, Fichte and Schelling (Berlin, 1979, 1999, Chapter 3). By the early nineteenth century the Counter-Enlightenment and its main arguments had become widely known internationally. Its sensitivity to cultural differences meant that it did not put forward a single method or theory – it was suspicious of principles claiming universal relevance. One can, nevertheless, identify core ideas that give advice on how social studies should be conducted.

The Counter-Enlightenment supported a pluralistic attitude: each society was seen as having its own distinctive character irreducible to any external checklist. Applying a universal template to all societies would deprive them of their uniqueness and overlook their defining qualities. The Enlightenment was criticised as being overgeneralised and oversimplified, based on blanket theorising and false analogies with the natural sciences. Instead of clumsy generalisation, the alternative was to respect local circumstances. Each society had a collective spirit plain to its members and to outside interpreters but distinct from the characteristics of the individuals involved. Only by acknowledging this could social studies make progress. Differences among societies were not insurmountable barriers that precluded mutual understanding, or else social studies would be impossible. The case for pluralism never went to a relativistic extreme whereby each society had a hermetic reality sealed off by an unbreakable wall. It remained feasible for members of one society to appreciate the customs, behaviour and beliefs of another. The Counter-Enlightenment held aloft the possibility of fruitful social studies, albeit by methods other than those of the Enlightenment.

When comparisons are made over time, pluralism translates into a historical specificity that treats each period as unique. From the Counter-Enlightenment perspective, human behaviour depends on the prevailing culture and institutions, which have evolved continuously during the course of history. Any attempt to discover universal behaviour and embody it in global theories would distort the humanities and underestimate the diversity of beliefs, values and institutions. Rather than building timeless theoretical systems, scholars should dedicate their investigations to particular historical periods. Societies separated by large stretches of time, even if they have the same physical location, should be treated as distinct. Studying historical societies would require an effort to understand the values, attitudes, customs and institutions behind individual behaviour and social interactions. Theorising should be careful about its historical limits.

Crucial to the Counter-Enlightenment was the place of the individual within society. Protests against the Enlightenment deplored the way it portrayed human beings as passive, mechanical automatons isolated from social relationships, emotions and feelings. The general theories and systems of the Enlightenment shackled the human will and saw people as material objects unable to act freely and subjectively. Abstract thought had supplanted our soul and robbed us of our character and identity. Cultural methods would devote greater attention to the complexity and diversity of human beings, with their capacities for emotions, empathy and creativity. This implied a stress on the individual, although our expressive potential could be realised only within society, not alone. Cultures and institutions were due to past creative acts by individuals and would in turn nurture the creativeness of future generations. People reached fulfilment within society and could be understood only through familiarity with their social circumstances.

For the Counter-Enlightenment, rationalism and empiricism were inadequate to explain human behaviour. Whatever their successes in the natural sciences, they would never be a sound basis for social sciences and, if adopted, would yield stunted, misleading outcomes. In place of rationalism and empiricism, the appropriate method for social subject matter was to seek an interpretative understanding of behaviour resting on an empathy with human agents in their social context. By making an interpretative effort, scholars could cross the historical and geographical boundaries between individuals and communities without claiming to have discovered universal principles. Many Counter-Enlightenment authors restricted themselves to commenting on social matters, so that (by default or otherwise) they allowed rationalism and empiricism to hold sway in the natural sciences. This yielded an anti-naturalism that kept natural and social sciences separate. Later in the nineteenth century, Wilhelm Dilthey formalised the division by identifying separate realms of natural science (*Naturwissenschaft*) and social science (*Geisteswissenschaft*). The differences were another example of diversity and pluralism – social sciences

*Table 1.1　Enlightenment and Counter-Enlightenment thought*

|  | Enlightenment | Counter-Enlightenment |
|---|---|---|
| Naturalism | Natural and social sciences are unified | Natural and social sciences are separate (anti-naturalism) |
| Method | Rationalist and empiricist methods apply universally | Social sciences require interpretative methods |
| Pluralism | Knowledge pertains to all societies | Knowledge is specific to a particular society |
| Historicism | Knowledge pertains to all periods | Knowledge is specific to a particular period |
| Values | Values are universal and set apart from factual knowledge | Values are plural and knowledge is not value-free |
| Causality | Causes are at a material or physical level | Causes can rely on motives or reasons ('reasons can be causes') |
| Evolution | Societies progress along a common, convergent path | No universal progress or convergence |
| Behaviour | Human behaviour is rational and predictable | Human behaviour may be irrational and unpredictable |

were not inferior to natural sciences, and the two branches of knowledge were merely adopting methods appropriate to their subject matter.

In the eyes of Enlightenment philosophers, the natural and social worlds followed a single, ordered pattern explicable through rational thought and observation. As reality was vast and science still in its infancy, a complete scientific account of reality had not yet been accomplished. Rigorous scientific method would ensure continuous progress, though, and knowledge was gradually accumulating towards completeness. Eventually science should reach the ultimate goal of universal knowledge. Counter-Enlightenment authors viewed this attitude as mistaken and deluded. For them, social reality was far too intricate and diverse ever to be uncovered by rationalist and empiricist methods alone, and study by these methods would be futile. The best way to proceed would be through pluralism, including interpretative methods, with a clear distinction between natural and social sciences. Table 1.1 summarises the differences between Enlightenment and Counter-Enlightenment.

Because it raised doubts about science, the Counter-Enlightenment has acquired an image as regressive and conservative (Mannheim, 1953). Its interest in historical societies seems backward looking, by contrast with the forward gaze of the natural sciences, and its sympathy with metaphysics and religion seems pre-scientific. Some aspects of the Counter-Enlightenment were indeed conservative, but it would be wrong to depict it as attempting to block political reform and scientific progress. The issue of political conservatism is complex and varies with individuals: many Enlightenment writers were linked with the *ancien régime* in France and politically conservative, whereas radicalism often drew upon Counter-Enlightenment sources (especially Rousseau). One cannot safely generalise here. Likewise, Counter-Enlightenment thought does not have to resist progress. If one looks at Table 1.1, the items in the right-hand column are a long way from enforcing a static, unchanging world view. In fact, the argument could be reversed by contrasting the pluralism, diversity and creativity of the Counter-Enlightenment with the monism, universality and closure of the Enlightenment. One should not attach labels and regard the Counter-Enlightenment as intellectually regressive and hostile to progress.

Another unfortunate connotation acquired by the Counter-Enlightenment is its apparent irrationalism. The querying of rationalist methods can easily be construed as a case for a wayward, emotive and anti-scientific approach. In the nineteenth century some offshoots of the Counter-Enlightenment did promote irrationality and nihilism (for example, the strand of German idealist philosophy that culminated in Nietzsche), but these views were not inherent in the Counter-Enlightenment. Its core arguments were to reject a universal, rationalist scientific method, rather than to abandon rationality. Advocacy of interpretative methods was a reasoned response to the nature of social studies, as distinct from the unthinking dogmatism of the Enlightenment. Rationalist theorising, in its proper context, could add to human knowledge but only as one method among others – it should be downgraded without being eliminated from all study. The Counter-Enlightenment did not repudiate Enlightenment goals and was still concerned with understanding social reality.

As the natural sciences grew in prestige during the eighteenth and nineteenth centuries, Enlightenment methods became established at the expense of alternatives. When social sciences were set up on a formal footing in the late nineteenth century, they mimicked the natural sciences and left little space for interpretative methods. Alternative views were commonest in history, anthropology and sociology but were scarce in economics, which provided barren soil for the Counter-Enlightenment. The upshot was a long-standing cultural critique of economics that started over two hundred years ago with classical economics and has lasted until the present.

## 1.3   THE ECONOMICS/CULTURE DIVIDE

Economics as a discipline dates largely from the eighteenth century, a period that witnessed the later stages of the Enlightenment, the continuing development of capitalist economic relations, and the early stages of the Industrial Revolution. Economic thought fitted in with the academic climate and became the purest expression of Enlightenment methods in their social application. Economists were eager to ally themselves with natural sciences. François Quesnay, who led the French physiocratic school, was a doctor by profession and based his economics on biological and mechanical analogies; in his view the best way to understand an economy was to dissect and analyse it as if it were a natural organism or a machine – his taste for mechanical analogies went as far as to plan an artificial human being (Schaffer, 1999). Adam Smith, acclaimed as the first modern economist, was a major figure in the Scottish Enlightenment, corresponded with French Enlightenment scholars and spent a period in France (Campbell and Skinner, 1982, Chapter 11; Ross, 1995, Chapter 13). The pioneer economists had a close personal and intellectual involvement with the Enlightenment, which shows through in their methods and theories.

Early contributions to the Counter-Enlightenment, such as the work of Vico, preceded modern economic theory. Once formal economics appeared in the later eighteenth century, it soon became obvious that general critiques of Enlightenment methods were germane to the new discipline. Economics epitomised the extension of Enlightenment ideas to the social sphere and attracted the ire of those who denied its arguments and methods. Dating back to classical economics, a cultural critique of economic thought has spanned the whole period in which formal economic theory has existed. As with the Counter-Enlightenment, the critique came from various sources and never grew into a concerted anti-economics movement or theory. It did, nevertheless, offer an alternative vision. For many of the critics, economic theory was an apologia for capitalism and to criticise one was to criticise the other. The Counter-Enlightenment led to the Romantic critique of capitalism in the early nineteenth century, which queried economic theory as well as capitalist economic relations.

Among the critical arguments was a belief that economic theory was overspecialised, oversimplified and overgeneralised; a better approach would be to integrate economic behaviour with the rest of human activity. Such arguments, because they renounced a separate discipline of economics, were resisted by economists anxious to set up their own scientific realm. Little dialogue took place between economists and their critics and few attempts were made to reconcile the differences. Economics developed separately, while the critical views were ignored or incorporated into non-economic disciplines. The gap between economics and its cultural critics widened with neoclassical economics in the late nineteenth century. By adopting a utilitarian individualism as the basis of its theory, neo-classicism distanced itself further from cultural thought and made it harder to bring cultural ideas to bear on economic theory. Cultural ideas have had influence in the humanities and other social sciences but in economics have been confined mostly to minority, heterodox positions. Even here, academic specialisation remains strong, so that heterodox economists have on the whole kept to standard disciplinary boundaries and made few references to the cultural literature. Most culturally based discussion has taken place outside economics.

The result has been an economics/culture divide allowing orthodox economics to define itself as a non-cultural subject. To portray the economy as cultural is to stray beyond normal disciplinary boundaries and cease to participate in mainstream economic discussion. As economics has grown into a profession, the economics/culture divide has been sanctioned and reinforced by institutional structures. Ever-increasing specialisation has reduced the likelihood of economists becoming fully conscious of culture. Although cultural approaches exist within social and cultural theory, they have no bearing on an economic orthodoxy that sees itself as a separate realm and claims a monopoly on economic theory. By default, culture has been delegated to other disciplines. In the current academic environment, it is quite possible to be an economist without ever mentioning the word 'culture' or thinking about cultural issues. The economics/culture divide has set up a boundary that seals economics off from culture and sanctions the neglect of culture by economists.

In cultural thought, the economics/culture divide has no validity. Economic behaviour is as cultural as any other behaviour and should be tackled through cultural methods. Capitalist economic development is thoroughly entwined with cultural changes and cannot be understood without considering them. Since economics has no special status as a separate social science, attempts to split the economic from the social or cultural will produce misleading and artificial results. A culture-free economic theory corrodes our ability to recognise the cultural context of economic activity and blunts our appreciation of cultural and institutional diversity. Progress towards a culturally informed economics requires breaching the economics/culture divide and returning to the previous, unresolved arguments between economists and cultural thinkers.

# 2. The meaning of culture

The word 'culture', never a technical term with a formal definition, has acquired many layers of meaning. In attempting to define culture, the anthropologists Kroeber and Kluckhohn famously came up with over a hundred different ways in which the word has been used; according to Raymond Williams, it is among the most complicated words in the English language (Kroeber and Kluckhohn, 1952; Williams, 1988). The difficulties in finding a neat definition are clear, and one might be inclined to avoid a word with such a potential for confusion. To do so would be hasty, as culture is too important to be overlooked. Efforts to expunge the word would be unsuccessful, for it permeates both everyday language and academic debate. If one knows its main uses, then a single definition is unnecessary.

The various meanings of culture testify to its subtlety and depth. Social sciences have complex, protean subject matter, and social or cultural theory should be correspondingly rich. As long as the meanings of culture do not get out of hand, its plurality can be beneficial and dissuade us from simplistic theorising. Yet a plethora of connotations may lead to inconsistencies: unless authors specify what they mean by culture, their arguments may be loose and imprecise. Possible misunderstandings include whether culture covers just the arts or a whole way of life, whether it is confined to ideas or embraces physical activities, whether or not it exerts a causal influence on the material world, whether it is purely descriptive or entails value judgements, and whether it is a state or a process.

Use of the word 'culture' generally falls under three headings: culture as a process, a way of life, and the arts (Williams, 1981b, Chapter 1). These three strands are the basis of the following discussion, which considers how culture has been defined and how its meaning has evolved. Early definitions saw it as a historical process and made no value judgements; later definitions saw it as a given way of life or narrowed it down to artistic activities evaluated as having special qualities. The shifts in meaning were not wholly accidental and reflected larger economic and social changes. Artistic definitions reaffirmed the economics/culture divide by suggesting that culture could be limited to the artistic sphere and kept away from the economic. After examining alternative views, the present chapter assesses how and why the concept of culture has changed and developed.

## 2.1 CULTURE AS A PROCESS

'Culture' began as a noun of process that referred to the way a person's beliefs and knowledge were formed and cultivated within society – this was its original meaning and its only meaning until the late eighteenth century. Etymologically, culture derives from the Latin *cultura* (cultivation or tending) and *cultus* (worship); it thus signifies husbandry, improvement and initiation into ongoing practices (Williams, 1988; Eagleton, 2000, Chapter 1). So defined, it deals with processes not end states. The related term 'cultivation' has been employed similarly, especially for applications to agriculture and natural resources. In modern usage 'cultivation' still denotes improvement and growth, whereas 'culture' no longer exclusively denotes a process and has other, static interpretations.

To view culture as a process brings out the social context within which people are being cultivated, so that culture can easily become identified with the context or end result of cultivation. The change of emphasis started in the eighteenth century, when Counter-Enlightenment authors compared human behaviour under different social circumstances. Herder, for example, was the first to use culture in the plural to refer to national and regional cultures coexisting at any given time (Williams, 1981b, Chapter 1). Emphasis switched from culture as a process to cultures as various end states resulting from different processes of cultivation. Interest in cultural relativities during the nineteenth century led to the static senses of culture becoming more common and outweighing its sense as a process. Nowadays culture mostly refers to states, though the original idea of culture as a process lingers on.

What are the consequences of viewing culture as a process? An immediate consequence is a stress on human development. Culture as a process occurs over time and refers to how individual beliefs, manners and customs are called forth and encouraged. Merely describing human behaviour would be inadequate to portray a cultural process, as it would not say why the behaviour arises and why it persists. For a society or economy to replicate itself, it needs a process whereby new members are introduced to its practices and enabled to participate in them, otherwise there would be no means of preserving common attitudes: innate differences between individuals would jeopardise social cohesion. Culture as a process provides the essential bond between individual and society.

Another consequence is that explanations cannot be wholly in individual terms. Individual behaviour depends on the outcome of cultural processes within a given social context; to ignore the context or depict it as the result of individual actions would misrepresent social behaviour. All people are born into pre-existing societies that mould and shape their development; no-one can develop in isolation. Culture as a process precludes any individualistic extreme but fosters individual development and growth. In most cases it should enhance our wherewithal for productive and creative activities, among which are some that may modify social practices, reshape institutions and transform the social context. Human behaviour need not be dictated by social constraints, and abilities cultivated within society yield the prospect of social change.

Cultural processes are relative to the surroundings within which individuals develop. Because no single cultural process applies everywhere, there must be a range of processes with different attributes and different end results. Even if human beings have biological features in common, their experiences growing up in varied cultural environments widen the differences among them. Culture as a process is the source of the many contrasts observed between cultures as end states – it explains the geographical and historical diversity of human behaviour. The ties with relativism and pluralism are strong (if not inevitable) and sustain the later, static views of culture.

## 2.2   CULTURE AS A WAY OF LIFE

The second main interpretation of culture came from the desire to compare the end states of cultural processes and draw historical or geographical contrasts. In showing that cultural processes bring diverse outcomes, it is convenient to reinterpret culture as a state not a process. Comparative studies often dwell on the customs and social practices in different societies without asking how these cultures emerged or how individuals were initiated into them. From the late eighteenth century onwards the static view of culture became commoner, until it became dominant in the nineteenth century.

At first the static view referred chiefly to the ideas and beliefs behind a society's way of life. Culture was the informing spirit that drives and motivates other activities – to understand a society required empathy with its spirit. Studies of national and regional cultures interpreted language, literature, the arts, religion and politics. Culture in this sense has an immaterial existence as the ideas and beliefs around which a society's institutions and activities are organised. Connections between culture and nature, visible in the analogies with agriculture and husbandry, are obscured.

Later static definitions, which appeared during the nineteenth century, treated culture more generally to include material production and day-to-day existence. A society's way of life took in all activities and attitudes, however mundane, and was no longer confined to the informing spirit.

Knowing a culture required understanding ordinary people as well as the philosophy of the intellectual elite. Ideas remained important, but interest swung back towards a material level, since much regular activity is bound up with material production. Growth of social sciences during the late nineteenth century promoted the comprehensive, way-of-life definition of culture found in anthropology and sociology.

The scholar who views culture as a state no longer looks at the cultivation of the individual and jumps straight to the results, namely socialised behaviour and customary practices at any given time. This abstracts from the temporal side of culture and makes it simpler to draw static comparisons among societies in different places or periods. Most comparative studies – the bulk of academic work on culture – define it as a state. Definitions of culture as state or process are distinct but not diametrically opposed, for a static way of life must emerge from a process of culture. A static method considers the end result of culture and passes over the details of how it was accomplished. Abstracting from cultural processes neglects the bonds between individuals and society: culture is examined at the social level alone, without considering agency–structure interaction.

## 2.3   CULTURE AS THE ARTS

In present-day usage, culture is often associated with the arts, especially the ones identified as serious and worthy ('high culture'). As in the way-of-life definition, culture is here a state rather than a process, the end result of the cultivation necessary if people are to appreciate the arts and participate in them. Unlike the other definitions, culture now has a specialised meaning and cannot be general – cultural activities can be distinguished from non-cultural, so that culture no longer refers to a whole way of life. The definition also acquires a normative cast, as culture is desirable and its absence a blemish: 'uncultured' becomes a pejorative term. Values are implicit in any cultural process, because the end result of cultivation should presumably be superior to the starting point. With culture as the arts, they come to the forefront and are made explicit.

Artistic definitions of culture have the side-effect of dichotomising cultural and economic matters. Economics, concerned with material production, distribution and consumption, gets classified as non-artistic activities distinct from culture. The humdrum, workaday world of economics provides the fullest contrast with the arts, which are viewed as leisure and an escape from the daily routine of work. Economics and culture, once dichotomised, are to be studied separately, do not impinge on each other, and require different methods. Artistic definitions of culture surfaced in the late nineteenth century, at a time when academic disciplines in the social sciences and elsewhere were becoming increasingly specialised. The same period saw the onset of neoclassical economic theory that assumes fixed preferences and pays little heed to culture as either process or state. Limiting culture to the arts widened the gulf between economics and cultural thought, while giving a pretext for orthodox economists to overlook cultural issues.

Separation of culture from economics is artificial, even when culture is defined as the arts. All artistic endeavours have a material aspect; professional artists support themselves by patronage or selling their work, and amateur artists need another way to make a living. As creative individuals, artists may strive for autonomy and free expression, but their work emerges from a particular social and economic environment. Attempts to set up a cultural realm apart from material life are misguided and hamper our understanding of both culture and economics. The retreat of culture into the arts reflected the growing specialisation of academic and cultural activities in the late nineteenth century – it demonstrated how the arts are beholden to economics while declaring the opposite.

The assumption that cultural activities are superior to non-cultural ones is also unhelpful, cutting across the wider, way-of-life definitions of culture and narrowing the relevance of cultural thought. Culture is reduced to being a stamp of approval awarded in line with the observer's tastes and used to circumscribe special activities. The intention may be to create a higher status for culture, but the effect is to place it within a ghetto and deny its relevance to ordinary life: as 'high culture' it may be debarred from the experience of the average person. The restrictiveness of 'high culture' contradicts the pluralism of the Counter-Enlightenment by endorsing only certain activities as culture and seeing the rest as non-cultural. Pluralism would not impose rankings and would allow culture to exist in many modes and guises. This is not to rule out all judgements about artistic quality – it means only that judgements should not be splitting cultural from non-cultural activities. If economics is to draw upon cultural thought, then the definition of culture must cover a society's whole way of life and cannot be confined to the arts alone.

## 2.4  THE EVOLVING DEFINITION OF CULTURE

Since the late eighteenth century the definition of culture has evolved with the growth of formal academia, on a path that has estranged it from economics. Two significant trends were the switch to static approaches and the increasingly specialised perspective; they were more or less sequential, as static methods arrived in the early nineteenth century, followed by greater specialisation in the late nineteenth century. Culture as a state gathered ground with comparative studies within new social sciences such as anthropology and sociology. Study of society usually proceeded from a snapshot of prevailing social relations, and theory was likewise based on given social structures. The terms 'culture' and 'structure', which began by referring to processes, were adapted to cover a fixed social state: culture was the end result of the formation of individuals, structure the end result of the formation of institutions and social relations. When anthropology and sociology became academic disciplines in the late nineteenth century, the static versions of culture and structure were officially recognised. Culture as a way of life was to overshadow culture as a process, even though the original meaning never disappeared.

The trend towards specialised definitions of culture had similar origins and was also bound up with new academic disciplines. Culture as a process had been general and applicable to any human activity. Counter-Enlightenment arguments were directed at social studies in the widest sense, with no limits on their relevance. The same was initially true of the static, way-of-life definition of culture, because a way of life covered all behaviour, customs and practices. By implication, any social science would require cultural methods, whatever the object of study. Economics, however, became committed to non-cultural methods with neoclassical theory in the late nineteenth century, creating a culture-free zone within social science. Under these circumstances, culture retreated to 'non-economic' territory. Anthropology and sociology, despite their way-of-life definitions of culture, steered clear of economics and concentrated on other matters. Specialisation encroached upon perceptions of culture when it started to be kept apart from practical affairs and confined to artistic pursuits. Seen this way, culture delineates the arts and has little relevance for anything else.

Evolution towards static and specialised meanings hemmed in the term 'culture' and reduced the leeway for cultural thought. Why did this narrowing down of culture take place? The main reason was the establishment of social-science disciplines that copied natural sciences in their theoretical and empirical methods. Studying human societies could be simplified by either abstracting from culture (economics) or opting for simpler, static definitions (anthropology, sociology). Full-blooded cultural thought, using interpretative methods, was sidelined and left to the humanities – it might be acceptable in 'soft' disciplines such as history but was too vague, subjective and imprecise to be tolerated in 'hard' social sciences. Expelled from mainstream social science, cultural thought sought refuge in specialised niches.

There is an irony here, for the foundation of social sciences was a classic example of culture as a process. It demanded institutions to define and formalise the new disciplines and demarcate them from non-scientific activities. Fledgling social scientists were shaped by a programme of training, which supposedly enhanced the ability to work creatively, conduct scientific research and improve our knowledge. The methods and theories of each discipline, developing gradually with further scientific work, were passed on to the next generation in order that the discipline could reproduce itself. This is readily compatible with cultural thought, but the social sciences had little time for cultural methods and played down culture in explaining human affairs; social scientists were trained and cultivated to model human behaviour as if it were aloof from culture. Such an odd outcome is not wholly surprising. The Counter-Enlightenment was a minority position within academic discourse and a response to the larger and prior Enlightenment. As the Enlightenment gained momentum and scientific disciplines were set up during the nineteenth century, it was perhaps inevitable that critical voices would be pushed to the margins. The doubts raised by cultural thought were irksome to new disciplines hungry for scientific credentials.

Cultural thought was never eliminated from social science but was restricted to minority groups. In economics, for example, cultural arguments were adopted by heterodox schools (notably institutionalism); in sociology the advocates of a cultural and historical perspective were outnumbered by a mainstream that preferred static, structural theorising. The early twentieth century was the high tide for positivism and a low ebb for cultural social science. By the late twentieth century the evident problems of positivism and natural-science emulation had prompted a revival of cultural arguments, in movements such as the New Left and postmodernism. The durability of cultural thought, despite vigorous efforts to institutionalise non-cultural methods, suggests that it does indeed have something to offer.

## 2.5 COMPARING DEFINITIONS

Culture, with its many definitions and meanings, has always been hard to pin down, but this can be an advantage. Its complexity gives it a subtlety that discourages oversimplified, reductionist theorising. Cultural thought has the richness needed to encompass diverse social and economic behaviour, along with the capacity for change. These are real benefits in social theorising, to be set against any drawbacks from vagueness or inexactitude. Even though culture has multiple definitions, one can speak

*Table 2.1    Alternative definitions of culture and their properties*

|  | Definition | | |
|---|---|---|---|
|  | Cultivation | Way of life | Arts |
| Process | Yes | No | No |
| State | No | Yes | Yes |
| Individualistic | Yes/No | No | No |
| Structural | Yes/No | Yes | Yes |
| Comprehensive | Yes | Yes | No |
| Normative | No | No | Yes |
| Comparative | Yes | Yes | Yes/No |

of a cultural approach without too much risk of confusion and draw a firm contrast with the non-cultural methods of economic orthodoxy. In identifying such an approach, it is helpful to look in more detail at the three main definitions of culture (cultivation, way of life, the arts). Table 2.1 compares them.

The first issue is whether culture should be a process (cultivation) or a state (way of life, the arts). Defining culture as a process gives it an active role in explaining how social behaviour and institutions came about and how they are reproduced. Culture provides the means by which individuals are socialised and able to participate in society; it enhances their personal capacities and creativity. Viewed as a process, culture can shed light on the relations between individuals and society, a question central to social science. Defining culture as a state is simpler and closer to common usage but does not relate individuals to society and focuses on the end product of cultivation at the social level. While useful for comparisons over time or space, a static definition is less useful for other purposes: the value of culture in social and economic analysis turns on its original meaning as a process.

A related question is whether culture engenders an individualistic or structural outlook. Cultural thought has been construed as both individualistic and structural. The individualism resides in the cultivation of individuals within society and the development of personal capacities: cultural methods have highlighted individual creativity in the arts, sciences, economic affairs and elsewhere. Cultivation occurs within a social context, and the process and end result are contingent on social roles and relationships: the individualistic aspect of culture cannot be separated from social structure. When culture is defined as a state, interest shifts away from the individual towards social relations and structures. In many recent applications culture has been structural, but it retains a latent individualism from its earlier usage. This stops short of methodological individualism and guards us from overestimating social structures and underestimating human agency.

Culture originally covered a person's entry into any social behaviour. Comprehensiveness was integral to the definition of culture as a process and carried forward to the way-of-life definition but was lost in the specialised definition of culture as the arts. An artistic view often sees some activities as more cultural than others, with the higher arts having the greatest level of culture and training, the lower arts a lesser level, and everyday, non-artistic life none at all. This may seem logical, but it understates the degree of socialisation in everyday activities. Even if some activities entail more cultivation than others, no human activities are free from their social context and independent from culture. To give culture a specialised definition is arbitrary and manufactures a false cultural/non-cultural gap. A wider definition of culture is essential if it is to contribute to economic and social theorising.

The earliest uses of culture carried no normative message and just described how individuals are introduced into social behaviour. One could not distinguish cultured from uncultured societies or pass judgement on individuals for lacking culture. While particular kinds of cultivation might be valued subjectively, the idea of culture was beyond valuation – it was simply a feature of any society. Neutrality was retained in way-of-life definitions of culture, which do not endorse one way of life in preference to others, but was discarded when culture became linked with the higher arts. If culture denotes approved artistic activities, then it has a normative slant and draws unflattering comparisons with other, non-cultural behaviour. The judgemental sense of culture is widespread in everyday language but best avoided in academic work.

Culture first entered academic discussion through comparative studies, and its comparative quality has been upheld. In its meaning as cultivation, it is open-ended and can bring about a vast number of different social practices. Likewise, culture defined as a way of life is consistent with varied social arrangements and lends itself to a pluralism or relativism based on cross-cultural comparisons. A cultural method denies any universal template for social and economic behaviour. Culture defined as the arts can also be comparative, but only if one refrains from writing off the 'lower' arts as non-cultural: normative judgements about the arts can twist and distort the comparative element in cultural methods. In most cases, though, cultural arguments permit pluralism.

The rest of this book sees culture as spanning all human behaviour and referring to processes as well as states. To define culture as the arts would block its broad application, separate it from economics and invite arbitrary value judgements. The following discussion uses the first two definitions of culture (cultivation, way of life), and for many purposes they harmonise with each other. When they clash, the original definition of culture as a process is preferred.

# PART II

# The cultural critique of economics

# 3. Early critical arguments (1800–1870)

The modern idea of culture, which predates both the Industrial Revolution and classical economics, originated in a critical response to the Enlightenment. The eighteenth century did host the early stages of capitalism, with major changes to agriculture and commerce, but the main wave of industrialisation was still ahead. By the early nineteenth century, the Industrial Revolution was at full speed, and cultural thought shifted towards economic affairs in a critique that has persisted ever since.

The shift came easily, owing to the close bonds between economics and the Enlightenment. All the pioneer economists, from the Physiocrats to Smith, Ricardo and Malthus, were rationalists and empiricists who dreamed of scientific progress and aspired to bring Enlightenment thought to bear upon society. They adopted an ahistorical posture, following the natural scientists, and claimed to have discovered fundamental principles applicable in all times and places. Most of these principles summarised the new, capitalist economic arrangements and presented a picture of growth and development. The lesson was that the same transformation would be beneficial everywhere and should be pursued as the means to generate economic prosperity. Such a universal template was inconsistent with the diversity and pluralism favoured by the Counter-Enlightenment and stirred up a critical reaction. Reservations about the Enlightenment were expanded into a critique of economic theory and capitalist development.

Authors in the cultural tradition did not, by and large, distinguish between economic theory and its practical consequences. They took it for granted that the new science of economics was the intellectual case for capitalism, so that economics and capitalism were partners – doubts about capitalism translated smoothly into doubts about economic theory. Once industrialisation had started in earnest, anxiety over the social effects of capitalism was accompanied by querying of economic theory. The arguments were entwined, and one cannot point to a separate critique of economics; most contributors to the cultural debate were not specialist academics and had no reason to pronounce on economic theory per se. Equating economic theory with capitalism would normally be unsafe, given that economics might take a non-capitalist form, but it tallies with the situation in the early nineteenth century. The ethos of the Enlightenment implies a disinterested quest for truth, yet economic theory was geared to markets, free trade and private enterprise – Smith, Ricardo and other economists were powerful advocates of the new capitalist society. Cultural critics realised that classical economics was apologetic to capitalism and treated it accordingly.

Early cultural criticism of economics can be dated roughly to the period between 1800 and 1870, when classical theory constituted the orthodoxy. A starting date of 1800 is late enough to allow for the origins of formal economic theory, while an end date of 1870 marks the onset of neoclassical economics and intensive academic specialisation. During this period, classical economics was subject to external challenges, often culturally based, coming from Romanticism and several other sources. Classical economists hardly acknowledged these challenges, and the few economists who accommodated cultural ideas were a small minority outside the mainstream. The same critical themes were reiterated for most of the nineteenth century, yielding a distinctive cultural tradition, and have retained their relevance. The present chapter discusses them and considers how they interacted with economic thought.

## 3.1   THE ROMANTIC CRITIQUE OF CAPITALISM

Romanticism as an intellectual movement flourished in the early nineteenth century, though its roots go back to the eighteenth century and its influence has lasted to the present day. It is usually linked with the arts but was never purely artistic and had wider philosophical origins (Schenk, 1966; Vaughan, 1994; Berlin, 1999; Brown, 2001). It began as a loosely coordinated set of beliefs and was only later extended to artistic practice: the assumption that it was exclusively artistic dates from later periods when definitions of culture were being narrowed down. Inspired by the Counter-Enlightenment, it projected the same style of thought into the industrial era. The difference between the Counter-Enlightenment and Romanticism was not their core ideas, which were essentially the same, but their applications: whereas the former was directed at the methods of the Enlightenment in a still proto-capitalist age, the latter was directed at capitalist economic development. The bugbear of Romanticism was not the deficiencies of scientific method but the social problems caused by market reforms and industrialisation.

Romanticism (like culture) has always been complex, and no single, tidy definition exists. Made up of various interrelated attitudes, it has a many-sidedness that does not lend itself to formal principles (and to seek them would collide with Romantic beliefs). The nearest one can get to a

*Table 3.1    Key ideas in Romanticism*

| | |
|---|---|
| Subjectivity | Emphasis on subjective, internal states of mind, as against objective, dispassionate knowledge |
| Emotiveness | Emotions have a place alongside emotion-free rationality |
| Organicism | Natural and social relations are an organic whole, rather than a mechanism built up of separate parts |
| Cultivation | People grow and develop within a social context that influences their nature and abilities |
| Creativity | People have a capacity for creative thought and actions, which is enhanced by the process of culture |
| Diversity | Human behaviour and societies are diverse and do not adhere to universal templates |
| Pluralism | Differences among individuals and societies are accepted and valued; the merits of historical and 'primitive' societies are recognised |
| Mutability | Natural and social relations are subject to change; nothing is permanent |
| Imperfection | Perfection is a desirable but elusive goal that has never been attained and never will be |
| Symbolism | Things have symbolic as well as practical value; symbols, metaphors, signs, myths, fables and folklore should be acknowledged |
| Rhetoric | Attention should be paid to styles of argument and discourse; communication and interpretation are significant matters |

definition is to trace key ideas that arise frequently in Romantic literature and art, as in Table 3.1.

The implicit world view is open-ended and resists uniformity or systematisation. Romantic thought can embrace individual creativity (and thus the capacity for change) but locates it within a social context and relates it to culture or cultivation. Current societies depend on the past, and to deny this would be disastrous. Attempts at reform based on ahistorical theories, in the manner of Enlightenment social thought, would be wrong-headed and counterproductive. The items in Table 3.1 are not specifically anti-capitalist. Romanticism and capitalism have intricate and ambivalent connections. One could, for instance, make a Romantic defence of capitalism by drawing upon its dynamic and creative attributes:

entrepreneurship, diversity in production and consumption, continuous unpredictable change, absence of universal planning, and so forth. Such a defence (which resembles neo-Austrian arguments) never prospered in the early nineteenth century, when capitalism was justified through classical economics on universal and ahistorical grounds. The new market-based economies were emblems of scientific progress, even though the Enlightenment was equally at home with economic and social planning as with the invisible hand. Faced with a close bond between capitalism and the Enlightenment, the Romantic Movement set itself decisively against both: it upheld the ideas of the Counter-Enlightenment but modified them to a critique of capitalism.

Participants in the Romantic critique were diverse literary authors, journalists, political commentators, historians and philosophers who were not economists but took an interest in economic development and its consequences. Their arguments, which ranged from overt critical analysis to allusive criticism in novels, poetry and other literary works, shared a disquiet about the harshness of capitalist development and a desire to find alternatives. The anti-capitalist aspects of Romanticism have not always been registered – it is often classed as a solely literary or artistic movement – though it provided staunch resistance to capitalism, modernity and classical economics (Grammp, 1973; Ryan, 1981; Löwy, 1987; Jackson, 1993; Löwy and Sayre, 2001; Connell, 2001). Because the Industrial Revolution started in Britain, much Romantic and culturally based criticism was produced by British writers (Williams, 1958a). Among the contributors to this tradition were Edmund Burke, William Blake, William Cobbett, Samuel Taylor Coleridge, Robert Southey, William Hazlitt, Thomas Carlyle, Charles Dickens, Elizabeth Gaskell, John Ruskin and Matthew Arnold. All these writers offered critical commentary on capitalism from a Romantic standpoint and contrasted it unfavourably with alternative social arrangements. Their preferred alternatives were far from uniform: some were conservative and lauded pre-capitalist conditions (Burke, Coleridge, Carlyle), others were radical and looked towards novel alternatives (Blake, Hazlitt). Participants in this critical tradition were united in their outrage at capitalism's social consequences, making many common observations and arguments, but differed in their policy proposals.

Three core arguments of the Romantic critique can be identified. First, capitalist development eroded traditional ways of life and trampled on religious and other beliefs that had lasted for centuries. Capitalism, with its ahistorical quality, showed little respect for the past or for social diversity – it was determined to impose a single mode of economic organisation everywhere, in order to maximise productivity and the gains from trade. Whatever the material benefits, the Romantics felt that the consequences would be spiritually and socially dire. Life would be stripped of its meaning, social bearings would be lost, and the richness of varied cultures would be replaced with vapid monotony. Second, Romantic authors hated the mechanistic side of capitalism. The quantitative bent of the Enlightenment had prompted the use of machinery, the organisation of production through the factory system, and the spread of strict timekeeping and fixed working hours. Such reforms were viewed as dehumanising and detrimental to life. Capitalism, for its Romantic critics, had an artificial nature founded on misguided efforts to quantify and systematise things in the name of efficiency. Third, the impersonality of markets and factory production was seen as weakening social ties and alienating people from their work. Cohesive societies were being supplanted by collections of atomistic individuals connected only by trade, contracts and work discipline. As workers lost control over their activities, their quality of life would suffer and they would become uninvolved in the outcome of their labour. These three arguments, taken together, are the kernel of the Romantic critique. From the many Romantic authors, the following discussion picks out a few who specifically criticised economics: Coleridge, Hazlitt, Carlyle, Ruskin and Arnold.

Samuel Taylor Coleridge was one of the first generation of English Romantic poets who in later life devoted himself to literary criticism, philosophy and social commentary (Holmes, 1982, Chapter 2). An early sympathiser with the French Revolution, he soon became disillusioned with radical politics and switched to conservatism (though he said that his basic values were unchanged). He is an important figure in the Romantic critique because he was well versed in German idealist philosophy and made conscious connections between British and German Romanticism. Throughout his career he opposed classical economics and utilitarianism (Winch, 1996, Chapter 12; Connell, 2001, Chapter 1). His social and political thought culminated in his last major work, *On the Constitution of the Church and State*, which defended a national culture anchored in tradition and rejected the 'mechanico-corpuscular' philosophy of Locke, Newton and other Enlightenment authors (Coleridge, 1830 [1972]). To escape such atomistic views, he proposed an 'enlarged system of action' founded on the cultivation of individuals within society. Precedence was to be given to the national culture, with commercial and economic activities organised so as not to threaten or dilute it; the method of sustaining it was to appoint endowed cultural guardians (the 'clerisy') who would protect, preserve and disseminate culture. His proposals did not replicate past institutions but were politically conservative in so far that they envisaged a hierarchical and paternalistic society.

William Hazlitt is today best known as an essayist and journalist but he wrote extensively on economic issues. Admiring Coleridge and Wordsworth, he had broad sympathy with Romanticism, though he remained a political radical and disowned the conservatism exemplified by Coleridge's later writings. He was critical of classical economics, and Malthus in particular, on both political and intellectual grounds (Winch, 1996, Chapter 11; Connell, 2001, Chapter 4; Grayling, 2000, Chapter 6). His main contribution was in rebutting the Malthusian population principle: he wrote a large volume dedicated to this aim (far longer than Malthus's original essay on population) and later summarised his critique in *The Spirit of the Age* (Hazlitt, 1807 [1930], 1825 [1991]). For Hazlitt, population was regulated not by the universal laws of the Malthusian population principle but by moral and cultural factors. Moral restraint as a preventive check on population had been acknowledged only grudgingly by Malthus; Hazlitt argued that moral restraint was observed widely in all societies and reduced the need for positive checks such as famine and disease. He queried Malthus's treatment of agriculture and argued that the capacity for economic growth and increased food supply was far greater than Malthus had claimed. Since the Malthusian population principle had been dovetailed into the Ricardian model, Hazlitt's commentary applied to the whole classical framework. The repudiation of universal laws, stress on culture, and recognition of growth and change are all consonant with Romanticism.

Thomas Carlyle wrote some of the most trenchant Romantic criticism (Morrow, 2006, Chapters 3–4; Welch, 2006). Influenced by Coleridge, he too was familiar with German Romanticism and forms another link between British and German traditions. In *Signs of the Times* and *Past and Present* he denounced the impoverished social relationships under capitalism and contrasted them with the stronger social bonds in pre-capitalist societies (Carlyle, 1829 [1971], 1843 [1918]). His aphoristic style yielded several well-known phrases: he dubbed economics the 'dismal science', was the first to speak of 'industrialism', condemned the commercial 'cash nexus', and described the nineteenth century as the 'Mechanical Age'. He was critical of how the mechanistic logic of capitalism permeated both the external social relations in markets or the factory system and the internal ways of thinking promoted by an obsession with material production. The attempt to codify thought and reduce it to its barest standardised essentials was, for Carlyle, especially pernicious. His social philosophy, like Coleridge's, was politically conservative: he harked back to pre-capitalist arrangements with hierarchical social structures topped by benevolent, paternalistic elites. In his later writings his elitism went to an extreme through a worship of the authoritarian heroic leader, the apotheosis of the creative Romantic individual. This authoritarian streak has tainted his reputation – he is often labelled a precursor of fascism – and reduced the impact of his social criticism. His concerns over social problems were well intentioned, though, and he had genuine sympathy for the poor and the working classes.

John Ruskin built upon Carlyle's arguments to provide an explicit Romantic critique of classical economics. Ruskin's reputation has been as an art critic, but he ventured into many other matters, including ethical and religious questions, political economy, social conditions, and the natural world (Batchelor, 2000; Henderson, 2000; Moore, 2005). His art criticism was sensitive to the moral dimension of art and related it to social context – high artistic standards came from individual creativity within a harmonious, well-ordered society (Ruskin, 1857 [1905]). Distress about social problems led him towards economic commentary, until he was eventually encouraged (by Carlyle) to write about classical economics. His views were published in a sequence of four essays entitled *Unto this Last*, which offers an eloquent rejoinder to orthodox economic theory (Ruskin, 1862 [1985]). Ruskin started by attacking atomistic individualism, as promulgated in the concept of rational economic man, and advocating an organicism that allows for social bonds and relations between people and the natural world. The mechanical and asocial attitudes in classical economics were, for Ruskin, dehumanising and neglected the true value of economic activities. To see work one-dimensionally as a means to the end of producing material goods was too narrow and ignored its role in encouraging self-fulfilment and fostering a collective consciousness. Ruskin was among the first to point out how advertising creates and manipulates wants in order to expand markets and permit continuous capital accumulation. He also anticipated environmentalism through his worries about the detrimental impact of industry on the natural world. In his view, all economic activity should be morally regulated and valued not by financial criteria but by its contribution to human life ('there is no wealth but life'). The vitriolic responses of economists, politicians and businessmen to *Unto this Last* led to the essay series being cut short (more than four had been planned). Ruskin tried to advance his critique by moving on (in *Munera Pulveris*) to a humanistic economics that constructed a new and broadly conceived theory of value (Ruskin, 1863 [1905]). Mainstream economists never took Ruskin's work seriously, and he was discouraged from further economic theorising. Economic orthodoxy sidestepped the issues he raised and, when it embraced neoclassical methods, moved further away from his position.

Matthew Arnold was another prominent cultural critic of capitalism in the mid-nineteenth century. As an author, literary critic and inspector of schools, he was engrossed by culture and how it bears upon social

conditions (Collini, 1994; Bennett, 2005). His main work in this area
was *Culture and Anarchy*, which presented culture as the remedy for the
adverse social effects of economic development (Arnold, 1869 [1932]).
Like the other cultural critics, he was troubled by the mechanical social
relations of capitalism, along with the acquisitive and philistine commercial mindset. Despite the material prosperity generated by industrialism,
the quality of life for all economic classes suffered because of the preoccupation with business, work and material production. The coarse fabric of a
commercialised society could be mellowed only by cultivating individuals
through a liberal, non-vocational education· Arnold championed a state
education system offering a liberal education to all citizens. He believed
that a common culture would be socially cohesive and limit the instability from economic and political individualism. Greater equality would
further enhance cohesion, and Arnold made a classic cultural argument
for egalitarianism (Arnold, 1878 [1986]). His accent on culture was in the
Romantic tradition, but he said less than the earlier authors about economics: he preferred to stay at the individual level, on the assumption that
cultivating individuals would yield immediate social benefits. The smaller
scope reflected the late-nineteenth-century trend towards artistic definitions of culture in a realm separate from economic affairs.

   Although the Romantic critique of capitalism soldiered on through
the nineteenth century, with contributions from many authors, it had
barely any impact on economics as a discipline. Social concerns raised by
Romantic critics did animate reforms and regulations introduced during
the Victorian era to soften the edges of capitalism, but they were snubbed
in the sphere of economic theory. Economists, aiming for a specialised
discipline, were reluctant to read the cultural critics and derided attempts
to formulate alternative theories. The body of cultural criticism, while
obviously related to economic thought, has not been accepted into the economic canon. Consider, for example, Schumpeter's lengthy and exhaus-
tive *History of Economic Analysis*. Schumpeter was aware of Romanticism
and mentioned writers like Carlyle and Ruskin but dismissed their
economic reasoning as unscientific and unworthy of serious discussion
(Schumpeter, 1954, Part III, Chapter 3). For him, cultural arguments
could at best be 'economic thought' (general opinion on economic issues)
but never 'economic analysis' (scientific study of economics). The attitude
of Schumpeter (who might have been expected to show more feeling for
history and culture) typifies the division that grew up between 'professional' economic theory and 'amateur' cultural critiques of economics.
Economists perceived cultural criticism as an external threat and refused
to give it credence or adapt their theories in response – they sought their
philosophical roots elsewhere, in utilitarianism, and drew inspiration from

natural sciences. The economic realm was sealed off from culture and developed non-cultural methods and theories.

## 3.2 UTOPIAN, MARXIAN AND OTHER CRITIQUES

Alongside the Romantic critique, various other critiques of capitalism and economic theory arose during the early nineteenth century. They had many similarities and voiced the same distaste for orthodox economics but differed in their politics, relationship to the Enlightenment, and cultural content. None had much purchase on economic orthodoxy, apart from inducing it to retreat further into its shell, though they had a bearing on heterodox economics and on later criticism. Three sources of critique are considered here: Utopian socialism, Marxian arguments, and early versions of social economics.

The defining feature of Utopian thought is that it offers a vision or plan for an ideal future state (Levitas, 1990; Kumar, 1991; Samuels, 2003). In the early nineteenth century, schemes of this kind were put forward by Robert Owen, Charles Fourier, Pierre Leroux, Claude Henri de Saint-Simon and many others. Utopians shared with Romantics a concern with social problems and a desire to improve the quality of life for working people. As a remedy they hoped to create new societies that would replace the market relations of capitalism with a planned and centrally regulated social order. The word 'socialism' was invented and popularised by Utopian writers around this time, in deliberate contrast with utilitarian 'individualism' (Williams, 1988; Hodgson, 1999b, Chapter 2). A difference from Romantic authors, who often looked back to pre-capitalist societies, is that Utopian plans were abstract and historically unspecific. The new visions of the future would supersede and outdo all current and past arrangements. Unlike Romantic thought, little reference was made to historical or geographical pluralism, so that the same blueprint could be applied anywhere. The way forward from capitalism would be to redesign society on socialist principles to yield equality, better living and working conditions, and greater social cohesion.

Utopian thought had an ambiguous relation with the Enlightenment and could either support or resist it. Owen, Saint-Simon and many other Utopians were adherents of the Enlightenment and sought a scientific reordering of society. Their rational, dispassionate planning exemplified the Enlightenment creed, even more so than the market-based arguments of classical economists. Utopians could appeal to the thoroughgoing application of science across all economic and social activities, with no need for the invisible hand invoked by Adam Smith. Scientific knowledge would permit the perfect central planning of social life, promising well ordered and equal societies, and would unravel earlier superstitions, myths and false beliefs. These arguments are far removed from Romanticism. Some Utopians were less strongly committed to the Enlightenment, however, and friendly to Romantic ideals. Instead of planning scientific reform, they elected to start afresh from a state of nature with communal living and greater freedom for individual creativity. Coleridge, for example, in his earlier career was involved in Utopian schemes for a 'pantisocracy' based on common property and universal participation in government. Fourier argued against the specialised labour promoted by economists and looked towards an unspecialised world in which everyone had diverse skills and varied, rewarding work. Notions of Utopia are manifold and may not imply a society planned from the top down.

Even when inspired by natural sciences, Utopianism usually had a cultural aspect. Paternalistic reformers such as Owen believed that, through education and better social conditions, they could improve the character of ordinary working people. For Owen, human nature was malleable and open to virtuous or malevolent external control – it was therefore imperative to shape and plan the social environment to ensure that people became good citizens with healthy attitudes (Owen, 1813–16 [1991]). Moulding of individual behaviour seems illiberal and authoritarian, yet it was aimed at enabling people to acquire new abilities and play a full role in society. It has an affinity with cultural ideas through the cultivation of the individual within a social context; it lacks the historical and pluralistic qualities of the Counter-Enlightenment, but it embodies culture. Utopians normally criticised atomistic individualism and took a collectivist view – individuals, having no fixed human nature, would grow and develop within a benign social order. Capitalist individualism, a recipe for social inequality and fragmentation, should be ousted by a new, cohesive society with a planned culture outside historical time and unconnected with previous traditions and cultures. The timelessness is at odds with cultural thought but the argument still rests upon culture or cultivation. Again culture forms a cornerstone for critical assessment of capitalism and economic theory.

From the 1840s onwards, Marx and his associates added another strand of critical thought. He was trained in German idealist philosophy and conversant with the Romantic critique of capitalism, having read Carlyle, so that his own critique was stimulated by Romanticism and borrowed many of its attributes. This side of Marx is salient in his early writings, notably the *Economic and Philosophic Manuscripts* (Marx, 1844 [1964]). His first assault on capitalism centred on how it dehumanises workers and alienates them from production, an argument repeating points made by Romantic authors. The mechanical quality of capitalist production and its ability to destroy traditional cultures was also noted by Marx (as it had been by the Romantics) and recounted in the *Communist Manifesto* (Marx and Engels, 1848 [1967]). Historical methods, vital for Marxism, had their origins in the Counter-Enlightenment and German idealist philosophy. Engels too came close to Romantic authors with his early studies of working conditions under capitalism (Engels, 1845 [1973]). The cultural dimensions of work (employer–employee relations, property rights in production, work intensity, working hours, work discipline, etc.) remained at the hub of Marxian reasoning, despite its evolution along a materialist path. Among the numerous influences on Marx, cultural and Romantic ideas were played down by later writers who announced Marxism's materialist and scientific credentials.

As a great synthesiser of other people's ideas, Marx drew not only from Romanticism but from Enlightenment materialism, classical economics and Utopian socialism. Fundamentally he wanted to keep faith with the Enlightenment and uphold its goals and methods. He adopted materialism and became a vehement critic of German idealist philosophy, despite his idealist background. Unhappy with previous Enlightenment scholarship, he never went so far as to join the Counter-Enlightenment: his critique of capitalism did not reach to a wholesale denial of the Enlightenment principles by which it was justified. On the contrary, he reworked the theories and methods of classical economics in an anti-capitalist vein. Having seen the radical potential of classical economics, he used it as the basis for his economic analysis; certain parts of the Ricardian system were abandoned (notably the Malthusian population principle), but the essence of the theory stayed intact. He derived his socialism from Utopians such as Saint-Simon, though he argued that socialism would emerge by revolutionary historical change rather than social planning. His anti-capitalist critique was distinct from Utopian ones yet still placed squarely within the Enlightenment tradition.

Marxian thought is broad and rich enough to attract many interpretations. Its materialism can nurture a mechanical account of history in which material forces dictate institutions and beliefs. A rigid base–superstructure model would rule out an independent effect of ideas and leave culture under the sway of material factors. This formalised historical materialism is suggested in the later work of Marx and Engels but reached its peak in the official Marxian doctrines after Marx's death. Marxism evolved in some decidedly un-Romantic directions, but its lineage was connected with Romanticism. The cultural and humanistic facets of Marx could never be eradicated and were to be revived in the twentieth century.

Romantic, Utopian and Marxian arguments all hailed from outside economics. Criticisms of capitalism from within economics were rare, since most economists supported markets, free trade and laissez-faire. Only a few were willing to depart from classical orthodoxy and raise doubts about capitalism. The most prominent example was the Swiss historian/economist J.C.L. Simonde de Sismondi, who in the early nineteenth century tried to reformulate economics on principles different from the classical school. Sismondi is known primarily as a historian, but in *New Principles of Political Economy* he expounded a non-classical, heterodox economics (Sismondi, 1827 [1991]). Among his innovations were the denial of Say's Law, a belief in the prevalence of unemployment from underconsumption, and a stress on the instability and cyclicity of capitalist production. Unlike many classical economists, he showed concern over the social consequences of capitalism and the turmoil created by its wilfulness. His policy recommendations were to forgo laissez-faire and resort to public regulation of the economy. Methodologically, he queried abstract Ricardian theory and argued for a historical and institutional stance. These views resemble the Romantic critique of capitalism and would, if fully developed, have sired an economics wholly different from classical orthodoxy. Sismondi has sometimes been regarded as founding a distinct tradition of social economics kept alive by later writers and lasting into the twentieth century (Lutz, 1999, 2002). While he did influence later critics, it remains difficult to identify a unified, Sismondian 'social economy' existing in parallel with classical 'political economy'.

The heyday of Romanticism in the early nineteenth century made only a shallow impression on economics. Classical economists, determined to be scientific, made few concessions to Romantic thought; the Romantics were mostly content to carp at classical economics from outside. A Romantic school of economics has been attributed to writers such as Adam Müller and Sismondi but was too disparate to sustain a thriving Romantic or neo-Romantic tradition (Vandewalle, 1986). Friedrich List, in *The National System of Political Economy*, argued for historical and cultural specificity at the national level (List, 1841 [1904]). He opposed laissez-faire and recommended that the State should oversee economic development; free trade, sacrosanct to the classical economists, should be replaced with protection wherever this would nurse new industries. The historical method, abjuring of abstract theory, and attention paid to national cultures is consonant with the Counter-Enlightenment and Romanticism. From the 1840s onwards, historicism was taken up by Wilhelm Roscher, who forged the German historical school that endured until the mid-twentieth century and played a major role in introducing historical specificity into economic analysis (Hodgson, 2001a, Part II; Milonakis and Fine, 2008, Chapter 5). Sceptical of abstract theory, the historical school opted for empirical methods as the foundation for a scientific economics – its goal, like that of

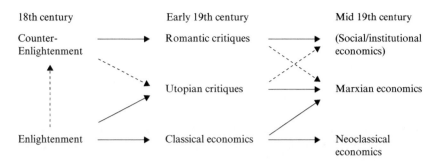

*Figure 3.1    Critical responses to classical economics*

the classical economists, was to attain scientific status. Strict empiricism brought a thinner perspective, so that the historical school made little headway in embracing cultural methods.

## 3.3    THE CULTURAL CONTENT OF CLASSICAL ECONOMICS

During the early nineteenth century the classical orthodoxy in economics was secure and well entrenched, but surrounded by criticism from Romantic, Utopian and Marxian sources. Figure 3.1 shows how these critiques interacted (solid lines indicate strong influence, dotted lines weak influence). The various strands of thought all sprang from the Enlightenment, even if some were reacting against it. Classical economics was the economic orthodoxy for the first half of the nineteenth century, eventually becoming an influence on both neoclassical and Marxian economics. Neoclassical theory took over as the orthodoxy from around 1870 onwards, and Marxian economics established itself as an alternative tradition. The Enlightenment also spawned Utopian critiques of classical economics that were another input into Marx's thinking. Cultural criticism of economics was linked with Romanticism, which was informed by the Counter-Enlightenment. Unwillingness to endorse the Enlightenment kept Romanticism and cultural thought on the fringes of economics: they stimulated social and institutional economics but were never to penetrate the economic mainstream.

Is classical economics innately anti-cultural, or could it be recast and refurbished to recognise culture? In recent years neo-Ricardian (Sraffian) economists have revived the classical economics of Ricardo and argued for its superiority over neoclassical theory (Kurz and Salvadori, 1998; Foley, 2001; Mongiovi, 2002). The classical framework is seen as being social and institutional, avoiding neoclassical individualism, and providing a

secure foundation for heterodox political economy, perhaps augmented
with Keynesian ideas in a classical/Keynesian synthesis (Eatwell, 1983;
Bortis, 1997). According to this perspective, classical economics has
much in common with institutionalism and stands apart from neoclassical orthodoxy. Since the institutions modelled are capitalist ones, it can
be construed as a historically specific theory at a high level of generality
but distinctive to capitalism. By summing up capitalist institutions and
showing how they contribute to economic reproduction and growth, classical economics could, the neo-Ricardians claim, purvey a full understanding of capitalism.

Do such claims hold water, or are they overstated? Early classical
economists made many historical and cultural references. Adam Smith,
for instance, based his conclusions on historical comparisons and practical examples: the index for *The Wealth of Nations* spans a huge breadth of
cases from ancient, medieval and modern times (Smith, 1776 [1976]). This
might suggest historical specificity, but he used historical examples to back
a universal programme for market-based society. His conclusions supported capitalist arrangements over all historical and geographical alternatives. Much the same can be said of Malthus who, in later editions of his
essay on population, offered plenty of historical illustrations. He too used
historical evidence for ahistorical purposes, to back his universal principle
of population. Far from engendering historical specificity, the early classical economists aimed to demonstrate absolute laws and principles.

Adam Smith had broader interests than many economists and wrote
extensively on non-economic subjects. His non-economic writings often
imply a more social, less individualistic attitude than his economics: the
prime example is his first major work, *The Theory of Moral Sentiments*,
which sets out an ethical theory reliant on sympathy with the interests of
others (Smith, 1759 [1976]). The contrast with the self-interest highlighted
in *The Wealth of Nations* prompted some commentators to identify the
'Adam Smith problem', the seeming contradiction between his moral and
economic arguments (Montes, 2003). To say that he had a split personality or dramatically changed his views would be mistaken, and the inconsistencies have been exaggerated: *The Theory of Moral Sentiments* was an
ethical treatise not immediately comparable with *The Wealth of Nations*.
Both books were written in the quest for absolute principles and have little
overlap with the Counter-Enlightenment.

The absoluteness of classical economics became clearer when David
Ricardo put it on a theoretical footing. As its title reveals, Ricardo's
*On the Principles of Political Economy and Taxation* lays down theo-
retical principles for a science of political economy (Ricardo, 1817 [1951]).
Historical examples are rare, and the goal is to construct a theoretical

model. Ricardian theory, the first formal foundation for classical economics, set the tone for later work in the orthodox tradition. Ricardo did not use mathematics directly, but his abstract theory opened the door for formal and mathematical theorising within the discipline. From Ricardo onwards, classical economics was seeking to replicate the theoretical models in the natural sciences and thereby widen its differences from historical or cultural approaches.

The Ricardian model portrays the causal factors behind investment and economic growth but in an ahistorical fashion. Implicitly it addresses the early stages of capitalism, yet it says nothing about the historical and institutional background. Factor shares are emphasised in Ricardian economics because they have an analytical function in determining profits and investment, not because they capture a particular historical period. All the defining features of the Ricardian system are timeless and universal – the law of diminishing returns, the Malthusian population principle, the iron law of wages, the wage fund doctrine, the principle of comparative advantage, and so forth. A single theoretical template is applied to every economy, and few concessions are made to diversity or pluralism. While individual behaviour receives little attention in classical economics, the tenor of the modelling suggests a deterministic, mechanical account. Ricardo was associated with utilitarians such as James Mill, whose rationalist view of ethics and human behaviour can be taken to underlie the classical position. The tie with individualism became far more obvious in the neoclassical era but had its origins in classical economics.

A belief that classical economics is historical and institutional seems to arise from the comparison with neoclassical methods. Unlike its later offshoot, classical economics is at least capable of being historical: it discusses development and growth (as against static resource allocation), is not founded on fixed individual behaviour, makes no assumptions about market-clearing equilibrium and conducts its analysis in terms of aggregated wages, rent and profit. Neo-Ricardian economists can plausibly argue that a classical model has more potential for historical and institutional analysis than a neoclassical one. This is not saying much, however, and depends on the limited comparison with neoclassicism. Romantic critics saw classical economics as palpably ahistorical and would be surprised to hear it defended for its historical aspects. A proper historicism came about only when classical economics was seized by Marx and set within the framework of historical materialism. When confronted with Marxism, most orthodox economists reacted against it and retreated into neoclassical theory. At best, classical economics is extendable towards culture and history, though this extension was never carried out by the classical economists themselves.

The uneasy relation between culture and classical economics is well illustrated by John Stuart Mill. As the son of the utilitarian writer and economist James Mill, he had a rigorous education that included a thorough grounding in classical economics and Benthamite philosophical radicalism. From the beginning he was brought up in the progressive climate of the Enlightenment, which combined support for capitalist economic development with a desire for liberty, democracy and social justice. His intellectual evolution was far from smooth, and in early adulthood he faced what he termed a 'mental crisis' caused by his first detailed study of Romantic and cultural arguments, especially Coleridge (Mill, 1873 [1989], Chapter 5; Capaldi, 2004, Chapters 3 and 4; Bronk, 2009, Chapter 2). The ensuing doubts led him to reconsider utilitarianism and classical economics: his views at this time are described in his essays 'Bentham' and 'Coleridge' (Mill, 1838 [1987], 1840 [1987]). Mill was supposedly a Benthamite utilitarian but, if anything, treated Coleridge more generously than Bentham and displayed a clear appreciation of Romantic thought while admitting the drawbacks of utilitarianism. This influence of Coleridge on Mill never converted him to Romanticism, but it kept him away from extreme individualism. While Mill is often seen as having invented rational economic man, he was acutely aware of the artificiality and narrowness of his brainchild.

Notwithstanding his doubts about classical economics, Mill did little to revise his economic theorising and remained faithful to core classical doctrines: his *Principles of Political Economy* restated the orthodox classical system, albeit in more socially sensitive language than other classical economists, and fenced off economic analysis from social matters (Mill, 1848 [1994]). When Mill was discussing property and distribution or commenting on socialism, he expressed ideas coloured by radical Utopian thought. His radicalism was overlooked because it was self-contained and aloof from his orthodox economic theory. With hindsight, Mill's failure to integrate his economic and social beliefs missed an opportunity for classical economics to learn from its cultural critics. Social matters were duly minimised and had little impact on the trajectory of economic theorising. In the long term, the single most enduring element of Mill's economics has been the concept of rational economic man. Whereas Mill used this abstraction tentatively, in a qualified and circumspect way, it is now brandished proudly and unreservedly by mainstream economists.

The potential for classical economics to be transformed in a social and cultural direction was perceived at an early stage without ever being realised within orthodox economic theorising. As early as the 1820s the Ricardian socialists (such as William Thompson, John Gray, Thomas Hodgskin and John Francis Bray) were drawing radical implications from classical theory and melding it with progressive, Utopian thought (King, 1983, 2003; Burkitt, 1984, Chapter 3). The classical model was easy to enlist for socialist purposes: factor shares and class-based analysis showed up the asymmetries and inequalities among social groups, a labour theory of value suggested that workers were the source of value and had a claim on the fruits of their production, and a focus on economic development raised the possibility of fundamental social changes as well as economic growth. The socialist interpretation of classical theory exploited its capacity to give a negative account of capitalism, in contrast with the positive account given by economic orthodoxy. This was visible in Mill's commentary on socialism and in Marxian economics.

Ricardian socialism brought an anti-Ricardian retort from conservative classical economists (Samuel Read, Samuel Bailey and Nassau Senior among others) who guided economic theory away from this dangerous territory. Anti-Ricardians dropped the labour theory of value and rejigged classical economics with alternative value theories resting primarily on supply and demand. The anti-Ricardian backlash shrank the (already slim) cultural content of classical economics and foreshadowed neoclassicism. From the 1870s orthodox economics transformed itself into a neoclassical form with a static, ahistorical and individualistic method.

# 4. Culture and the social sciences (1870–1950)

The late nineteenth and early twentieth centuries saw the rapid growth of economics, sociology, anthropology, psychology and other social sciences. Often the boundaries between them were variable, though conventions emerged to draw clear (if arbitrary) demarcation lines. Ultimately each developed a professional organisation and institutions, together with core theories and methods. One thing that they had in common was the desire for scientific status and the prestige that went with it. The humanities (history, philosophy, literary studies, etc.) were less driven by scientific ambitions, but they too acquired professional structures during this period.

Cultural methods did not fit comfortably into the new academic disciplines. An immediate problem was the tendency for social sciences to mimic natural sciences by adopting rationalism or empiricism. The Counter-Enlightenment and Romanticism had warned against this, but in the scramble for scientific kudos the warnings were overlooked. Cultural thought, which raised doubts about the feasibility of social science, was unpalatable for those aspiring to scientific status. Ever increasing academic specialisation was itself an artefact and symbol of the modernity that cultural critics of capitalism had resisted. The advance of the social sciences seemed to mark the eclipse of the Counter-Enlightenment and a wholesale rejection of its arguments.

The eclipse was partial, as cultural thought influenced several new disciplines. Cultural ideas were difficult to erase and reappeared (consciously or otherwise) in the writings of social scientists. Any social sciences interested in understanding human behaviour, analysing institutions or comparing different societies gravitated towards cultural thought. Anthropology had culture (usually defined in a static sense) as a core concept and was happy to acknowledge its importance. Some disciplines generated internal cultural critiques, with a minority favouring a cultural approach. Cultural thought found a niche in social sciences, even if their aims and methods were modelled on natural sciences.

Economics was the social science least receptive to cultural thought. In the late nineteenth century, neoclassical theory replaced classical and brought with it a static, timeless, individualistic method that squeezed out any inklings of culture. The narrower scope was confirmed in the shift of title from political economy to economics, implying a discipline separate from politics, sociology and everything else. The isolated world of neoclassical theory had no room for culture; as economists became more specialised they confined discussion to their professional circle and excluded cultural and other critics. Cultural arguments could get a foothold only outside the mainstream, in the heterodox schools. Marxian economics overhauled the Ricardian model and, despite a sometimes doctrinaire materialism, accommodated history and culture. Institutionalists, reacting against neoclassicism, were pleased to embrace culture, history and institutions, as were the German historical school. Heterodoxy kept cultural thought alive within economics but could do little to redress the anti-cultural bias of neoclassical orthodoxy.

## 4.1   THE EMERGENCE OF NEOCLASSICAL ECONOMICS

Neoclassical economic theory is usually traced back to the marginal revolution of the 1870s, when various theorists (notably Jevons, Marshall, Menger and Walras) arrived independently at similar principles (Screpanti and Zamagni, 2005, Chapter 5; Milonakis and Fine, 2008, Chapter 6). For a while the new methods coexisted with classical ones, but they spread quickly and soon usurped the classical system. By the early twentieth century economic orthodoxy had become neoclassical, and the old Ricardian model was forgotten. The exact relationship between classical and neoclassical economics has been a vexed question. Both terms were coined by critics (classical by Marx, neoclassical by Veblen) and were not used by orthodox writers. The term 'neoclassical' suggests continuity with classical economics, yet the early neoclassical economists proclaimed their differences from the classical school (Aspromourgos, 1986). Neoclassical economics jettisoned the Ricardian model and shared only a few features with classical thought.

Ambiguities over the classical/neoclassical relation derive largely from the dual personality of classical economics. Formal classical theory was at a macroeconomic level and evaluated the causes of economic growth. As growth depended on investment and capital accumulation, which in turn depended on the profit share in national income, it was necessary to consider economic classes and the factor distribution of income. The analysis was class-based and said little about rational individual behaviour or individual interactions through markets. Notions of equilibrium revolved around equalised profit rates, without the market clearing that became a totem of neoclassicism. At a microeconomic level, classical economists talked about specialisation and free trade, as well as endorsing Benthamite utilitarianism. Classical arguments for laissez-faire had an individualistic flavour, and John Stuart Mill was the (reluctant) inventor of rational economic man. The classical school can be viewed as having implicit individualistic foundations that were never visible at the Ricardian surface. Individualism had ancestry in the classical period but came to dominate economic theorising only during the neoclassical era.

Under the sway of neoclassicism, dynamic or historical theorising about economic development gave way to static theorising about resource allocation. The social attributes of classical economics, with its appeal to economic classes, shrivelled before a rigorous individualism. Classical theory could be eclectic about the motives behind people's behaviour; neoclassical theory was individualistic. The shadowy utilitarian substructure of classical economics had been made overt and, instead of being integrated with the Ricardian superstructure, had dislodged it. Henceforth, orthodox economics was to have a microeconomic slant.

Neoclassical economics went on to exclude every hint of cultural thought. If one were asked to design a social theory that neglected culture, then it would be hard to improve upon neoclassicism – culture in all senses is banished. The individualistic method, based on fixed preferences and instrumental rationality, rules out the original definition of culture as the cultivation of the individual within society. Individuals in a neoclassical model undergo no such process, and the source of their preferences, values and beliefs is beyond the ken of economic theorising. Neoclassicism has a static, absolute form that evades history and hampers comparison with pre-capitalist societies. Historical specificity is ignored, national and regional differences are passed over, and the same economic principles are supposedly applicable in all circumstances. Culture defined as a way of life, which seeks to capture historical and geographical variations, has no place in the absolute neoclassical universe. The third main sense of culture – the arts – is barred from economics by disciplinary divisions: economic behaviour is seen as being different from artistic activity, which lies outside economic science. Far from responding to cultural ideas, neoclassical theory has resolutely non-cultural foundations.

The early neoclassical economists showed an awareness of social issues in their broader opinions and attitudes. Alfred Marshall wanted economics to be a tool of social progress and contributed to the establishment of welfare economics. He was unwilling to barricade economic theory from other disciplines and felt, in particular, that analogies with biology would be useful (Thomas, 1991; Hodgson, 1993a, Chapter 7). Léon Walras, whose general equilibrium theory is viewed as the pinnacle of neoclassical purity and elegance, took an interest in social questions and showed sympathy for socialist ideals (Jaffé, 1975; Cirillo, 1984; Jolink, 1996, Chapter 2). For Marshall and Walras the neoclassical model was an abstraction that illustrated features of economic behaviour but did not represent the whole of economics. By the early twentieth century the initial circumspection had been lost, and neoclassical theory congealed into fixed principles. Unlike the previous classical orthodoxy, neoclassicism was axiomatic – it claimed to have exposed the fundamentals of all economic behaviour. Once neoclassicism took over, economics was perceived in static, neoclassical terms as addressing resource allocation. Alfred Marshall had defined economics as the 'study of mankind in the ordinary business of life' (Marshall, 1890–1920 [1961], Book I, Chapter I); by the 1930s, Lionel Robbins could define economics as dealing with scarcity and choice, so that anything else would no longer qualify (Robbins, 1937). For the first time, economics was being defined through its (neoclassical) methods, not its object of study.

Perfect competition became the benchmark for orthodox theorising. Market-clearing equilibrium was associated with allocative efficiency, and the theoretical case for markets swung towards their allocative properties rather than their effects on growth or innovation. With perfect competition as the reference point, other economic arrangements could be modelled only as imperfections bringing a loss of allocative efficiency. Ricardian theory was ditched, and orthodox economics now pivoted on absolute neoclassical principles relevant in all times and places. Other approaches, if they were to be deemed acceptable as economic reasoning, would have to comply with the neoclassical world view. An example of this is the fate of the many theoretical innovations from the 1920s and 1930s – the 'years of high theory' – which included imperfect and monopolistic competition, Keynesianism, early Sraffian economics, input–output techniques, various attempts at modelling growth and economic cycles, and the first trial uses of econometrics (Shackle, 1967). These innovations, prompted in part by the interwar depression, were often at odds with neoclassical theory and sufficiently general to provide the raw material for a shift away from neoclassicism. The shift never happened and orthodoxy held firm: failing to unseat neoclassicism, the innovations were swallowed by it. New theories were tolerated if compatible with core neoclassical doctrines but not allowed to challenge or replace them.

## 4.2 HETERODOX ALTERNATIVES TO NEOCLASSICISM

During the period when orthodox economics went neoclassical, several heterodox schools of thought emerged as alternatives, among them

Marxian economics, institutionalism and the German historical school. They were able and willing to accommodate history and culture: the following discussion examines their cultural content.

## Marxian Economics

In theorising about the economy, Marx used Ricardian ideas and acknowledged his debts to Ricardo. From a heterodox perspective, he inherited the classical mantle, while neoclassical economics broke with the classical school and forged a different tradition (Dobb, 1973). By discarding the Malthusian population principle and bringing out the historical nature of development, he improved the prospects for a cultural approach. Yet his reliance on classical economics imposed limits on this, as did his disdain for Romantic anti-capitalism. Marx never doubted the methods of the Enlightenment; he shared with classical economists a yearning for scientific status and had little time for the 'unscientific' delusions of Romanticism, German idealist philosophy and Utopian socialism. His early work, which had a humanistic and cultural quality, was counterbalanced in his economics by the legacy of the Ricardian model. He was awake to cultural matters, but his economic theory did not emphasise culture and was prone to reductive, materialist interpretations.

Marx's later career, dominated by the writing of *Capital*, saw him turn away from his earlier interests in order to formalise his economics. Some authors have claimed to identify an 'epistemological break' in the mid-1840s that separated the early 'humanist' Marx from the mature 'scientific' one (Althusser, 1969). Such views can only be speculative, and there is little evidence of a sea change in Marx's opinions and method. *Capital* was just the first volume in a planned series that would span all human behaviour and social relations (Marx, 1858 [1973]). The missing parts of the larger project would presumably have diluted the apparent supremacy of economics in his later work and said more about culture. Many additions made by Marx to the Ricardian system increased its social and cultural content: examples are the concept of the labour process, the distinction between labour and labour power, the variability of productivity, and the potential for alienated labour. Through these additions he allowed for diverse economic and social arrangements within capitalism. Never a dogmatic materialist, he avoided any crude determinism that subordinated everything to economic forces.

Marxian writers in the next generation were less careful about avoiding determinism and produced theories with a reductionist complexion. Keen to consolidate Marxism and establish its scientific status, they simplified its core arguments and removed its subtleties and qualifications. After Marx's death in 1883, Engels was left to edit and publish the last two volumes of *Capital* and other unfinished work. He had collaborated with Marx from the outset and knew about the humanism of the early Marx, but in his later life put forward the base-superstructure model as a stylised Marxian doctrine. This framework, endorsed as authentic by Engels, was taken up by Marxian theorists in the late nineteenth century: Kautsky, Plekhanov and Labriola offered pared-down, mechanistic brands of historical materialism (Kautsky, 1887 [1925]; Plekhanov, 1895 [1961], 1897 [1976]; Labriola, 1896 [1908]). The new, 'scientific' Marxian theories were approved by the Second International and are sometimes described as Second International Marxism. They were to underlie the official doctrines of the Soviet Union and became synonymous with an unbending Marxian materialism. The formalised Marxian theory had the unfortunate consequence of narrowing it and moving it further away from cultural thought.

The Marxian tradition was diverse, though, and alternative views were always present. An early example is William Morris, who was committed to Marxism but refused to give economics priority over culture and art. He began as an adherent of the Romantic critique of capitalism, having been influenced especially by John Ruskin, and was a central figure in the Arts and Crafts Movement (Thompson, 1955; McCarthy, 1994; Upchurch, 2005). He retained his Romanticism but (unlike Carlyle and Ruskin) denied that fundamental social change could be effected through paternalistic reform. By the late nineteenth century it was obvious that capitalism was deeply entrenched and that the chances of restoring pre-capitalist working methods by reformist means were minimal. Morris turned instead towards socialism as the best hope of replacing capitalism with a more humane way of working and living. He studied Marx's writings, entered British radical politics, and wrote much on artistic, social and political questions (Morris, 1882, 1888). Although his writings remain within a Marxian frame, his main concerns were the alienating and impoverished texture of life under capitalism – these were issues discussed by the early, humanist Marx but omitted from later, official Marxian doctrine. For Morris, socialism could not be separated from art and culture: its purpose was to raise the quality of life by giving people rewarding and varied work, extending the arts into everyday life, and improving the living and working environment (Morris, 1883–94 [1915]). After a peaceful socialist revolution, the changes were to be accomplished not by social planning but at a local level by participation of ordinary people in reshaping their living and working conditions. His ideas, which had no leverage on the practice of Marxism, were to return with the New Left in the late twentieth century.

From the 1920s onwards, Marxian authors began to query Second International Marxism and argue for a less deterministic and 'scientific' outlook. Karl Korsch and György Lukács interpreted Marxism not as a science of society but as a critical philosophy promoting revolutionary change (Korsch, 1923 [1970]; Lukács, 1923 [1971]). A critical Marxism should attend to the class consciousness of the proletariat, a question that invokes culture through the formation of beliefs within society. To concentrate solely on material production would be inadequate: thoroughgoing Marxian analysis should deal with cultural matters in their own right, not just as appendages to the economy. Much the same argument was made by Antonio Gramsci, whose imprisonment meant that his work remained unpublished until the 1970s (Gramsci, 1971). For Gramsci, Marxian thought should avoid imitating the natural sciences and aim for a comprehensive philosophical and cultural critique of capitalism that would pave the way for revolution. The Frankfurt School, led by Max Horkheimer and Theodor Adorno, expounded an anti-positivist Marxism. In their view, the Enlightenment itself should be opened up to critical scrutiny for its inherent conservatism in searching for general laws and appealing to universal reason (Horkheimer and Adorno, 1944 [1973]). True progress would be possible only when the constraints imposed by the Enlightenment had been challenged and overthrown. The kinship between the Frankfurt School and the Counter-Enlightenment is clear, though the Frankfurt School remained loyal to Marxism.

In the early twentieth century, official Marxian doctrine took on a rigid materialism that reflected broader intellectual trends towards positivism. Marxian writers felt it necessary to make scientific claims and prove the superiority of their own science over bourgeois versions. The Marxian tent was big enough to house alternative views sensitive to cultural matters, and a more critical and reflective strain of Marxism stood alongside the official doctrine. Between 1870 and 1950 the critical voices had only a limited impact, but they were to make a bigger impression with the New Left in the 1960s.

## Institutionalism

The American institutionalist school came to fruition with the writings of Thorstein Veblen in the late nineteenth and early twentieth centuries (Hodgson, 2004, Part III). Unlike Marxian economics, it departed from the classical heritage of Ricardo and sought to rebuild economic science on different principles. Nor did it connect with the Counter-Enlightenment or Romanticism; it had its own critique of orthodox economics, and parallels with earlier arguments remained implicit. It differed from the Counter-Enlightenment in its wish to uphold Enlightenment methods and put economics on a scientific basis. A theme of its critique was that orthodoxy had never quite been scientific enough – in this respect it was concordant with the late-nineteenth-century trend to set up new social sciences.

While culture was crucial for institutionalism, its founding ideas owed little to the cultural tradition. Veblen took his lead from Charles Darwin: he aimed for an evolutionary science of economics and rejected neoclassical orthodoxy because it had failed to accomplish this (Veblen, 1898). He made links with biology and the natural sciences, as against the humanities, and wanted to expand upon the achievements of evolutionary theory. The resulting materialism and naturalism contrasted with the idealism of the Counter-Enlightenment and the Romantics. Institutionalists travelled towards cultural matters from a materialist and evolutionary starting point.

Another source of ideas was the pragmatist philosophy of C.S. Peirce, John Dewey and William James (Mirowski, 1987; Liebhafsky, 1993; Webb, 2002). Pragmatism was friendly to science but adopted a practical, rule-of-thumb approach rather than a strict empiricism or rationalism. The emphasis on practical results and workable solutions meant that pragmatists did not chase absolute knowledge and were satisfied with approximate truth. Their appreciation of the difficulties of social science concurred with the Counter-Enlightenment and encouraged pluralism. Interpretative methods were a trait of pragmatism that accorded well with cultural thought; in appealing to pragmatism, institutionalists were following ideas that meshed with the cultural critique of capitalism but were not actually a part of it. Pragmatist accounts of human behaviour rested largely on the instinct–habit psychology of William James, which was a cornerstone of Veblen's theory (Waller, 1988; Hodgson, 2004, Chapter 7). James combined biological and natural behaviour (instincts) with behaviour influenced by the social and institutional environment (habits). Habits are consistent with the cultural tradition, though they carry a passive connotation at odds with the active creativity applauded by Romanticism. Pragmatist theories, resting on instincts and habits, can be married with concepts of culture but chiefly in its static sense as given customs and routines.

The institutionalist notion of culture was similar to the anthropological one, with culture defined to include all human behaviour that varies across societies and is not biologically fixed (Mayhew, 1994). Since culture covers a whole way of life, economic behaviour must then be cultural. Contrary to the absoluteness of neoclassical economics, institutionalists tailored economic analysis to the context under investigation: in the same way that anthropologists had studied pre-industrial societies, economists should study the customs, beliefs and practices of modern industrial capitalism. Institutionalists hoped to understand how individuals participate in and reproduce economic institutions. The need to observe different cultures pulled them towards empirical study, and they are sometimes seen as hardened empiricists, but many (such as Veblen, Commons and Mitchell) were openly dedicated to finding suitable economic theories. Although a few institutionalists succumbed to the craze for positivism in the early twentieth century, most have recognised the importance of both theoretical and empirical research.

Veblen excoriated the neoclassical school and its individualistic reductionism. For him, neoclassical economics neglected the social origins of economic behaviour: to model human beings in abstract terms as making continuous optimising decisions was to deny the prevalence of habits and social norms (Veblen, 1898). Neoclassical theory could not explain individual preferences, the bedrock of its analysis, and was nonchalant about this, having dropped preference formation from the subject matter of economic science. Theory based on fixed preferences promoted a timeless, static view that depended on oversimplified equilibrium models and could not encompass evolution. Veblen's critique, pointing out the sterile atomism of orthodox economics, has affinities with earlier critiques by Romantic writers, but he was not a Romantic. Guided by Darwinian thought, instinct–habit psychology and the anthropological sense of culture, he tried to reformulate economics as an evolutionary science and remained optimistic about scientific methods in general.

Where does institutionalism stand in relation to the cultural critique of orthodoxy? The resemblance between Veblen's arguments and those of cultural critics might tempt one to regard institutionalism as the offspring of the cultural tradition. This would be somewhat misleading, for the real influences came from elsewhere: a primary goal was to be Darwinian, hence institutionalism's alternative title as evolutionary economics. The Counter-Enlightenment and Romanticism had an effect, filtered through anthropology and pragmatist philosophy, but it was weak and indirect. Adherents of the cultural tradition tended to be fellow-travellers of institutionalism, on the periphery of the school but not fully belonging to it. The best example is John Hobson, who was a lone author and 'economic heretic' writing on economic and social matters without ever holding an academic post (Hobson, 1938). His distinctive beliefs were based on the evolutionary ideas of Herbert Spencer and the organic social philosophy of John Ruskin; he replaced Spencer's competitive individualism with a social and cooperative outlook (Hobson, 1898, 1902). The appeal to Ruskin and the cultural tradition unites Hobson with Romantic anti-capitalism and contrasts with Veblen's Darwinism. He was following in a (sparsely populated) line of social economics consonant with institutionalism but separate from it (Lutz, 1999, Chapter 4). Institutionalists, seeking an evolutionary science, were unmoved by the apparently non-scientific Romantic writers. This creates an anomaly: institutionalism harboured culture as a core concept yet drew little on the cultural critique of orthodox economics.

## The German Historical School and Austrian Economics

The German historical school, with origins going back to the 1840s, pre-dated the arrival of neoclassical economics in the 1870s. Its arguments about the need for historical specificity were directed at classical econom-ics but were transferable into the neoclassical era and, if anything, gained in relevance. During the late nineteenth century the historical school developed into an alternative to orthodoxy, centred on Germany with off-shoots in Britain and the US. It can be divided into two periods through a distinction between the older and younger historical schools (Hodgson, 2001a, Part II; Tribe, 2003). The older school, led by Wilhelm Roscher, was critical of Ricardian economics and classical laissez-faire policies. The younger school, led by Gustav Schmoller and Werner Sombart, began in the 1880s and opposed Austrian and neoclassical economics, with which it engaged in methodological debate (the *Methodenstreit*). Both the older and younger historical schools were internally diverse but stalwart in their case for historical specificity and dislike of jejune, foolhardy theorising.

Despite the critique of orthodoxy, the historical school was ambivalent towards cultural thought and the Counter-Enlightenment. Its case for his-torical specificity chimed with the cultural relativism of previous German thinkers such as Herder. It resisted the rationalism and universalism of orthodox economists in favour of a cautious, piecemeal approach. While not anti-theoretical, it was unhappy with orthodox theories and reluctant to formulate an alternative. Castigating utilitarianism and laissez-faire was in tune with Romantic anti-capitalism, as was the argument for policy intervention at the national level. The historical school could easily be viewed as part of the cultural tradition, but in key respects it diverged from cultural methods.

A major difference arose with empiricism. Having fought shy of abstract theorising, the historical school relied on empirical research as its guar-antor of scientific status. Although it should have been compatible with pluralistic theorising, few attempts were made to theorise. Empiricism crowded out interpretation or imaginative reconstruction of the past. The stringent empirical focus contrasted with cultural thought, which was willing to countenance interpretative methods and creative theorising. The historical school's accent on observation lured it towards a static view of culture; it could say little about culture as a process, which would have required portraying how individuals and society are related. Theory of this type was missing, and the potential for a cultural economics stayed unfulfilled.

The German historical school was opposed methodologically by the Austrian school founded by Carl Menger. For Menger, economics should base itself on abstract theorising that summarises the essence of economic behaviour. His building block for theory was the rational individual who economises and uses scarce resources optimally; economics could safely begin with this behaviour and construct larger models and theories without case-by-case empirical research. Data collection would cast only a dim light on economic systems, which were best illuminated through pure theorising. The ahistorical and individualistic method resembled that of neoclassical economics and, in its early years, Austrian economics was a subset of the neoclassical school. It had distinctive views about capital, thanks to Böhm-Bawerk, but remained in league with neoclassical thought. During the *Methodenstreit*, which took the local form of a dispute between German and Austrian economics, the Austrian school was speaking on behalf of the new, neoclassical economic orthodoxy.

Compared with neoclassicism, the early Austrian school had small differences of detail that were magnified in later Austrian economics. Menger's individualism rested on the subjectivity of individual judgement, not the objective image of rational economic man preferred in neoclassicism. This caused Austrians to beware mathematical modelling and take up interpretative methods aimed at empathising with individual behaviour. For the Austrians interpretation meant finding ideal types and did not fully acknowledge social and historical context, but it at least branched out from rationalism and empiricism. Menger and the Austrian school showed a greater interest in institutions and evolution than was usual in neoclassical economics. Even though Austrian analysis started with the individual, it recognised how institutions might come spontaneously from individual behaviour and influence how the economic system functions, as in Menger's speculation about the origins of money (Menger, 1871 [1981], Chapter 8). Here a cultural aspect to economic reasoning becomes possible, albeit restricted by individualism. The peculiarity of Austrian thought was to be brought out by later writers, such as von Mises and Hayek, but it was only after the 1940s that (neo-)Austrian economics matured as a heterodox school. In its early period, Austrian economics was a variant of neoclassicism and allied with economic orthodoxy.

The current dominance of individualistic theorising within orthodox economics has given the impression that the Austrian school won a decisive victory in the *Methodenstreit*. This was not how it seemed at the time, and the methodological debates had no neat outcome: both sides maintained their positions until well into the twentieth century. The demise of the German historical school in the 1940s was due to political events rather than intellectual failure – its perceived German nationalism ruled out any revival in the post-war period, and the path was left clear for German economics to become neoclassical. Ironically, the Austrian 'victory' underpinned neoclassical hegemony, while the neo-Austrians were relegated to being a heterodox school.

## 4.3   CULTURE IN OTHER SOCIAL SCIENCES

Economics was joined in the late nineteenth century by other social sciences, all of which emulated natural sciences. As positivism expanded, the space for cultural and interpretative methods diminished. Yet cultural ideas managed to cling on within many social sciences and humanities; their survival in a harsh climate proved their resilience and vitality, as well as providing a platform for the revival of cultural thought in the late twentieth century. The following discussion considers how culture was treated in sociology, anthropology, psychology and history.

**Sociology**

The term 'sociology' was coined by Auguste Comte in the mid-nineteenth century and applied to his views about social evolution. Wedded to Enlightenment aims, he sought to fill a gap in existing sciences and spread scientific thought to the humanities (Thompson, 1976). For Comte, all societies evolved from theological and military organisation to the scientific and industrial organisation of modernity. The purpose of his sociology was not only to understand modern society but to accelerate social evolution. Sociology should go further than disinterested study and actively promote science. Comte also coined the term 'positive philosophy', the forerunner of positivism, which expressed his faith in an empirical and analytical scientific method. His universalism and total devotion to science were at the opposite pole from the Counter-Enlightenment.

The fathering of sociology as an academic discipline, without its Comtean mission, is often accredited to Émile Durkheim. While in the tradition of Comte, his sociology had the more modest aim of standing alongside other social sciences. The main topic was modern industrial societies, which he modelled as organic systems made up of interrelated parts (Thompson, 1982, Chapter 3). Each individual fulfilled a role that contributed to the functioning and sustenance of the social system. The analogy was with a biological organism that depended on its internal relationships and was irreducible to its component parts. Once a social system was operating smoothly it had no reason to change, so that Durkheim's perspective tended to be static – he viewed organic societies as the end result of an evolutionary process but did not foresee other stages of evolution. His organic and structural theory formed a contrast with neoclassical economics. The structural emphasis did not bring him anywhere near a cultural approach, however, as he used positivistic methods and glossed over cultural variation and diversity.

An alternative sociology, more attuned to cultural ideas, was flowering among German writers such as Ferdinand Tönnies, Georg Simmel and Max Weber. Sociology thus acquired a French/German division that echoed earlier divisions over the Enlightenment and Counter-Enlightenment: German sociologists queried the application of rationalism and empiricism to social matters, ascribed more importance to culture, and were less happy to give a positive functional interpretation to modern industrial society. Tönnies introduced the well-known distinction between community (*Gemeinschaft*) and association (*Gesellschaft*) (Tönnies, 1887 [2001], 1925 [1971]). For him, pre-capitalist societies had common values, social solidarity and personal relationships, whereas capitalism had impersonal markets, social dislocation and self-interested behaviour. Communities were dissolving into looser aggregations of individuals connected only by formal contractual bonds. Tönnies viewed these changes regretfully and adopted a tone similar to Romantic anti-capitalism. Durkheim and his followers were preoccupied with social structures and their functional consequences; German sociologists looked towards the cultural and social changes wrought by capitalist development. Simmel, for example, wrote exhaustively about the ramifications of an economy organised around monetary transactions among anonymous agents (Simmel, 1907 [1990]). With these differences of perspective, sociology was more pluralistic than economics and more receptive to cultural arguments.

Max Weber was the chief rival to Durkheim. He was acutely aware of historical and cultural variation, forever comparing and classifying social behaviour, but he also wanted to give sociology a methodological and theoretical foundation. Following the German idealist and cultural tradition, he argued that social sciences were distinct from natural sciences and required their own procedures. The appropriate method, according to Weber, was to seek interpretative understanding (*Verstehen*) which could then inform sociological theory. To understand ideal types of behaviour within a particular historical context would permit further theoretical modelling. Ideal types were a compromise between the ahistorical generality of natural sciences and the piecemeal fragmentariness of historical research – Weber was bidding to create a value-free scientific sociology without losing sight of cultural relativism and historical specificity. His interpretative method sucked him towards individualism, so that he is often described as a methodological individualist. He did nonetheless allow for context and never went to an atomistic extreme (Swedberg, 1998, Chapter 6; Hodgson, 2001a, Chapter 9). Weber's individualism has been exaggerated through comparisons with Durkheim's highly structural theory.

Weber was employed as an economist for most of his career and wrote a great deal on economic topics. His stance with respect to the *Methodenstreit* was complex and ambiguous. The comparative and historical side of his work, evident in all his writings, would seem to put him squarely in the German historical camp, and he had intellectual contact with members of the younger historical school such as Schmoller and Sombart. His efforts to provide theoretical foundations for sociology could have done the same for the historical school of economics. This was not to be, and Weberian theory has been construed as coming closer to economic orthodoxy. The ambiguities arise from his ideal types for economic behaviour – he named formal rationality as the ideal type under capitalism, differentiated from the tradition-centred behaviour of pre-modern societies (Weber, 1921–22 [1968], Chapter 2). Formal rationality, when coupled with individualism, looks like the individualistic theory championed by neoclassical and Austrian economists. Despite his historicist beliefs, Weber can be viewed as backing the Austrians in the *Methodenstreit* and contributing to subjectivist and individualistic economics (Parsons, 2003). Though he rejected ahistorical methods, he sanctioned formal rationality as the basis for analysing modern capitalism. The breadth of his research, along with the frequent obscurity of his prose and terminology, has spawned many accounts of his true meaning. His economic theory did not cohere into a system and bore only a superficial resemblance to neoclassical economics: it led towards what would today be called economic sociology (Swedberg, 1998). Regrettably, his individualism offered apparent support for an exclusively individualistic economics, thereby legitimising the economics/sociology division.

During the early twentieth century, sociology needed to map out its subject matter. A general study of society would have to examine economic and cultural questions, but this might encroach on other disciplines. In order to be self-contained, sociology specialised in a 'non-economic' and 'non-cultural' domain. Concepts of individual rationality were assigned to economics, cultural issues to anthropology or history. Sociology opted for static, timeless methods that hinged on social structures and depicted human behaviour as being structurally determined. Culture was oblique to its main interests.

## Anthropology

Of all the social sciences, anthropology has been the most culturally alert. In studying the whole of humankind, it addresses primitive and pre-industrial societies as well as modern industrial capitalism. By its nature, anthropology must be comparative and sensitive to geographical and historical diversity. The sheer width of its subject matter overlaps with other social sciences and brings difficulties in setting disciplinary boundaries: research into a way of life must include economic activities and social structures, entering the realms of economics and sociology. This problem has been resolved (arbitrarily) by anthropology investigating pre-industrial societies and leaving the modern world to other social sciences.

Although it had many precursors, anthropology as a discipline was founded in the mid-nineteenth century (Eriksen and Nielsen, 2001). Early studies were based on evolutionary ideas current at the time and discerned common patterns of human development. Lewis Morgan, for example, proffered a materialist analysis resting on economic organisation: a society evolves from 'savagery' in the hunting/gathering era to 'barbarism' in the agricultural era to 'civilisation' characterised by cities, industry and formal government (Morgan, 1877 [2000]). His judgemental terminology associates evolution with the passage from an unproductive, primitive society ruled by kinship ties to a modern, prosperous industrial state with elaborate institutions. The materialism mirrors that of Marx but omits class conflict and views capitalism in a flattering light. Marx's evolutionary scheme was essentially a materialist anthropological model grafted on to Ricardian economics – the bonds between Marxian thought and anthropology were always close and have remained so (Bloch, 1983; Donham, 1999; Elardo, 2007). Other evolutionary theories were due to Edward Tylor, whose materialist vision was similar to Morgan's, and James Frazer, whose idealist model foresaw transitions in belief systems from magic to religion to science (Tylor, 1871; Frazer, 1890). All these schemes located different societies on a single evolutionary path to scientific and industrial progress. In the Enlightenment spirit, they took it for granted that accumulated scientific knowledge would guarantee economic and social advancement.

Evolutionary anthropology predicted a unified, predetermined pattern of social and cultural development. Even if societies had different starting points, they were expected to converge on the same end point that yielded optimum economic arrangements. Responding to this implicit monism, an alternative anthropology grew up in Germany and followed a pluralistic, cultural approach. The key figure here was Adolf Bastian, who demurred at a single course of evolution and instead argued that cultural evolution could take multiple and divergent paths (Eriksen and Nielsen, 2001, Chapter 2). Anthropology should therefore be comparative and highlight cultural diversity without fitting each society into a prior evolutionary category. The pluralistic school was labelled 'diffusionism' from its belief that cultural evolution was diffuse and multiform, with no common origins or destinations. Eschewing a grand evolutionary scheme, diffusionists studied each culture or society on a case-by-case basis.

By the early twentieth century, anthropology was influenced by sociological theorists, especially Durkheim. Evolutionary arguments lost ground to static analyses of the social structures in a given society and the functions they performed. Anthropological explanation took on a functionalist cast, parallel with the functionalism in sociology and other disciplines. Marcel Mauss and Alfred Radcliffe-Brown promulgated a structural-functionalist anthropology that connected social structures with their functions and was allegedly applicable across many societies. The emphasis was on the institutional roles people play, as against ideas or beliefs. Bronislav Malinowski formulated a different version of functionalism, which espoused methodological individualism and theorised in terms of individuals rather than social structures – it explained social arrangements by their functions for individual members of society. Both versions of functionalism avoided stipulating a single evolutionary scheme but introduced the drawbacks of structural-functionalist sociology.

Cultural methods, in the tradition of Bastian, were upheld by Franz Boas, a German-trained emigrant to the US. Each culture, for Boas, had to be considered on its own merits through detailed empirical research without an overarching theoretical framework (Boas, 1904 [1982], 1940). By contrast with structural-functionalism, he looked beyond social structures and individual behaviour to ideas and beliefs – studying social relations was insufficient, and culture in a wider sense had to be addressed. The contributions of Boas and his followers (notably Alfred Kroeber) gave rise to the US school of 'cultural anthropology', which was an alternative to the prevailing functionalist accounts. Kroeber went on to make major contributions to clarifying culture and asserting its importance (Kroeber and Kluckhohn, 1952). Cultural anthropology was perceived as a sub-discipline, despite the centrality of culture for any anthropological research.

Like other social sciences, anthropology had internal debates about the role and significance of theory. General theoretical systems confronted historical specificity. This division gradually intensified until it came to a head in the formalism/substantivism debate from the 1940s onwards, a quarrel reminiscent of the *Methodenstreit* in economics. Formalists claimed that economic behaviour in all societies had common properties explicable through orthodox economics. Following Malinowski, they supported neoclassical economic theory as a means of explaining economic behaviour regardless of the society under investigation (Firth, 1951; Herskovits, 1952; LeClair, 1962). Substantivists denied the universal relevance of neoclassical theory and reaffirmed the importance of historical circumstances. They studied economic cultures separately, given that individual behaviour, social relations and belief systems could differ dramatically from modern developed societies (Polanyi, 1944, 1957; Dalton, 1961; Sahlins, 1974). Karl Polanyi viewed economic activity as an 'instituted process' – he included capitalism in this assessment and argued that markets did not appear spontaneously but required careful planning and deliberate structural changes. The formalist/substantivist debate lingered on into the 1970s and (as with the *Methodenstreit*) had no decisive outcome (Lodewijks, 1994; Wilk, 1996, Chapter 1; Billig, 2000). Anthropology, often seen as the epitome of a cultural discipline, has experienced bitter disagreements about general theorising and cultural relativism.

**Psychology**

Among the non-economic social sciences, psychology has had the lowest cultural content. Several reasons for this are immediately apparent. As the study of the human mind, psychology starts at the individual level and broaches social issues only when they impinge on the individual. It also has a larger physiological element than other social sciences through its analysis of mental processes within the brain. Its biological basis means that it straddles the distinction between natural and social sciences, raising doubts as to whether it can be classified as a social science. Empiricism and experimental methods have preponderated, while cultural matters have been marginal.

The earliest formal studies in psychology were undertaken towards the end of the nineteenth century (Schultz and Schultz, 2007; Mandler, 2007). German scholars were in the lead, but their work had little to do with German cultural and idealist thought. Gustav Fechner and Wilhelm Wundt wanted a science of the mind with experimental and quantitative methods – their template was the natural sciences, as is evident in Fechner's description of his work as 'psychophysics'. The credit for founding psychology as a discipline is normally given to Wundt, who set up the first experimental laboratory, edited the first professional journal and wrote the first major textbook. For Wundt, psychology entailed the empirical study of human consciousness, with the aim of reducing this to its components. Introspection (or internal perception) was approved as a valid empirical method. Systematic observation could supposedly dismantle consciousness and reveal its universal properties. Later authors, such as E.B. Titchener, were to develop this into a 'structural' psychology that sought to identify the structures behind all human thought. Little was said about cultural relativism or social influences, and the target was to discover universal characteristics. In his later career, Wundt attended to cultural matters through the 'folk psychology' of the arts, language and customs. He accepted that this could not be handled experimentally and would require methods akin to the humanities. His cultural writings, a significant proportion of his total output, have been overlooked and had little effect on psychology as a discipline.

A different perspective emerged with the instinct-habit psychology of William James, who reacted against Wundt and Titchener. As a Darwinist, James moved away from static structures to place psychology within an evolutionary setting. He emphasised the practical consequences of human thought, rather than its components, and paid heed to the physical and social environment. His theorising made a distinction between conscious, reflective thought and unconscious habit or instinct. Conscious thought was needed to tackle and overcome new problems and challenges: it permitted human beings to adapt to new environments, giving them an evolutionary advantage over animal species. Habits and instincts maintained existing behaviour patterns when adaptations were not required: they stabilised behaviour and allowed regular activities without the distraction of conscious thought. Psychologists would have to study unconscious as well as conscious mental processes and unmask the evolutionary purpose of both. Explanation was to be functionalist, in so far that mental processes were explained by their evolutionary functions in sustaining human behaviour and social relations. Such reasoning implied that psychology should consider the social context of human thought and seek functions within that context. James's practical ethos accorded with his pragmatist philosophy and provided theoretical backing for institutional economics (Lawlor, 2006; Barbalet, 2008). His interests were too wide for him to be just a psychologist, though he wrote a psychology textbook (James, 1890). A functionalist school of psychology was established in the US and persisted until the mid-twentieth century but was not destined to become the orthodoxy.

The early twentieth century saw the rise of behaviourism and decline of structural and functionalist psychology. Behaviourism, exemplified by the work of Watson, Pavlov and Skinner, shifted away from the study of consciousness towards the study of observed behaviour. Introspection was criticised as being subjective and unreliable – in its stead came experimental methods. Psychology became stuck firmly in empiricism, at the expense of theory and introspection. Behaviourists dismissed consciousness as 'metaphysical' (despite its prominence in earlier psychology) and carried out stimulus–response experiments. Culture, social context and the growth of the individual were all excluded. Social influences on behaviour were reduced to external stimuli that could be observed to produce conditioned responses – behaviour was viewed as passive and mechanical, with no cultural enhancement of an individual's capacities. The new behaviourist orthodoxy drove psychological research further away from cultural issues.

The potential for a more cultural psychology rested with alternatives to behaviourism. Noteworthy here was the German school of *Gestalt* psychology that arose almost simultaneously with behaviourism in the early twentieth century. *Gestalt* psychologists retained the idea of consciousness and treated it as irreducible. Since the whole of human thought was different from its parts, psychologists had to study the overall form (*Gestalt*) of consciousness and make no attempt to break it down to components or mechanical relations. While not overtly cultural, *Gestalt* psychology permitted the possibility of human consciousness developing within society. To be compatible with culture as a process, psychology has to examine how individual consciousness grows and evolves through interaction with the social environment. These questions were to be seriously investigated only in the second half of the twentieth century with the appearance of cognitive psychology. During the late nineteenth and early twentieth centuries, psychology had an experimental and behaviourist bias that obscured its connections with culture.

**History**

Historical study long predates social sciences. Before the Enlightenment, scholars had written about history without feeling obliged to declare scientific principles. Enlightenment thought presented a challenge because it downgraded historical detail and local circumstances. Cartesian rationalism incited the quest for theoretical systems applicable in all times and places; historical events were trifles that could entice us to mere description and a failure to explain. History would have to adhere to scientific methods or be demoted to lesser status and lack the imprimatur of scientific research. The relation of history to science has been contentious, with friction between those who want to reshape history as a science and those who value its independence.

After the Enlightenment, historical study had two contrasting strands. The first was the attempt to base history on empirical research. Enlightenment thought in its later phases had turned away from Cartesian rationalism towards the empiricism of Locke and Hume, which was more amenable as a basis for historical study. Hume had worked as a historian, and his empiricism seemed to merge history with scientific method. The second strand saw fundamental differences between history and natural sciences. Many Counter-Enlightenment authors (such as Vico and Herder) had undertaken historical studies and, in doing so, realised the gulf between the humanities and natural sciences. History, for them, should not be studied as if it were a natural science. The distinctiveness of history resided in the use of interpretative methods to understand human behaviour within its social context. Copying natural sciences would be futile.

The empiricist strand developed during the eighteenth and nineteenth centuries with the ambition of creating a scientific history equivalent to natural sciences but less reliant on abstract theorising (Haddock, 1980, Chapter 7; Burke, 2005, Chapter 1; Gunn, 2006, Chapter 1). By resorting to empirical methods, the need for prior theory could be eradicated and rationalist objections to history overcome. Scientific history was inductive, such that particular observations were collated and facts ascertained before general laws and principles were derived. In practice, scientific historians devoted most of their efforts to gathering data and hesitated to go further and generalise. The formal method did not require them to make value judgements or interpret historical behaviour – it was enough to accumulate detailed information and trust that this might allow future progress. Empiricism encouraged smaller scale historical work in order to fill gaps in factual information and chronicle past events. The most voluminous empirical research was done by German historians such as Leopold von Ranke and Theodor Mommsen who produced massive tomes on narrow empirical topics not previously covered by historical research. They inspired the German historical school in economics and had the same attitude towards theory – while not opposed to general theorising, they were loath to go beyond observation and reach theoretical conclusions. The strict empiricism meant that their work stood apart from the German cultural and idealist tradition.

The other main strand of historical thought listened to the Counter-Enlightenment and avoided empiricism (Collingwood, 1946; Haddock, 1980, Chapters 8 and 9; Smith, 2007, Chapter 4). History was seen as having special qualities requiring open-mindedness, pluralism and an imaginative understanding of past societies. In Germany, Herder, Fichte, Hegel and others wrote idealist accounts of history that kept their distance from natural sciences. Hegel divided history from nature, viewing history dialectically as being propelled by the opposition of ideas – only by knowing and accepting this could we study history effectively. In the late nineteenth century various philosophers of history proposed an anti-naturalism whereby history was separate from natural science and had its own methods: examples were Heinrich Rickert, Wilhelm Windelband and Wilhelm Dilthey in Germany, F.H. Bradley and T.H. Green in Britain and Benedetto Croce in Italy. While they differed in their arguments, they agreed that history should be set apart from natural sciences and from any social sciences that copied them. For the anti-naturalists, history was not a social science in the sense claimed by economists and sociologists, but stood at the forefront of the humanities in using methods suitable for the study of social behaviour.

During the late nineteenth and early twentieth centuries, when the new social sciences were imitating natural sciences, many historians followed another road. They defended cultural thought and gave it a presence within academic discourse, so that it could not be easily stigmatised as amateurish or idiosyncratic. Some historians went further and confined interpretative methods to history (see, for example, Collingwood, 1946, Part V). The implication was that, outside history, the methods of the natural sciences could resume. Cultural issues are relevant for all social studies, however, and to align interpretative methods with history alone would overstate the uniqueness of historical study and give too much credence to the artificial borderlines between academic disciplines. Rather than retreating into history, interpretative methods should be used wherever they are needed.

# 5. Theory divided: economic, social and cultural (1950–present)

The period since the 1950s has brought a huge expansion of social sciences within the boundaries established previously. Each discipline has garnered many sub-disciplines, but attempts to cross boundaries have been rare, even when topics have overlapped. Truly interdisciplinary work remains scarce, and social sciences have theorised separately, often duplicating arguments. As before, the desire to copy natural science is unremitting and encourages formal empiricism, quantitative techniques and mathematical theory. The core doctrines of most social sciences have continued to be non-cultural.

The second half of the twentieth century did, nevertheless, see a reaction against the positivistic extremes reached in the first half. From the 1960s onwards, dissatisfaction with positivism induced a revival of cultural thought within radical philosophy, the New Left, structuralism, postmodernism and cultural studies. The new ideas were reminiscent of the Counter-Enlightenment and Romanticism, a connection recognised by some authors though not by all. Renewed cultural thought gained many supporters during the late twentieth century and had a bearing on social sciences. While the attention paid to culture helped redress its earlier neglect, the consequences were variable and could not overcome disciplinary divisions.

Orthodox economics, true to its neoclassical ethos, had little time for cultural ideas. The post-war period was marked by the conversion of existing theories into mathematical form and the spread of quantitative techniques; both trends were further exercises in natural-science emulation. Unmoved by the resurgent cultural thought, orthodox economics swung in the opposite direction towards mathematics, econometrics and a militant individualism (evident in the New Right). Other social sciences proved readier to rethink their theories and take a pluralistic attitude. By the late twentieth century the rejuvenated interest in culture had engendered new fields such as cultural studies and cultural theory, which have been cordial to cultural thought. The present chapter examines these developments in more detail: it first considers the mathematisation of economics, before discussing the revival of cultural thought and emergence of cultural studies.

## 5.1   THE MATHEMATISATION OF ECONOMICS

The salient feature of post-war economics was the growth of mathematical methods, leading to what has been termed a formalist revolution (Blaug, 1999; Weintraub, 2002). Pioneered by John Hicks's *Value and Capital*, the mathematisation of neoclassical theory was completed by Paul Samuelson's *Foundations of Economic Analysis* (Hicks, 1939; Samuelson, 1947). Econometrics was refined and standardised by the Cowles Commission in the 1940s and 1950s (Epstein, 1987; Morgan, 1990). The twin influences of mathematical theory and econometrics were to transform orthodox economics. Earlier mathematically trained economists such as Marshall and Keynes had avoided mathematical reasoning, which they viewed as being obscurantist and impolite to the general reader. In contrast, axiomatic and mathematical language was now the hallmark of rigorous theorising to be used wherever possible. From the 1950s, mathematical methods rolled out across the whole of economic research and teaching until they became the norm. Post-war economics has not otherwise undergone radical change – the neoclassical synthesis deflected the potential threat to orthodoxy of Keynesianism, and other major developments (such as game theory) were absorbed into the neoclassical paradigm. The ease with which neoclassical theory lends itself to mathematical expression has reinforced it and undermined alternatives less amenable to mathematics.

Mathematical models were taken up with a minimum of debate or dissent – there was no equivalent of the *Methodenstreit* and no organised body of anti-mathematical economists (Beed and Kane, 1991). Ever since the Counter-Enlightenment, many people had argued against the mathematisation of social science, but these arguments were ignored in the rush to use mathematical techniques. Economic methodology fell out of fashion, and it became widely held that methodological discussion was fruitless and redundant. Effort that could have been devoted to methodology was devoted to econometrics and mathematical theory. Outside economics the post-war period saw lively debate in the philosophy of science, much of which raised doubts about mathematical social science, but orthodox economists disregarded this literature (Beed, 1991). They remained shackled to positivistic methods at a time when the philosophy of science had moved on.

Only a handful of economists voiced serious concerns about mathematical and econometric techniques. Among them was Keynes, whose work on probability and uncertainty made him sceptical of econometrics. His objections were fundamental – he described econometrics as 'black magic' or 'statistical alchemy' and criticised its 'pseudo-analogy' with natural science – and sufficient to throw doubt on quantitative methods (Keynes,

1939; Lawson, 1985a; Pesaran and Smith, 1985). Even though Keynesian economics has often been linked with the birth of econometrics, Keynes himself was critical of econometric estimation; for him, economics was a moral science that should not make ill-judged attempts to mimic natural sciences. John Hicks too was dubious about econometrics, notwithstanding his application of mathematics to economic theory (Hicks, 1956, Chapter 1, 1979). Sensitive to the historical nature of economics, he was willing to have mathematical models as a theoretical abstraction but reluctant to approve their translation into quantitative form. Keynes and Hicks were responsible for the staple content of post-war economic textbooks (aggregate demand analysis; the IS-LM model; indifference curves; constrained optimisation methods), yet neither of them believed that these models were estimable or usable for quantitative policy planning. Their warnings went unheeded as econometrics and mathematical methods burgeoned.

In the absence of methodological debate, why did post-war economics turn so enthusiastically towards mathematics? There were few intellectual reasons for this beyond the perennial desire to imitate natural sciences (Drechsler, 2000, 2004; Hudson, 2000). The turn could have been made much earlier, since the mathematical techniques imported into economics were long familiar to natural scientists: constrained optimisation had been applied in early-nineteenth-century physics, regression analysis in late-nineteenth-century biology. Arguably, the neoclassical project was trying to remodel economic theory in the mould of physics, but economists were slow to take up the associated mathematics (Mirowski, 1989; Ingrao and Israel, 1990). The main reasons for the mathematical turn seem to have been pragmatic and institutional rather than intellectual: a display of mathematical skill could strengthen expert status, create an aura of scientific precision, and distinguish the work of professional economists from that of amateur commentators and laypersons (Katzner, 2003). Those without the necessary skills were compelled to retreat from economic discussion, allowing it to become self-contained and safe from external scrutiny. Mathematics gave a veneer of objectivity, so that economic theory could appear to be technical, value-free and above awkward issues of political economy (Lawson, 2003, Part IV). Once mathematical economists came to occupy senior posts, a cumulative mathematisation could begin. Mathematical fields of study were regarded as the most prestigious, and the Nobel Prize introduced in the late 1960s was usually awarded for mathematical theory or econometrics. The syllabus of economics degrees shifted towards mathematical content (with econometrics elbowing aside methodology), until mathematical techniques were part of the 'toolkit' of any well-educated economist. Abstract mathematical theory came to signify 'advanced' work, even when its practical relevance was less than obvious. Literary economics became vulnerable to rebuke as being old-fashioned, soft and imprecise in comparison with the modern, hard and rigorous methods of mathematical economists.

Heterodoxy was more sympathetic to a non-mathematical perspective but was overpowered within the economics profession. Post Keynesians, who sought to preserve Keynesian ideas as a clear alternative to neoclassicism, were marginalised from mainstream discourse centred on the neoclassical synthesis. The same was true of other schools of heterodox thought: Marxian economics, never fully accepted as respectable social science, operated independently as a cross-disciplinary tradition; the German historical school was irretrievably damaged by its ties with nationalism and did not survive into the post-war era; the American institutionalists found it tough to compete with the apparent technical sophistication of the economic mainstream. Heterodox economics did not lose ground because it was defeated in academic debate or because the mainstream had stunning empirical and predictive successes. The crux of the matter was institutional: neoclassical orthodoxy was well suited to the post-war political climate and could be reproduced and fortified through the appointments and promotions system, the editing of journals and the training of new generations of students.

The sidelining of heterodoxy and dominance of neoclassicism guaranteed that cultural approaches were ruled out. Neoclassical theory, as it flourished in the post-war period, eliminated culture or history from economic analysis. The split between economics and culture, present since the origins of modern economics, had finally been made official and institutionalised. From the 1960s onwards, the institutional (if not intellectual) triumph of neoclassical economics led to calls for the 'economic way of thinking' to be exported into other disciplines and for all human behaviour to be investigated using neoclassical, rational-choice theories (Tullock, 1972; Becker, 1976; Hirshleifer, 1985). Rather than recognising the limits of neoclassicism, the aim was to trumpet its virtues and spread a culture-free neoclassical method across all social sciences. That such an aim could be taken seriously showed how far orthodox economics had become detached from cultural thought.

## 5.2   DISCIPLINARY DIVISIONS

Other social sciences did not embrace mathematics with the same fervour as economists and remained non-mathematical. Use of mathematics did enter certain sub-disciplines (such as mathematical sociology) but never went as far as it did in economics. This asymmetry allowed orthodox economists to enjoy a putative superiority in adopting precise scientific methods contrasted with the woolliness of lesser disciplines. Mathematical theorising became the cynosure of orthodox economics and bolstered the tendency for economics to be defined by its theories not its subject matter. All disciplines saw a large expansion of formal theory during the post-war period. Each discipline stood alone and had its own theories, career structure, departments and journals. Separate theories and methods confirmed the divisions among disciplines.

With orthodox economics dedicated to individualism, other disciplines chose structural theories. In the 1940s, sociology swayed towards the structural-functionalism of Talcott Parsons, which portrays human behaviour as role determined and governed by social structures (Parsons, 1937, 1951). Parsonian theory was the sociological mainstream until the 1960s, abetting the dichotomy between individualistic 'economic' approaches and structural 'sociological' ones. This division, convenient to both disciplines as a boundary, was not entirely accidental. Parsons, who had received a wide-ranging education in economics and sociology, should have been well aware of the potential for structural/institutional methods in economics and for individualistic/interpretative methods in sociology. His later academic work was skewed by the need to define and demarcate sociology – he made a gentleman's agreement with economists to stay away from 'economic' approaches and use structural, role-based theorising (Ingham, 1996; Hodgson, 2001a, Chapter 13; Milonakis and Fine, 2008, Chapter 12). As with the Robbins definition of economics, sociology was to be defined by its methods: it was granted academic territory on condition that it should quit the territory of economics, which was abandoned to neoclassical theory (harming the institutional alternatives to neoclassicism). Structural-functionalist sociology was a less robust orthodoxy than neoclassical economics and lost this status in the 1960s, to be replaced by greater pluralism. Yet the Parsonian economics/sociology division has lingered in the image of economics as being individualistic and sociology as being structural.

Strong divisions between disciplines have restricted interdisciplinary discourse and deterred reflection upon method. Any pluralism has had to be internal to each discipline and accommodated with the orthodox position, if such orthodoxy exists. Economics has been the least pluralistic social science through its efforts to set up neoclassical theory as a body of core principles. The post-war period has seen endless variations on the neoclassical model, but the basic assumptions have stayed intact and delineate the 'economic method'. Heterodox economists have criticised orthodoxy without being able to sap its institutional supremacy. Since economics has been equated with neoclassicism and taught in this way to generations of students, those wishing to pursue alternative ideas must depart from orthodoxy and impair their career opportunities as academic economists. Other social sciences, such as sociology, anthropology and psychology, have not had the same commitment to a single orthodox position. Orthodox economists might dismiss this as incoherence, but it shows willingness to think critically and query assumptions. A problem with internal arguments within disciplines is that they frequently cover the same ground in different conceptual language, especially when addressing questions of structure and agency common to all social sciences. These private debates would benefit from greater cross-disciplinary discussion.

On the whole, cultural thought has not been well catered for in social science and struggled to find acceptance. Orthodox economics offers the least fertile soil, as its neoclassicism abstracts from culture: a cultural method in economics would imply leaving the mainstream. In other disciplines, cultural thought has found a place alongside less cultural alternatives. Sociology, despite its structural image, has seen renewed interest in Weberian interpretative methods and a boom in non-reductionist social theory. Anthropology too has preserved its interpretative cultural branches in the vein of Boas and the substantivists, which stand beside formalist and individualistic branches. With the growth of cognitive psychology in the 1960s, psychology began to ask how social context moulds the individual. These cultural elements proceeded independently, without much sense of common cause, and forged separate concepts and terminology. Cultural methods became fragmented and partitioned to fit into a few enclaves within the non-economic social sciences, where they were tolerated. No social science has settled on cultural thought as its orthodox standpoint.

A thoroughgoing case for the importance of culture needs to be free from disciplinary boundaries. In the nineteenth century, before modern social science, the case was made by literary and social critics outside academia. Today non-academic voices would be unlikely to get a hearing – without the kudos of science they would be rebuffed as amateurish, inexpert and unprofessional. Recent arguments for a cultural approach have come from academic authors unhappy with disciplinary boundaries and conventional social science. These arguments, taken together, have revived cultural thought within the last fifty years or so.

## 5.3 THE REVIVAL OF CULTURAL THOUGHT SINCE THE 1960S

The first half of the twentieth century marked a peak in the desire for codified scientific methods and grand, universal theories: examples of this were logical positivism in the philosophy of science, theoretical system-building in economics, sociology and anthropology, and behaviourism in psychology. By the second half of the century, the intellectual environment had changed. Attempts to find a single, watertight scientific method had failed, and supposedly universal theories were flawed. Dissatisfaction roused a search for alternatives; the late twentieth century witnessed a return to cultural and relativistic thought which crossed disciplinary boundaries and challenged scientific orthodoxy. While the effect of the cultural revival has differed across disciplines, the general outcome has been to increase awareness of culture. Cultural ideas have still not penetrated mainstream social science (especially in economics) but they are more secure than they were in the early twentieth century. Three sources for the cultural revival can be identified, namely scientific methodology, the New Left, and postmodernism.

**Scientific Methodology**

Philosophers of science have always wanted a universal, absolute scientific method that could uncover truth in any field of enquiry. This was a lodestone of the Enlightenment and motivated natural and social sciences. During the nineteenth century, formal scientific methods acquired the label 'positivism' through their quest for positive, value-free knowledge untarnished by subjectivity, prejudice, superstition or metaphysics. Positivist goals were seen as a prerequisite of science, even though positivism was never clarified. A strenuous effort to define positivism was made only in the early twentieth century with the logical positivism of the Vienna Circle (Ayer, 1959; Hanfling, 1981). Explicitly aimed at unifying science, it applied tight logical analysis to the empiricism that underlay scientific work. Among its principles were the primacy of observation as the source of knowledge, the need for formal logic in deriving knowledge from observation, the belief in a global methodology for all scientific disciplines, and the rejection of metaphysics. Once systematised, it would reveal the fundamentals of scientific method and differentiate scientific from non-scientific work. Through logical positivism and its offshoots, the early twentieth century was the summit of endeavours to realise a universal scientific method.

Difficulties quickly became apparent, and no consensus was ever to be reached on unified scientific practices. Logical positivism suffered internal setbacks that could not be resolved, such as the failure to find conclusive ways to verify or falsify statements, the uncertain status of scientific laws or theories not open to observational tests, doubts surrounding the impartiality and neutrality of observation, and limits to explanations from empirical correlations. Its adherents gradually diluted it into milder forms that were less insistent on every scientific statement being empirically testable and allowed greater leeway for theorising and speculation. The best known internal critique came from Karl Popper, who was to have a big influence on orthodox economic methodology (Popper, 1959, 1965; Caldwell, 1982, Chapter 4). Popper worried about the obstacles facing inductive methods, given the impossibility of verification, and chose instead to champion deductive methods based on falsification. Science should formulate bold hypotheses independently of prior observation and then test them empirically – successful theories would pass the tests and escape being falsified. Though packaged as a critique of positivism, Popper's beliefs were still positivistic. He placed a heavy weight on empirical tests and sought a single method for all sciences; his writings have a positivistic scent, notwithstanding his professed opposition to positivism.

More comprehensive critiques of positivism emerged in the 1960s with the 'growth of knowledge' tradition (Caldwell, 1982, Chapter 5). Philosophers of science became interested in the social and cultural context of scientific research, as against the abstract and unified methodologies of the positivists. The chief stimulus here was Thomas Kuhn's work on scientific revolutions (Kuhn, 1962). According to Kuhn, science progresses through a sequence of theories that are usually stable but occasionally challenged and overthrown in scientific revolutions. A scientific community defines itself around a common paradigm or set of beliefs and practices which reigns through prolonged periods of 'normal science' and changes only after a crisis or revolution that forces a rethink about basic tenets. Scientific revolutions occur not through abstract verification or falsification but through subjective and disorderly argument. The ultimate success of a scientific revolution depends on the merits of the new theories but also on the social relations and institutions behind scientific debate – revolutionary ideas survive and prosper only if they can interrupt the reproduction of the previous orthodoxy and upset existing hierarchies within scientific disciplines. From this viewpoint, scientific method rests upon the social and cultural backdrop of scientific practice, not a list of stylised principles evoking an ideal seldom if ever attained in reality.

Kuhn's social and cultural emphasis switched towards a historical/relativist view and away from absolute rules of scientific method. Uneasy about the relativism, Imre Lakatos tried for a compromise between Kuhn and Popper. He adapted Popper's falsificationism and, instead of applying it to individual theories, applied it to groups of related theories termed 'scientific research programmes' (Lakatos, 1970). According to him, a scientific research programme is progressive if it generates new theories open to formal empirical tests and confirmed by these tests; it is degenerative if it has a merely defensive strategy designed to protect existing theories by revising them in response to new empirical findings. Science should be organised around progressive research programmes and forsake degenerating ones that perpetuate outmoded orthodoxies. Lakatos offered advice about how research should proceed, while noting the social context and historical specificity of particular research programmes. The purported compromise between absolute and relative aspects of science has not been generally accepted, and the prescriptive side of Lakatos has attracted much criticism. Difficulties arise from the categorisation of progressive and degenerative research programmes, which is prone to subjectivity, and the reliance on falsification, which is vulnerable to the same criticisms as Popper's methodology.

The strongest sally against positivistic science can be found in the writings of Paul Feyerabend, who went as far as to deny the value of any formal method (Feyerabend, 1975, 1987). Scientific progress, for Feyerabend, has never been accomplished by slavery to methodological principles; on the contrary, creative scientific work has been anarchical and either indifferent or hostile to prevailing methods. To formalise and codify scientific method would be counterproductive because it would choke off creativity, thin out the range of scientific enterprise and condemn fruitful theories to non-scientific status. Feyerabend discarded positivist goals and took a historicist and relativist stance. Science, if defined too narrowly, could suppress diverse thought, slow down intellectual progress and impose a dull uniformity on human activities – the liberal alternative would be to abandon method and dismantle the fences around scientific work. The complexity of the real world means that oversimplified procedures are unhelpful and hold back the acquisition of knowledge. Scientific rules are part of a particular cultural attitude, derived from Enlightenment philosophy, which lays down its own values universally and eradicates alternatives.

During the late twentieth century, philosophy of science moved away from positivism towards culture and historical context. Most of the literature addressed the natural sciences, but the issues were equally germane to economics. Curiously, as the natural sciences gave up on positivism, orthodox economics ignored the warnings and reaffirmed its loyalty to positivistic methods (Caldwell, 1982, Part 2; McCloskey, 1983; Beed, 1991; Hands, 1993). Anxious to be a hard empirical science, it favoured Friedman's predictive instrumentalism and Popper's falsificationism (Blaug, 1992, Chapter 4). The anti-positivist literature was either bypassed or met by calls to tighten existing formal methods so as to close loopholes and achieve greater rigour. Acknowledgement of the wider methodological debates has been left to heterodox economics and the non-economic social sciences.

## The New Left

The New Left was a radical political and academic movement that began in the late 1950s and thrived in the 1960s and 1970s. It was born out of dismay at the political alternatives on offer during the Cold War – the seed was the reaction of European academics to the Suez crisis and the Soviet invasion of Hungary in 1956 (Thompson, 1960). Searching for new forms of radicalism, these academics lost faith with the orthodox social sciences of the West and the official ideologies of the East. Always diverse, the New Left had no single theory or doctrine and to do so would have gone against its core beliefs. In general usage, it is identified with the political activism of the 1960s, but the present discussion concentrates on its academic work, which had two main threads: the first was humanistic and sceptical of universal, ahistorical theory; the second was theoretical and sought theoretical alternatives to orthodoxy. Both argued for the relevance of culture, though they treated it in sharply different ways.

The humanistic thread originated with British writers in the late 1950s – the key authors were Raymond Williams and E.P. Thompson. As a left-wing literary critic, Raymond Williams brought out and extended the critique of capitalism embedded in the English literary tradition; *Culture and Society* was a classic account of how English literature has grappled with the social and cultural consequences of capitalism (Williams, 1958a). His own critical views, an updating of earlier cultural critiques, emphasised how new media have instilled a uniform, docile mass culture (Williams, 1981a, 1989a). To remedy this would require a 'long revolution' to liberate people from debased mass culture and improve their capacities to live fuller, more rewarding lives (Williams, 1961). Amid all his work was the ubiquity and pervasiveness of culture and its role in shaping our experiences. The historian E.P. Thompson wrote a revisionist biography of William Morris, in which he gave pride of place to Morris's oft-neglected radicalism (Thompson, 1955). Much influenced by Morris, he went on to propound a humanistic and cultural variant of radical history. His magnum opus was *The Making of the English Working Class*, which traced the cultures behind class consciousness and resistance to capitalism (Thompson, 1963). For Thompson as for Williams, fundamental social change would come only from cultures capable of standing outside and challenging capitalist institutions and belief-systems. Academics, if they were to comprehend this, should be studying and debating cultural matters.

A possible weakness of such cultural radicalism is that it seemed to hark back to the Romantic anti-capitalism that Marx had rejected as idealist and reactionary. Marxian theorists could rubbish cultural arguments for being blind to material production as the driving force behind economic and social change. In reply to accusations of idealism, Williams moved in his later writings towards cultural materialism, an explicitly materialist view that included the material circumstances of cultural reproduction (Williams, 1977, 1980). He continued to assert the centrality of culture in social change but recognised that culture relies on material reproduction if it is to survive. Ideas and culture could have an independent effect on economic and social change, although a culture must ultimately be sustained by material production. Cultural materialism ensured that New Left cultural critiques complied with Marxian doctrines and avoided idealism, while stopping short of a reductionist causal materialism. The theoretical content of the cultural arguments remained quite low, and beyond a limited materialism it was not felt necessary to theorise about how culture is linked to economic and social changes.

The second thread of New Left thought wanted a formal theoretical analysis as an alternative to orthodoxy. Universal in scope and internationalist, the arguments drew on the Western Marxist tradition of Lukács, Gramsci and the Frankfurt School. Many of these ideas went as far back as the 1920s but had remained largely unknown and came to prominence only during the 1960s and 1970s. Herbert Marcuse and Erich Fromm, who reiterated and extended the Frankfurt School approach, were influential at this time (Marcuse, 1964; Fromm, 1956, 1961). Another element was the structuralism applied to Marxian thought by Louis Althusser. Structuralism had started in linguistics through the argument that language has an independent structural form distinct from the things it refers to, so that culture and language may have only a loose, fluid connection to the material world. Theory must therefore tackle language and culture as topics in their own right, without subordinating them to economics or other factors. Althusserian Marxism was a reworking of structuralist ideas that fitted them within a Marxian scheme (Althusser, 1969; Althusser and Balibar, 1970). According to Althusser, culture has relative autonomy as a structural level within a larger stratified framework; it is not determined wholly by material forces and plays a major part in supporting social classes and hierarchies. His analysis was universal, ahistorical, anti-humanist and allegedly scientific. In the distinction between the early 'humanist' Marx and the late 'scientific' one, Althusser claimed to be following and augmenting the late Marx. Althusserian Marxism, by attempting to integrate culture into Marxian theory, became the dominant school of New Left theorising.

The humanistic and theoretical threads of the New Left, despite their shared radicalism and interest in culture, had many disagreements. An obvious difference was in attitudes towards natural sciences: the humanists detested imitation of natural science, whereas the Althusserians hoped to preserve and renovate Marxian scientific socialism. Some New Left scholars undertook historical and literary study, whereas others opted for general, timeless theory. Vigorous conflicts sprang up within the New Left, best illustrated by E.P. Thompson's lengthy polemic against structuralist Marxism (Thompson, 1978). The disagreements could never be reconciled, and the two sides of the New Left were eventually to feed into cultural studies, post-structuralism and postmodernism. Yet the New Left was united in its arguments for the importance of culture; the internal clashes were only about how culture should be handled.

New Left thought had a big impact on social science and cultural studies, but economics was an exception as few New Left writings were addressed directly to economic issues. Orthodox economics remained neoclassical and resisted the New Left – the political disquiet of the 1960s triggered a shift by many economists towards the New Right, monetarism and neo-liberalism. Far from welcoming a cultural approach, orthodox economics became the fountainhead of political opposition to the New Left. The 1960s saw heterodox developments, with radical economics as a new field of study, but even here the input of the New Left was minor. Much of radical economics followed the ongoing Marxian tradition, not the ideas of New Left writers. Cultural thought did enter a few strands of heterodox economics, such as the Regulation School, which found inspiration in Althusserian Marxism, and Braverman's critique of scientific management (Braverman, 1974; Lipietz, 1993). New Left interest in culture also helped animate radical institutionalism (Dugger, 1988, 1989; Dugger and Waller, 1996; Stanfield, 1995). Heterodox economics had an affinity with the New Left, but there was no cohesive New Left economics to set against the neo-liberalism of the New Right. The anti-cultural bias in orthodox economics meant that few economists appreciated or reflected upon New Left ideas.

**Postmodernism**

By the 1980s the doubts about positivism had crystallised into what became known as postmodernism. As the name implies, postmodernism aims to grasp the characteristics of modernism and go beyond them. Modernism has been notoriously hard to define, given that it never really existed as a single intellectual movement and took many guises. The word 'modern' first appeared in the English language during the sixteenth century, when it was used to distinguish modern from ancient and medieval times; 'modernity' can be linked with the Enlightenment and capitalist economic development, but 'modernism' is more recent and refers (retrospectively) to intellectual trends of the late nineteenth and early twentieth centuries (Williams, 1989b; Pippin, 1999, Chapter 2; Gunn, 2006, Chapter 5). Broadly speaking, modernism engages with the modern world (modernity) that has arisen from capitalism and the associated scientific and technological changes. Modernist thought rejected previous traditions and customs in order to break with the past and imbibe the special, ahistorical qualities of modernity (Berman, 1983; Harvey, 1990, Chapter 2). In the sciences, modernism has seen attempts to tie down the principles of scientific method, as exemplified by the logical positivists; in the arts and humanities, it describes those movements ('-isms') which symbolise and portray the fragmentary, rootless nature of life in modern capitalist societies. Modernist thinkers varied in their attitudes to capitalism but concurred on the changes it had brought about and the need to acknowledge them in intellectual and artistic work.

Postmodern arguments go further by querying the ability to place a logical structure on the modern world; they dwell on the problems of modernism without necessarily being anti-modernist (Jameson, 1991, Chapter 2). Instead of trying to control the fragmentation of contemporary life, postmodernism accepts it as a feature of modernity and comes to terms with it. While still fully cognisant of modernity, postmodernism responds to it differently. Central to postmodernism is the reaction against the scientific and artistic projects of the early twentieth century. Faith in our ability to marshal modernity and tame it into smooth, continuous social improvement has eroded. The record of warfare, political unrest, global inequality and environmental damage in the twentieth century has shaken earlier assumptions about the benefits of economic and technical change. Grand narratives of scientific progress derived from the Enlightenment have been interrogated and criticised (Lyotard, 1984; Touraine, 1995). Postmodernism turned away from sober modernism and took on a light, irreverent tone. With science no longer on a pedestal, non-scientific thought could be rehabilitated. Historical styles of art and architecture, scoffed at by modernists, resurfaced in an unsystematic, haphazard fashion. The formalisation of everything into scientific language was defied and replaced with informality and pluralism. Universal schemes were set aside in favour of localisation and diversity.

Postmodernism has had no theoretical basis as such but has run in parallel with relativistic theorising, as in the passage from structuralism to post-structuralism (Jenks, 1993, Chapter 7; Milner and Browitt, 2002, Chapter 4). Although structuralism could model culture through linguistic structures and social conventions, it retained positivistic values by seeking deeper meanings and truths. The post-structuralism of Derrida and Foucault moved further towards relativism by denying that texts had a fixed meaning or authorial voice and pointing to the indefinite capability for re-interpretation – in Derrida's terminology, any text could be deconstructed to show its failure to establish its declared meaning. The openness of meaning raised the possibility of manipulation and control, as stressed by Foucault, and gave a reminder of how difficult it was for academics to uncover truth. Another example of relativism was the revival of pragmatist philosophies that cast doubt on absolute knowledge: Richard Rorty, for instance, demolished any single, objective reality that could be the foundation for science (Rorty, 1980, 1991). Disillusionment with twentieth-century science led to arguments against objective scientific truth.

Like scientific methodology and the New Left, postmodernism has made little impression on orthodox economics. There may be some postmodern glimmerings but, if so, they are tacit and unremarked by orthodox economists themselves (Ruccio and Amariglio, 2003, Chapter 3). Heterodox economists have been more attentive to postmodernism and asked how it relates to the economy. From the viewpoint of Marxian and Regulation approaches, it reflects economic and social changes (Fordism to post-Fordism) bound up with information technology (Harvey, 1990; Jameson, 1991; Boyer and Saillard, 2002). Postmodernism is a symptom of the increased diversity, decentralisation and fluidity of society in the post-Fordist era. Such views confirm its significance and tie it to economic development but afford it little autonomy and see it as the next stage in the ongoing materialist account of history. Whether postmodernism can be given an adequate materialist explanation is a moot point, and any coupling between postmodern thought and prevailing economic conditions is inevitably complex.

Postmodern relativism and diversity have a kinship with the earlier ideas of the Counter-Enlightenment and Romanticism. In its strongest forms, postmodernism has relativised reality and undermined the Enlightenment belief in disinterested scientific study. The writers of the Counter-Enlightenment never went this far, as their critiques left space for study of society by alternative methods. Sceptics about postmodernism have viewed it as a defeatist or escapist overreaction to the difficulties of the late twentieth century, which has exaggerated the shift away from modernity (Callinicos, 1989; Eagleton, 1996). Many postmodernists have been the disappointed radicals of the 1960s and 1970s who, when faced with the onslaught of the New Right and neo-liberalism in the 1980s, retreated into idle musings about language and culture (Eagleton, 2003). What seems to be a fundamental critique of the Enlightenment may be failing to get to grips with current political changes and, by default, endorsing and sustaining them. Relativistic extremes prevent not only science but social criticism. Playfulness and skittishness may blunt one's critical faculties and jeopardise one's understanding of reality.

## 5.4 CULTURAL STUDIES AND CULTURAL THEORY

The revival of cultural thought has brought the emergence and growth of cultural studies (Inglis, 1993; Turner, 2003). Now a separate field, it has argued for the pervasiveness of culture but (unlike anthropology) looked at modern developed societies. It has sought to elude cultural elitism by investigating popular culture, together with the role of the media in creating and propagating this. Paying heed to technology is unavoidable here, since popular culture requires material dissemination (press, television, radio, telecommunications, Internet, etc.). The prime topic of interest has been the mass media, and media studies are now a specialised area within cultural studies. Other topics have been the divisions, fragmentation and diversity in modern societies, and the issues broached by feminism, multiculturalism and post-colonialism. By the late twentieth century cultural studies had swelled into a new academic discipline with its own journals, departments, courses, and sub-disciplines.

Cultural studies has encouraged theorising about culture, which is often designated as cultural theory to be set alongside economic theory and social theory. Major influences on cultural theory have been the Romantic critique of capitalism, the Marxian tradition (especially Gramsci and the Frankfurt School) and structuralism/post-structuralism (Jenks, 1993; Swingewood, 1998; Milner and Browitt, 2002; Barker, 2007). Cultural theorists have the same dilemma as the New Left: they could either be suspicious of abstract theories or construct novel theories to accommodate culture. They have met the dilemma in different ways, yielding a bifurcation between humanistic and structural varieties of cultural studies (Hall, 1980). Most cultural theory tends towards the structural position, having sympathised with Althusserian Marxism and post-structuralism, but no single model is supreme. To sunder cultural theory from social or economic theory would be an error, given that culture must depend on social behaviour and material production. The questions posed by cultural theory resemble those posed by social or economic theory, and rigid boundaries between them would be arbitrary and unhelpful.

Within cultural studies, the bonds between economics and culture have come to the fore in what has been termed the political-economy approach (Garnham, 1977, 1979; Golding and Murdock, 1991; Mosco, 1996; Maxwell, 2001; Calabrese and Sparks, 2003). The general outlook, influenced by Marxism, regards cultural practices as based in material production and subject to the historical processes of economic development. An overriding concern is the rise of mass media in the twentieth century and the way that they have reproduced and legitimised the prevailing institutions and class relations (Schiller, 1973, 1989). The media are studied as commercial entities inside modern industrial capitalism. A drift towards concentration and centralisation has brought the pre-eminence of a few global corporations with interests in the press, television, telecommunications and other media. The political-economy approach examines the ownership and management of these corporations, as well as their editorial policies, commercial/advertising practices and relations with governmental and other organisations. Their activities are liable to shape society at large, in so far that they control the flow of information to the public and determine how this information is presented. A 'consensus' can be fabricated merely by repeating a particular viewpoint in the media, while shunning alternatives or portraying them negatively. Material forces underlie the analysis, but it allows for the top-down moulding of standardised beliefs and behaviour. The materialism harmonises with heterodox economics, especially its Marxian and institutionalist variants.

In recent years, various authors have argued that current economic and technical changes will yield a cultural transformation towards the 'information society' (Lyon, 1988; Webster, 2002). The arguments have a materialist flavour through the appeal to advances in technology such as microelectronics, computing, telecommunications and the Internet. Economically, the information society should replace manual work in manufacturing with non-manual work in service industries that use information technology. Traditional hierarchical business organisation should be supplemented by looser personal relations or networks made possible by improved communications (Castells, 2000). The new technologies, though materially based, are viewed as switching us from physical manufacturing into an immaterial or virtual realm of information and services. An information society should enhance the role of the media and increase their range and diversity as new information sources become available. The changes wrought by the informational revolution are predicted to be on a scale equivalent to the Industrial Revolution of the eighteenth and nineteenth centuries. Some have doubted the impact of information technology and the likelihood of an information society or 'new economy' (Garnham, 2000; May, 2002; Henwood, 2003). Among the problems are the continued importance of manufacturing industries, the low profile of the information sector at the macroeconomic level, the modest contribution of information technology to productivity growth, the tendency for the virtual economy to be subject to short-term booms and busts, and the prominence of low-skilled service employment unrelated to information technology. One should be cautious in drawing conclusions about a transformed way of life, but the debates about an information society do at least relate economics to culture.

The economically based strands within cultural studies have whipped up tensions with those who wish to focus on the media and popular culture: the political-economy approach has been viewed as diverging from the core domain of cultural studies (Garnham, 1995, 1997; Grossberg, 1995; Kellner, 1997). These tensions have yielded an economics/culture divide within cultural studies similar to that within other disciplines (Robotham, 2005, Chapter 1; Peck, 2006). Critics of the political-economy approach see it as economically reductionist and subordinating cultural studies to Marxism. The preferred alternatives are postmodernist and post-structuralist theories that allow culture to be autonomous and studied separately from the economy. An idealist angle replaces a materialist one, even if the idealism is covert. The political-economy approach has also been chided for overemphasising class divisions and underestimating the other differences discussed in feminism and post-colonialism. Cultural studies should, the critics claim, avoid making economic arguments and stick to popular culture, which forms an object of study in its own right – to invoke economics is to be insufficiently cultural. Erecting a wall around cultural studies would demarcate it from other disciplines but hamper a complete understanding of culture. A strict economics/culture divide is as detrimental to the study of culture as it is to the study of economics.

Cultural studies has had to fight for acceptance as an academic discipline. Close scrutiny of popular culture makes it vulnerable to criticism for being trivial, chatting about ephemera and failing to address serious intellectual problems. Its terrain could be covered by sociology, anthropology, history and economics, so that a new cultural discipline might be deemed superfluous. Defying the opposition, it has expanded and seems set to be institutionalised as a permanent, full-scale academic subject. Even though some of the doubts may have substance, it should be welcomed as giving durability to the revival of cultural thought. With cultural studies in place, academic work is more likely to appreciate culture and less likely to brush it aside.

To have a branch of study dealing with culture is, all the same, somewhat anomalous and ratifies the overspecialisation within modern academia. Most authors belonging to the cultural tradition distrusted specialised disciplines and would not have wanted the treatment of culture to follow the same route. On practical grounds, cultural studies may need to carve out and protect its own province in order to survive in the current academic environment, but this has no intellectual warrant and goes against cultural thought. The existence of cultural studies sanctions the narrowness of 'non-cultural' social sciences – orthodox economists can justify their neglect of culture by claiming that it lies beyond their remit and should be discussed elsewhere. A discipline of cultural studies suggests that culture and economics are separate. Although detailed study of culture is valuable, it should ideally be spread across all social sciences and not held apart as a specialised subject. Cultural studies and cultural theory have added new disciplinary boundaries and given institutional form to the economics/culture divide.

# 6. Common themes

The cultural critique of economics has lasted for two hundred years without ever being organised programmatically; given the diversity of cultural thought, no single set of principles can encompass it. Cultural criticism never went by fixed principles and defended a pluralism that ruled out dogmatic prescriptions about method. One can, nevertheless, discern common themes that were widely articulated. The present chapter summarises these themes and assesses their consequences for the economics/culture divide.

## 6.1 THE MAIN ARGUMENTS

Cultural critics of economics have made many arguments. The style, manner and language of the criticism are by no means uniform, and the preferred alternatives to orthodoxy do not converge on any specific ideal. Rather than purveying another theoretical system, cultural critics pointed to how human behaviour and social relations differ from their portrayal by orthodox economics. The most important arguments are considered below.

**Culture as a Process**

In its origins, cultural thought referred to a process of cultivation, whereby individuals acquire their beliefs, values and personal capacities from their social surroundings. A cultural method implies that all people grow up within a social environment and do not have a fixed, unchanging character from birth. Theorising should examine the institutional and cultural context; any notion of natural economic behaviour should be rejected. If people do have distinctive economic behaviour, then the economist should be asking how and why this came about.

**Relativities**

Cultural methods avoid timeless and universal theorising. Diverse economic arrangements should not be forced into a predetermined model that oversimplifies them and obscures their diversity. Theorising should be relative to local circumstances and not expressed in an unqualified form on the implicit assumption that it applies everywhere. If a theory claims wide applicability, then the onus is on the theorist to explain why and tell us about any limits. The intricacy of modern economies suggests that few theories could have universal relevance.

## Realism

Despite its relativistic tendencies, cultural thought in its original form was clear that we could investigate culture. The Counter-Enlightenment, though critical of social studies copying natural science, was an offshoot of the Enlightenment and had the same objective, that is, a quest for disinterested knowledge. The aim was to find the right method for social studies, not to denigrate or nullify them. Later cultural thought, especially in its postmodernist dress, has pushed relativism further and denied any objective reality independent of scientific investigation. Anti-realism muddies the waters and threatens the rationale for academic study. Postmodernism has drifted away from the initial goals of cultural thought, which were to acquire knowledge about social behaviour.

## Imperfection

A hallmark of cultural thought is a reluctance to believe in perfect individual or social states. Diverse human behaviour overwhelms any ideal template and quashes any delusions that we are evolving on a path to perfection. This attitude shares the humility of medieval philosophy, in which only the supernatural could be perfect, but dispenses with the supernaturalism and leaves human activity open-ended. At most, perfection should only be a mirage that drives human endeavours but is unattainable and remains far distant (a view termed the 'philosophy of the imperfect' in nineteenth-century literature). If ever perfection were reached, then creativity and diversity would fade away. Enlightenment thought, by contrast, took perfection seriously and made practical, Utopian proposals for ideal social organisation: perfection was seen instrumentally as a target not yet attained but attainable through scientific knowledge and social reform. Such proposals have been alien to cultural thought, which regards them as oversimplified, judgemental, and destructive of human variety.

## Subjectivity and Creativity

Accepting that individuals are formed within society does not mean that their actions are socially determined. The process of culture, within a specific social context, builds up individual capacities to do new things, play constructive roles in society, and think creatively. People are subjects not objects and should not be modelled as reacting predictably to external stimuli. Culture goes beyond replication of a way of life and indoctrination in belief systems and social practices. Those who undergo a process of culture have the potential to change the course of future social development. Culture is vital not only to the reproduction of economies and societies but to their growth and evolution.

## Social Construction

Cultural thought has rested on the premise that social reality is independent of the activities of the investigator but not of human activities as a whole. Institutions have been created by past generations and are reproduced and transformed by current generations. Many components of an economy are socially constructed: firms, households, markets, governments, money and accounting systems are social artefacts and should be depicted accordingly. This contrasts with the natural forces and real economic variables in neoclassical theory. From a cultural perspective, all economies combine material and socially constructed elements.

## Rejection of Individualistic and Structural Reductionism

If culture is a process, then economic and social theorising needs to take in both individual behaviour and social institutions. Reductionist explanations founded wholly on individual agents or social structures are one-sided and inadequate. The cultivation of individuals within society guarantees that individual and social levels of analysis are intertwined – agents rely on society for their capacities to act, while society can be reproduced and transformed only through agency. An economic or social theory that is culturally aware should be non-reductionist and give no primacy to agency or structure.

## Layering

Economics, by virtue of its subject matter, must deal with production, distribution and consumption. Unavoidably it has a material dimension and cannot proceed entirely in terms of ideas, beliefs or values. Culture, on the other hand, has often been given idealist interpretations that separate it from the material world. In practice, culture in all its definitions (process, way of life, the arts) needs material support. The co-presence of ideas and material factors brings a layered or stratified theory with various layers that coexist and interact. Cultural thought should not rest on ideas alone, nor should economics rest solely on material objects. Theorising should be rich enough to have multiple layers, in order to examine how ideas, institutions and personal relations jointly affect economic life.

## Emergence

Even if theorising is layered, it can still be drawn towards reductionism whereby one layer takes precedence over the others. Cultural thought, when it views culture as a process, asserts the interdependence of social and individual levels – individuals are sculpted and cultivated within society but, as a result, have the creative capacities to implement social changes. Material welfare is a prerequisite for human agency without dictating human actions or denying free will. A layered, non-reductionist framework suggests emergent powers: any layer can exert causal powers that depend on other layers but are not reducible to them. Higher layers such as ideas or institutions are not wholly explicable through lower layers such as individual agency, material production or human biology. Cultural methods permit social sciences that are rooted in the material world without imploding into biology or other natural sciences.

## Distrust of Mechanistic Analogies

Human behaviour cannot be understood through axiomatic models on the pattern of Newtonian mechanics, Benthamite utilitarianism or neoclassical economic theory. Far from being machine-like, people display complex and volatile behaviour that may show little consistency or rationality. To use mechanistic theory is to draw a false analogy with physics or engineering: it compresses human behaviour and fails to provide a theoretical system to cover all economic activity. Cultural approaches keep their distance from physics and other natural sciences, avoid portraying behaviour mathematically, and promote alternative methods better suited to social studies.

## Symbolism

Cultural thought has been receptive to symbolism, in contrast with the scientific tradition that has played it down and minimised it. Denial of symbolism began with Enlightenment contempt for the medieval period, which had used symbols to represent the supernatural. Banishing religion meant that this symbolism was redundant, and rationalism attached theoretical concepts directly to their intended objects rather than symbolically. The Counter-Enlightenment tolerated symbolism not for its connections with the supernatural but for its role in shaping social relations and cultural identity: to understand a society and its members, one had to study and know its symbols. Postmodernism has argued that, as societies become richer and material needs are fulfilled, consumption activities are motivated increasingly by symbolic value.

## Power and Authority

Culture implies that personal capacities are only partly biological and depend on cultivation within a social context. The ability to do things is bestowed by family background, national culture, education, life experiences, and access to social positions. In a hierarchical society, cultural processes reflect the pre-existing hierarchy: people born into a given rank are socialised to participate at that rank. Culture reproduces unequal power and authority by preparing some people to govern and others to obey. Many cultural thinkers (such as Coleridge, Carlyle, Ruskin and Weber) have looked towards the leadership of talented, educated and charismatic individuals whose capacities derive from their (cultivated) personal characteristics and from their position in the hierarchy. Culture and concentrated power do not have to be bedfellows – there are egalitarian and democratic cultures – but any exercise of power has a cultural side to it. The power in cultural thought contrasts with the atomistic, powerless, invisible-hand theorising of orthodox economics.

## Evolution and Dialectics

As cultural methods are historical, evolutionary or revolutionary change is ever present and must be acknowledged. No consensus has arisen on causality, but most explanations in the cultural tradition have had a dialectical flavour that appeals to arguments, conflicts and tensions. Historical development does not adjust tamely to some distant, eternal equilibrium: on the contrary, it is messy, unpredictable and punctuated by frictions among ideas, individuals, interest groups, social classes, nation states and empires. Revolutionary changes are more sudden and discrete than evolutionary ones, but both are the outcome of tensions and would not occur in a harmonious steady state. Changes are cumulative, history never repeats itself exactly, and knowledge may be no guarantor of continuous social progress.

## Interpretative Methods

From a cultural perspective, because people engage self-consciously with their social context, human behaviour is too subtle and elaborate to be explained by rationalism or empiricism. Rationalism has no purchase on the thoughts and feelings of a person in a given social setting; empiricism is fixated on the observable surface of events and neglects the inner world of human agents. These deficiencies can be remedied, in part, by interpretative methods where the social investigator seeks to empathise with and understand the behaviour of people in a specific time and place. Although the Enlightenment debunked such methods as being unscientific, they are embraced by cultural thought as an appropriate response to the plenitude and intricacy of human behaviour.

### Pluralism of Method and Theory

Cultural diversity brings a corresponding need for diverse methods and theories. Rationalism and empiricism do not exhaust our methodological resources and should be augmented by interpretative and other approaches. Discriminating between theories cannot be reduced to unified rules or procedures, and assessment must turn on wider arguments and debates. Even though human behaviour does have general features, its cultural variants are too disparate to be contained by a single theoretical model; theory should be plural and tailored to local circumstances.

### Scepticism about Disciplinary Boundaries

No human activities can be accurately described as non-cultural. Economic activities are imbued with culture, from production to distribution to consumption, and inseparable from any cultural sphere of the arts or humanities. Cultural methods are germane to all academic disciplines and cannot be confined to the humanities. Pluralism of method would forbid the tying of a discipline to a single method or theory. Space would be left for alternative schools of thought; no single method or theory would have a monopoly. Disciplinary boundaries, if required at all, should be based on the object of study rather than the methods used. Particular methods and theories, no matter how popular they become, should not be allowed to hijack a discipline and redefine it in their own terms.

## 6.2   ECONOMICS VERSUS CULTURE?

The chasm between orthodox economics and cultural thought did not come from economists appraising and rejecting cultural ideas. Its main source was their unqualified servitude to the Enlightenment, which led to a tacit denial of cultural arguments. As the scientific formalism of economics has waxed, so has its distance from cultural thought. A decisive step was taken when neoclassical economics was installed as the orthodoxy – the static universality and rational-choice individualism excluded culture from economic theory. The laissez-faire beliefs of many economists made them hostile to Romantic anti-capitalism and unlikely to listen to its concerns. Mainly by neglect, orthodox economics has found itself far removed from culture.

By the mid-twentieth century, the Robbins definition of economics as the scientific study of scarcity and resource allocation had narrowed its scope as a discipline. Economists perforce followed neoclassical principles. The severing of economics from culture was now institutionalised: choosing cultural methods meant that one could not be an economist. The assumptions and axioms of orthodox economics debarred culture and prevented any shift in a cultural direction. Despite the mushrooming of economic research since the mid-twentieth century, this blinkered view has held firm and dictates how orthodox economists perceive themselves. For them, culture is not an active issue, since considering it would take them outside the domain of economics. With cultural questions being overlooked or left to other social scientists, economics and culture have become dichotomised.

The economics/culture divide is itself cultural. Economic orthodoxy has become channelled into a development path of ever-increasing specialisation and allegiance to formal theoretical and empirical methods. As a child of the Enlightenment, economics was always going to tread the route of rationalism and empiricism; conceivably, it might have developed along different lines, as the cultural critics would have wished, but alternative views were unable to make inroads against the accumulating strength of established doctrines. Neoclassical dominance, once attained, could be perpetuated through the institutions of economics. The apparent neoclassical superiority was not justified by methodological debate and says nothing about how economics should be studied. If we define economics through its subject matter as against its methods, then there is no reason why we have to eschew cultural arguments. Culture, defined as a process or way of life, includes economic activities – an economics/culture barrier can only deform and impoverish economic research.

Economists have little excuse for being ignorant of culture. As Part II has recounted, orthodox economics has attracted much cultural criticism that offers alternative ideas and values. Is there any chance of belatedly introducing culture into economics? Heterodox economists have rued the anti-cultural bias of orthodoxy and proved willing to acknowledge history and culture: the heterodox literature indicates how economics could be different. Also relevant is the post-1960s revival of cultural thought, which shows up many inadequacies and lacunae in modern economics. Recent social and cultural theory could supply alternatives to neoclassicism as a foundation for economic theorising. Heterodox and non-economic literatures provide guidelines as to how economics could overcome the economics/culture divide and reintegrate itself with culture. Part III considers how economics might learn from cultural criticism of its methods.

# PART III

# Implications of the cultural critique

# 7. Relativism and realism

Cultural thought, with its comparative and historical temper, has the reputation of being relativist. If academic work must always be case-specific and fitted to local circumstances, then absolute knowledge seems to recede. Limits or qualifications in theorising are often perceived as faults, and relativism has pejorative connotations among scientists. The apparent relativism of cultural thought has made it seem imprecise, loose and subjective by contrast with the exact, rigorous and objective natural sciences. Repeated allusion to problems caused by relativities can easily be interpreted as denying the possibility of science.

To label cultural thought as relativist is an oversimplification, given the many and varied guises that relativism can take. Cultural ideas are not relativistic in every sense of the word, and one should be careful about the relativities in question. The mere act of comparing or qualifying does not yield a nihilism that threatens scientific study. Relativism may be essential for successful research, especially in social sciences; attempts to find absolute theories may be inappropriate and hinder scientific progress. Long discussed in philosophy, relativism and realism have frequently been ignored or obscured by natural and social scientists. Orthodox economists have dealt in absolutes and said little about the specificity of their theories and models.

The present chapter considers how cultural thought can sponsor relativistic but not anti-realist economic theory. While some writers within the cultural tradition have been anti-realist, this is not inevitable and derives largely from postmodernism. Many cultural writers were clear that human societies formed a real but complex object of study that was capable of being understood. Likewise, the scepticism of cultural thinkers about natural-science emulation in social studies need not imply that they reject social science. The goad for cultural arguments was the perceived inadequacy of prevailing methods of study and the feeling that scholars could do better. As the rest of this chapter argues, social sciences founded on an explicit and cautiously defined scientific realism are compatible with cultural methods.

## 7.1   THE RELATIVISM OF CULTURAL THOUGHT

Culture in its original sense as cultivation takes place within a particular social setting. Once cultivated, a person possesses beliefs, values, habits and capabilities that are localised and differ from those of people raised elsewhere. Some facets of human development are biological and vary little among individuals or groups. Biological factors may change on an evolutionary time scale and show small differences across human populations but can be safely regarded as fixed in most social studies. The same cannot be said for cultural factors: to assume fixity and universality would be to overlook culture and social context.

Definitions of culture as a way of life or the arts are also historically and geographically specific. A way of life is the end product of culture as a process and differs from those generated by other cultural processes. Each way of life is characterised by unique institutions, behaviour and social relations. In order to know about a way of life, one should compare and contrast it with others. Culture defined as the arts embodies specificity, owing to the many artistic endeavours and their dependence on society. A paternalistic judgement to single out the approved 'higher' arts would limit variation by excluding 'lower' arts; embracing popular culture would permit variation on a scale similar to culture as a way of life. In all its definitions, culture brings a comparative, locally grounded approach.

A cultural method means that one accepts relativity over time and place: one should be explicit about historical and geographical context (to be mute suggests a claim to universal relevance). The appropriate type of relativism is historical and geographical specificity. Cultural thought, because it revels in diverse behaviour and institutions, does not seek universal behaviour applicable in all times and places. Though some behaviour patterns may be commoner than others and come closer to generality, it would be unwise to see any as universal. General theorising remains possible but must proceed warily and allow internal variations among cases or categories. Ambitions for a definitive, universal theoretical model should be waived in favour of more modest and localised theories.

Cultural relativism may not extend to knowledge or truth: theorising about a particular society can still provide absolute knowledge. Relativism can meet with complex objects of study without hurting our ability to understand them. Diverse social behaviour makes it hard to acquire knowledge in social sciences, yet the potential for knowledge stays intact. A major aim of the Counter-Enlightenment was to find methods suitable for social studies that would uncover truth and illuminate human behaviour. Relativism is here in the service of knowledge, not inimical to it. For cultural thinkers, absolute theory fails to shed much light on human societies, whereas relativistic and interpretative methods have a better track record in achieving this. The purpose of cultural relativism is to savour and comprehend the rich, multifaceted nature of human life.

Cultural thought should not be construed as throwing away scientific goals or saying that social science is impossible. Early authors in the cultural tradition agreed with the goals of the Enlightenment and had no wish to denigrate scholarly enquiry. Unimpressed by Enlightenment social studies, they looked for alternative methods and never renounced objective truth (Berlin, 1991a). Stronger brands of relativism, in which truth does come under question, date from the recent revival of cultural thought, rather than the original work in the cultural tradition. The wholesale relativism among some postmodernists stems principally from other, distinct traditions within philosophy. It is important to distinguish types of relativism and ask whether they are inherent in cultural thought.

## 7.2  TYPES OF RELATIVISM

Relativity means that something can be understood only in relation to other things, not in isolation. There are no restrictions on what we are relating, and relativism may have several dimensions. Comparisons in one dimension need not imply comparisons in another, so that academic discourse may combine relativistic and absolute aspects. To speak baldly of relativism (as in much philosophical literature) risks confusion: relativism itself is a relative concept and can be treated adequately only by considering different types (Harré and Krausz, 1996; O'Grady, 2002; Baghramian, 2004). The types below are the most widespread.

### Spatial

Spatial relativism occurs when an object of study shows geographical variations that must be noted in academic research: a universal, one-size-fits-all theory would be unsatisfactory. Theoretical and empirical work has to be tailored to the case in hand and make no claims about other cases. Local knowledge is paramount, and global results have to be justified by proving relevance across many locations. General theories must earn their generality by being warranted through comparative analysis.

**Temporal**

Here the object of study varies over time, and academic work is historically specific. Appeals to universal human nature or institutions are avoided for the sake of case-by-case historical research. Theories should be qualified by the period to which they refer. As with spatial relativism, general properties may emerge from comparative study but must be shown to apply in all cases.

**Ontological**

Ontology, as a branch of philosophy, deals with the nature of being or reality. Ontological relativism envisages a relativised reality that varies with social context. The reality of an object of study is no longer absolute but filtered through scholarly and other activities: it becomes meaningless to refer to a predetermined reality independent of human actions. Under ontological relativism, scientific study loses any reference point, and multiple realities hold sway across different academic work. The problems exceed those in temporal and spatial relativism – instead of just being complex and variable, the object of study has no solid existence beyond the actions of the investigator.

**Epistemological**

Standing alongside ontology, epistemology is the branch of philosophy concerned with how we acquire knowledge. Epistemological relativism implies that we have no unique method of knowing things – different methods are required in different circumstances. The methods for natural sciences might differ from those for social sciences, and pluralism might be beneficial in most areas of study, as against a single formula or system. Diverse methods should not be equated with multiple realities, and epistemological relativism is separate from its ontological counterpart. One can argue for plural methods while still upholding an absolute ontology that exists independently of human investigation.

**Semantic**

Much relativistic discussion in recent years has been about language and the meaning of words. Under semantic relativism, meaning is wrapped in language and does not exist in general or absolute terms. Translation from one language into another must bring loss of meaning. Each language facilitates internal conversation among those who belong to the language community but blocks conversation with those outside it. There is no universal language or perfect medium of communication.

## Moral

For a moral relativist, ethical questions cannot be answered absolutely. With no universal standard or benchmark, the moral worth of an action can be judged only by the values of a particular society or historical period. Actions applauded as virtuous in one time and place could be condemned as immoral in others. Moral relativism deters the outside observer from imposing absolute moral rules or principles – actions within a given society are subject to the morals of that society.

## Aesthetic

Relativistic ideas are also prevalent in the realm of art and aesthetics. An aesthetic relativist makes no universal artistic judgements and lets each society set its own standards. Some aesthetic judgements may coincide across societies, but others may differ – objects deemed beautiful in one historical era may be decried as crude or ugly in later eras (and become vulnerable to destruction). Under aesthetic relativism, one cannot have an ultimate yardstick of artistic value.

The types of relativism above are logically distinct and may not coexist. Relativists usually subscribe to more than one type, but few endorse every type. Relativism is sufficiently complex that it cannot be caged within a simple relative/absolute dichotomy. Most people are relativists in certain areas but not in others.

Does cultural thought have to be relativistic? The definitions of culture in Chapter 2 entail spatial and temporal relativism. If academic work addresses a particular way of life or the cultivation of individuals within a social context, then it must have historical or geographical specificity. Matters are hazier with the other types of relativism. Semantic, moral and aesthetic comparisons are all consonant with cultural thought and often accompany it. Comparative study of cultures encourages sensitivity towards differences of language and meaning, moral values, and aesthetic judgements. Cultural methods may well foster semantic, moral and aesthetic relativism. None of this is obligatory, and to make cross-cultural comparisons one may need absolute values. One can acknowledge cultural differences while still believing in general meanings, ethical principles or aesthetic standards. Cultural methods should not be taken as a sign of semantic, moral or aesthetic relativism.

The ties between culture, ontological relativism and epistemological relativism have been troublesome. Cultural thought has speculated about the internal practices and methods of science without insisting upon ontological or epistemological relativism. Diversity in the object of study hampers academic work but leaves intact the possibility of uncovering truth or acquiring knowledge. As Ernest Gellner put it, the singleness of Man is not required for the uniqueness of the World or Truth (Gellner, 1985). To be ontologically or epistemologically relativist is to go beyond what is necessary for a cultural approach. The only types of relativism essential to cultural thought are spatial and temporal; all the others are optional.

## 7.3   REALISM AND THE NATURAL SCIENCES

The attitude of orthodox economics towards relativism has echoed that of the natural sciences: relativism has been cold-shouldered, as it seems antiscientific, negative and downbeat. For any aspirant scientist the ultimate goal has been absolute knowledge confirmed by empirical tests and robust against fundamental challenges. Making concessions to relativism of any type qualifies a theory by limiting its range and casting aspersions on its validity. Extreme relativism could topple the natural and social sciences and reduce them to the same level as casual speculation. In an 'anything goes' relativism, they would cease to exist as the sole fount of knowledge and their professional standing would be jeopardised. Orthodox economists in both classical and neoclassical eras have kept away from relativistic ideas that might ruin their scientific ambitions.

If science is to be justified and defended from relativistic extremes, then it needs an object of study anchored in reality. This implies scientific realism, which has been discussed at length in the philosophy of science (Psillos, 2003; Devitt, 2005). Definitions of scientific realism have varied, but most have held that the object under investigation must exist independently of the actions of the investigator and be explainable through scientific study. Crucial is a single reality, as against a nullity or multiple realities. Scientific realism has an explicit ontology making presuppositions about the reality being studied. Ontological relativism is rejected, and science can look towards a reality that may be complex and elusive but remains knowable. It would be nice if reality was neat, tidy and stable, but this is not strictly necessary for scientific realism. What counts is the uniqueness of reality, not its fixity or simplicity.

The need for realism may seem obvious but has been overlooked by scientists, who have dwelt on the practice of science. Apathy about ontology comes from the Enlightenment view of metaphysics, religion and supernatural explanation. Ontology was seen as a throwback to pre-scientific thought, and ontological statements were felt to be unreliable, for they had no licence from rationalism or empiricism. The emphasis switched away from ontology towards epistemology and formal scientific methods. By this logic, scientists should not waste their time pondering ontology – a vice of ancient and medieval philosophy – and instead get on with their research. Once ontology had been ousted, the nature of the reality being studied could no longer be considered. In their zeal to bury religion, scientists excluded themselves from an explicit realism that could have underpinned scientific work.

Denial of metaphysics drove a wedge between Enlightenment philosophy and day-to-day science. Many scientists have behaved as if they are investigating real objects of study which, with rigorous scientific research, can be uncovered and explained. This amounts to tacit realism, even though the Enlightenment has supposedly banned metaphysics and refused to make presuppositions about reality. Most scientific work is far from being relativist, and an unspoken realism is readily apparent. Scientists who repudiate explicit realism fall back on implicit realism from the methods they use. Since sciences have well-defined epistemologies and officially sanctioned practices, the missing reality can be inferred from the ways in which it is studied. Epistemology stands in for ontology and reveals the qualities of the reality under examination.

Natural and social science has often been empirical and used observation as the gauge of theories or models. A theory is judged successful if it has observable content and performs well in empirical tests, preferably under experimental conditions. Observation becomes the arbiter of whether a scientific model accords with reality – if it matches our observations, then it is realistic. This has been termed empirical realism, as it lets empirical results decide what is real and what is not real (Bhaskar, 1986, Chapter 1). Empirical realism, seldom overt, keeps science away from the spectre of relativism: it does without metaphysics and shrinks reality down to items which are observable and empirically testable. Unobservable items cannot be real.

The other main strand in natural and social sciences, less prominent but still significant, is rationalism. Many scientists are loath to call themselves rationalist, but the esteem attached to pure theory suggests rationalist proclivities. In a rationalist method, a theory is deemed successful if it builds on accepted axioms to produce, through logical reasoning, a larger set of outcomes. The implicit realism is conceptual, as it assumes that logically watertight theories can give access to reality. As with empirical realism, conceptual realism is rarely admitted but provides a buffer against relativism. A problem is that reality becomes subservient to theory and has no independent existence – things incapable of theoretical modelling cannot be real.

Implicit realism in science creates a tension between a de facto ontology and the abandonment of metaphysics. The tension need not affect everyday activities of scientists, who can do their research without worrying about philosophical foundations, but it poses difficulties for the philosophy of science. How can science be justified if it has no real object of study? Can it go ahead without realism? Two basic answers to these questions have emerged in the philosophical literature – the first is anti-realist and continues to deny ontology, the second restores ontology and argues for explicit realism. Neither side in this debate is hostile to science, and both claim to be justifying it.

Anti-realists follow the Enlightenment tradition of being suspicious of ontology and metaphysics; they see no profit in unproven statements about reality and give precedence to the practicalities of science. For them, acquiring and applying knowledge outstrips uncovering a pre-existing reality. Scientific research effectively creates and opens up its own reality without the need for ontology. We should instead focus on epistemology in the attempt to understand scientific practice. Various philosophers have downgraded or relativised ontology – their arguments differ, but they agree on the vapidity of ontological assumptions (Quine, 1969; Dummett, 1978; Putnam, 1981; Rorty, 1991). Anti-realist sentiments have often been viewed as cultural or linguistic, associated with the 'growth of knowledge' literature and the renewed interest in scientific discourse. The ontological relativism of anti-realists is, however, distinct from and stronger than the spatial and temporal relativism of cultural thought: although many writers on culture have been attracted to anti-realism, the link is by no means automatic. As a philosophical basis for science, anti-realism has the disadvantage of arousing a thoroughgoing relativism of the kind usually shunned by scientists. It has to justify and defend science on the pragmatic grounds of accumulating know-how and practical skills, as opposed to unveiling reality. This goes against the grain of much Enlightenment thought, which may have written off supernatural explanation but still aspired to a disinterested understanding of material nature.

As an alternative to anti-realism and largely in reply to it, some philosophers of science have taken a different tack and proposed an explicit realism (Harré, 1970; Hesse, 1974; Bhaskar, 1975, 1986). For the realists, ontological relativism cannot justify science and should be replaced by stronger ontological presuppositions that posit a reality existing independently of scientific activity. An ontology of some sort lurks beneath all science – if it is not explicit, then it will be implicit in the methods of investigation. Announcing ontology is healthier than denying it and allowing a stunted and unappealing account of reality to creep back through one's methods. When ontology is denied, epistemology fills the gap and distorts the investigator's perceptions of reality. The outcome is the 'epistemic fallacy', whereby statements about being are analysed in terms of statements about knowledge (Bhaskar, 1989, Chapter 2). Since knowledge and being are not distinguished, they become merged and confused. The practical and hard-headed anti-realists fail to escape ontology and end up with an implicit ontology more restrictive than the ones adopted by the realists. Authors in the realist camp have championed open and unrestrictive ontologies that can accommodate a variety of methods. While having an absolute foundation, scientific realism is compatible with epistemological relativism. Indeed, realism should relieve epistemology from its anti-realist burden of adjudicating the nature of reality and let it be more adventurous. Under scientific realism, metaphysics returns in a mild, naturalistic form that bars supernatural explanation but leaves room for science to investigate a pre-existing reality.

## 7.4 REALISM, ECONOMICS AND CULTURAL THOUGHT

Orthodox economics has mimicked natural sciences in seeking absolute knowledge and universal theories. With no explicit ontology, the nature of reality has to be deciphered from methods of study. Given that pure theory is often viewed as the apex of economic research (especially when stated in axiomatic, mathematical form), the implicit realism may appear to be conceptual, as if theorising alone can lay bare reality. This position, which has little open support, can be detected in arguments for mathematical theorising free from empirical tests or practical uses (Debreu, 1984, 1991). Many orthodox economists are shy of discussing methodology and query its value, but the methods patronised by orthodox textbooks are empirically based and falsificationist (Blaug, 1992; Dow, 1997). Much effort has been devoted to spreading quantitative methods through the teaching of econometrics; whether economic theories ever do stand or fall by econometric testing is unclear, but this is how economics is said to progress towards objective knowledge. The implicit ontology is empirical realism, such that observation gives access to reality (Lawson, 1995). Problems with empirical tests are widely recognised, though the response is usually to aim for improved econometric techniques and apply them more vigorously rather than raise doubts about empiricism.

The implicit ontology of heterodox economics is less straightforward, owing to greater pluralism of method. Heterodoxy, like orthodoxy, has mostly played down metaphysics and made no explicit assumptions about reality. The accent on case studies and empirical research in much heterodox literature tilts towards empirical realism; a few heterodox authors have seen falsificationism as the criterion by which heterodox theories can be proved superior to orthodox ones (Robinson, 1977; Eichner, 1983). More generally, heterodox economists have been alert to the weaknesses of positivism and taken a cautious and pluralistic line (Caldwell, 1982; Hodgson, 1988, Chapter 2; Beed and Beed, 2000; Dow, 2002). Despite the temptations to be anti-realist, the desire for absolute knowledge has curbed the relativism of heterodox economics and discouraged it from rejecting realism. The old institutionalism, inspired by pragmatist philosophy, has sometimes had an anti-realist hue. Pragmatism shifted away from the disinterested quest for truth towards a search for workable, useful knowledge that may or may not be realistic: this permits scientific activities that do not strive for absolute truth and are happy with approximation. Recent postmodernist versions of pragmatism have been ontologically relativist and parted company with realism. Institutional economics could be flirting with a relativistic extreme, but the relations between institutionalism, pragmatism and anti-realism are fluid and ambiguous (Samuels, 1991, 1993; Hoksbergen, 1994; Kilpinen, 2003; Gronow, 2008). Heterodox interest in the rhetoric of economics has led to a rhetoric/realism contrast being made, although it now seems to be appreciated that the contrast is false and that rhetoric should not be mistaken for anti-realism (McCloskey, 1985; Mäki, 1988, 1993; Peter, 2001). Anti-realist sympathies hover around some heterodox thought without being typical of the heterodox literature: most heterodox economists have been implicitly realist.

The attitude of cultural thought towards realism has also been variable. Early cultural thinkers wanted reliable ways of understanding society and human behaviour – they were realists, even if they said little about ontology or metaphysics. Their methods differed from those of the Enlightenment and engendered different forms of implicit realism. Vico, for instance, based his 'new science' on interpretative methods directed at the man-made world; any other objects of study could never be fully understood. This yields an interpretative realism (or subjective conceptual realism) in which real status depends on our ability to interpret subjective thoughts and actions. Items not created by human beings are unfathomable and 'unreal'. Vico's implicit realism comes from an adherence to interpretation as the only valid method, but most cultural thinkers have been pluralists who allow for methods other than interpretative ones. Postmodernism has mixed cultural thought with anti-realism, though this is far from compulsory. On the whole, cultural thinkers have tended towards implicit realism.

The key issue here is whether the relativism in heterodox economics and cultural thought can be married with social science. Can we take on board the cultural critique of economics while hoping for a reformed but still scientific study of society? The question is addressed in the recent literature on scientific realism, which was applied first to natural sciences and then to social sciences (Keat, 1971; Harré and Secord, 1972; Bhaskar, 1979; Outhwaite, 1987; Sayer, 1992). For realists, scientific activities should rest upon a presupposed reality consistent with the methods being used. If an ontology is not declared, then it will be tacit and often take a narrow, degenerate form. A pluralist method should have an open, non-reductionist ontology that can coexist with epistemological relativism and give a rationale for scientific study.

Realist writers have set out a critical realism extending across natural and social sciences (Bhaskar, 1978, 1979; Sayer, 1992). The aim is to combine a naturalistic science with sensitivity towards the problems unique to the study of human behaviour and societies. The social ontology must be broad enough to envelop social-scientific research: Bhaskar adopts the transformational model of social activity, which has an open-endedness that defies individualistic or structural reductionism and carries no prior commitment to any single research method (Bhaskar, 1979, Chapter 2, 1983). Because ontology is now explicit, use of certain methods no longer dictates the perception of reality. Social sciences can have methods different from the natural sciences and still be naturalistic; one can invoke cultural thought without resorting to an anti-naturalism that splits social and natural sciences.

From the 1980s onwards a number of heterodox authors have been arguing for realism in economics, and the critical realist framework has been seminal (Mäki, 1989; Lawson, 1989, 1997, 2003; Fleetwood, 1999, 2001; Lewis, 2004). According to critical realists, the positivistic methods of orthodox economics are unsuitable for social studies. Mathematical theorising and deductive empiricism, copied from natural sciences, have grown incrementally with little or no discussion as to whether they are appropriate for economics. Critical realists rethink the foundations of the discipline by making ontology explicit and then recommending methods consistent with that ontology. Acceptance of the complexity of economic subject matter, along with its differences from natural sciences, would lead to methods far more pluralistic than those of economic orthodoxy.

In a social science, the central ontological problem is the nature of society and its relation with human agents. Orthodox economics has no explicit ontology, but its methodological individualism decides the humour of its theories and offers a particular image of society. The outlook is reductionist as it boils all explanations down to the individual level and removes any causal role for social structures or institutions. Individualism has an affinity with empirical realism, for individuals are observable units whose physical and material interactions are susceptible to empirical study. As with empirical realism, methodological individualism compels economists to operate on a single analytical level and ignore depth or stratification. Critical realists argue for a stratified ontology with individuals and social structures mutually dependent. By clarifying this, they are no longer imprisoned by methodological individualism. The deeper and richer vision of society relaxes arbitrary constraints and expands the range of theories and methods that can be used.

A non-reductionist social ontology should dissipate anti-cultural bias. The original definition of culture as a process embodies the formation of individuals within society: social structures shape individual behaviour but simultaneously enhance individual capacities and reinforce human agency. This complex interaction between the individual and society mirrors the social ontology of critical realists. Individualistic reductionism is shelved, and one can examine how individual preferences are formed within society. One can also contemplate cultural differences in economic behaviour and the historical evolution of the economy. An explicit social ontology can sustain greater pluralism, so that theorising and empirical research can be augmented by interpretative methods. The critical realist view of economics, though it seldom mentions culture, reiterates many points made by the cultural critique. It can bring to the fore cultural arguments without bowing to ontological relativism and querying science.

Sceptics about critical realism have cavilled at its philosophical foundations, its presupposed ontology and its paucity of specific and detailed theorising. Authors writing in a pragmatist tradition see theory as descriptive not explanatory: causal holism, for example, follows Quine in tying economic theory to description and eschewing statements about ontology or explanatory goals (Boylan and O'Gorman, 1995). For critical realists, causal holism has an unwelcome empiricist slant through the weight it places on observation as the measure of descriptive success (Fleetwood, 2002). Other authors have felt that critical realists impose unnecessary philosophical foundations and choose a particular social theory as the ontology, thereby granting 'ontological privilege' to one theory over others (Albury et al., 1981; Benton, 1981; Layder, 1985; Chalmers, 1988; Baert, 1996; Cruickshank, 2004; Vromen, 2004; Ruccio, 2005). An assumption of ontological status for a disputed theory could be a brake on further theorising and legitimise a theoretical orthodoxy. The social ontologies selected by critical realists are, however, designed to be general and non-reductionist – their aim is not to set up an orthodoxy but to guard against individualistic and structural reductionism. Another sceptical argument is that critical realists have made no headway with renovating economic theory and been sidetracked by philosophy and methodology (Graça Moura and Martins, 2008). Too much time has been spent on preparing the ground for social science ('underlabouring') and too little on critical analyses of modern capitalism, such as those within the Marxian tradition (Gunn, 1989; Nielsen, 2002; Fine, 2004, 2006). The belief that a methodological critique on its own can be 'emancipatory' and have profound social and political benefits seems overblown and unconvincing (Sayer, 1997a; Hodgson, 2006a). Yet critical realism does not theorise about particular economic problems or other subject matter – there is no single critical realist approach to economics. The goal is more modest, namely to provide a philosophical frame within which critical social sciences are possible. The need for further theorising at a specific institutional level is duly conceded.

Arguments against realism have overstated its theoretical and methodological claims, which are deliberately minimal: the point of realism is to presuppose an ontology, not to smuggle in particular theories or methods. Realism respects the rationale of science (the quest for objective, disinterested knowledge) but looks for a middle ground between culture-free positivism and extreme relativism. It can evade all-encompassing relativism by being ontologically absolute but epistemologically relative. Even if social sciences have the same ambitions as natural sciences, they have different subject matter which depends far more heavily on human behaviour and social relations. In a social science, opportunities for controlled observation are slim, and other methods are required. Empirical study has to take uncontrolled forms, and in some cases may not be feasible. People's private thoughts and motives are not observable but may be open to imaginative reconstruction and interpretative methods. These activities, characteristic of the humanities, can find a refuge within pluralistic social sciences based upon explicit realism.

# 8. Idealism and materialism

Any cultural approach to economics must ask how culture relates to material production. Does culture determine the economy, or is it the other way round? No agreement has been reached on this question, and various accounts have coexisted. Whereas idealist ('cultural') views give causal priority to ideas and beliefs, materialist ('economic') views give it to material production. An idealist/materialist dualism reflects and feeds the divisions between culture and economics. The usual assumption is that economics, concerned with material production and consumption, should be predisposed towards materialism and wary of idealism. Orthodox economics, with its neglect of culture, has been quiet about such matters, although by default it falls on the 'economic' side of the argument. Heterodox economics, with a richer theoretical background, includes 'cultural' as well as 'economic' views.

Cultural thought has often been idealist, underlining the causal influence of ideas and beliefs. The narrowest idealism restricts culture to just the prevailing beliefs or ideology, as distinct from institutions and material production. Culture then becomes the informing spirit of a way of life but remains separate from the social structures and physical activities on which a society depends (Williams, 1981b, Chapter 1). To define culture thus is at odds with the definitions in Chapter 2, which do not limit culture to ideas and beliefs. A broad perspective on culture should avoid equating it with ideas and show how it interacts with institutions, social structures and material nature. This leaves causality open and makes no presuppositions that culture exists separately from the material realm or has a causal influence upon it. Despite the brotherhood between cultural thought and idealism, a full treatment of culture should penetrate beyond ideas and beliefs.

The following discussion examines idealism and materialism, their bonds with the cultural tradition, and their place within economic theory. Idealism has been peripheral to economics, but some authors have put forward idealist theories of economic development. An alternative canon of idealist and humanistic economic thought can be discerned, though it is spasmodic and confined mainly to heterodoxy (Reinert and Daastøl, 2004). Materialism has reigned in orthodox economics, Marxian theory and institutionalism. The apparent idealism/materialism conflict broaches the problem of whether idealism and materialism are polar opposites. If one has doubts about strict idealist or materialist causality, then alternatives such as cultural materialism offer a way of housing culture in the material world without giving causal precedence to material or cultural factors.

## 8.1  IDEALISM, THE CULTURAL TRADITION AND ECONOMIC THEORISING

The term 'idealism' in philosophical usage normally refers to the belief that objects of knowledge rest on our perception of them and do not exist independently of the mind. So defined, idealism is ontological and gives priority to human thought in explaining natural and social phenomena. Causal idealism is weaker than ontological in so far that it lets matter exist independently of thought: the idealism comes from the causal potency of ideas, and all events and outcomes are caused through thoughts, beliefs and intentions, not material forces. The economic literature has seldom addressed ontological idealism, as economists have largely ignored ontology. Causal idealism is harder for economists to ignore and, if accepted, has major implications for the causality behind economic development.

The idealism/materialism debate, which dates back to ancient times, has never been resolved. Idealism in its modern forms is due to Immanuel Kant, who founded the German school of idealist philosophy (Pinkard, 2002, Part I). He identified closely with the Enlightenment, but his work had a big impact on the Counter-Enlightenment and Romanticism because he traced the boundaries of the Enlightenment and spelled out the areas where it could not reach – unlike some others at the time, he refused to make exaggerated claims about the universal value of the new scientific methods (Beiser, 2000). His circumspection was to fuel Counter-Enlightenment arguments wishing to go further in denying the relevance of Enlightenment thought. Several aspects of his philosophy were to prove fertile, among them his separation of the moral and spiritual from the natural, his view of the individual as a free agent, and his case for direct understanding (the 'synthetic a priori'). He was dissatisfied with cultural thought, decrying Herder's writings as loose and undisciplined, but did much to inspire the neo-Kantian philosophy that justified cultural methods.

Later German idealism differed from Kant in the lesser emphasis on reason and greater emphasis on creativity and freedom of expression. Kant remained loyal to Enlightenment values: for him both the moral and natural realms, though separate, were under the rule of reason, and

freedom for the individual could be exercised only by rational deliberation. As idealism evolved, the role of rationality was reduced and replaced
with notions of will power, creativity and resistance to Nature. Fichte and
Schelling presented the essence of the free agent as self-expression and the
self-determination of ends, which could transcend natural constraints.
Their arguments were cultural, for individual creative capacities were
unique to a particular social setting. Fichte went on to meld the individual will to the collective spirit of a culture, nation or religion, so that
they were interdependent and not always clearly distinguished. Idealism
could now be dislodged from the Enlightenment and associated with the
Counter-Enlightenment and Romanticism. Allied at first with liberalism,
the new strains of idealism summoned up darker trends towards irrationality, hero-worship and reckless nationalism (Berlin, 1991b). By the mid-
nineteenth century, idealist philosophy stood abreast with cultural thought,
to the extent that they were often viewed as synonymous.

The augmented, culturally charged idealism bred idealist theories of
history and anti-naturalistic arguments about the separation of sciences
and humanities. Idealism, by celebrating the creative will of the individual
or collective, gave priority to ideas over material or natural forces as
the prime mover of historical change. Nature provided resources to be
exploited but had no final control over human behaviour. An understanding of history required empathy with individual motives and sensitivity to
the cultural context of human action. With such a vital part being played
by individual creativity, rationalism and empiricism were inappropriate for the humanities. Idealism shifted away from its Kantian origins
towards cultural methods. The outcome was a dualism between the material reality studied by the natural sciences and the social reality studied
by the humanities, as in the anti-naturalism of Dilthey, Rickert and
Windelband. The humanities became separated from the natural sciences,
and the idealist natural/moral division was translated into a sciences/
humanities division. Few of the nascent social sciences were to heed these
arguments: against idealist advice, they copied natural sciences and took
up methods earmarked for the natural realm.

Orthodox economics was oblivious to idealism, and theorists did not
consider the influence of ideas on the economy. Idealism was unattrac-
tive to classical and neoclassical economics, as it declared the significance
of ideas and conscious planning in guiding economic change. Orthodox
economists, from Adam Smith onwards, preferred invisible-hand doctrines about spontaneous markets that supposedly emerged without the
need to plan or design them. Markets were depicted as being natural
and unconditional on social planning or theoretical schemes. Although
Enlightenment thought could acquire an idealist complexion in Utopian

blueprints for social reform, this did not extend to orthodox economists, who assumed that laissez-faire would generate the best results. Such views, expressed verbally by Smith and Ricardo, were formalised through the individualism, market-clearing equilibrium and welfare theorems of neo-classical economics.

Heterodox economics has shown more sympathy for causal idealism without subscribing to it openly. The causal power of ideas has been enlisted on a piecemeal basis by arguments that point to how beliefs, concepts and values can steer economic change. When interpreted loosely in this way, idealism has surfaced repeatedly in heterodox discussion and taken several forms. In some cases it has been at the collective level as a national spirit behind economic development (Weber) or as public policies to regulate the economy (Polanyi, Keynes); in other cases it has lauded the creativity of the individual inventor and entrepreneur in catalysing economic growth (Schumpeter).

A famous example of an idealist theory is Max Weber's argument about religion and capitalist development (Weber 1904–5 [2002]; Swedberg, 1998, Chapter 5; Hamilton, 2000). While scrupulous not to be dogmatically idealist, Weber rejected materialism and accepted that ideas and culture can influence the economy. According to him, the rise of Protestantism in the sixteenth and seventeenth centuries spread the work ethic and commercial sense that nourished capitalism. The Catholic Church had regarded work as a necessary evil, with little intrinsic value, and frowned upon activities devoted to money making for its own sake. Protestantism, especially in its Calvinist form, began to see work as having intrinsic value. To work hard and make money came to be an ethical imperative, so that being idle and aimless was a dereliction of duty and neglect of one's vocation. For Weber, the new ethics of Protestantism dethroned a religious morality that would have stifled capitalist development. Under the new values it was easier to sustain capital accumulation, new working practices and market trading. Religion created a climate of opinion receptive to capitalism and prepared the ground for dramatic changes in economic organisation. Weber did not claim that Protestantism actually caused capitalism, but he listed it as a significant causal factor among others. His views, controversial from the outset, were reiterated by Tawney (1926) but did not enter orthodoxy and remain on the fringes of economics.

From the orthodox perspective, Weber's thesis is annoying: it brings religion into economics, breaches disciplinary boundaries, raises awkward questions about preference formation, and talks about ethics and duties when explaining economic behaviour. The incompatibility with orthodox analysis has meant that it has been set aside by the mainstream economic literature. Heterodox economists have fewer qualms about an idealist argument, which would stand or fall on the interpretative and empirical grounds of whether Protestant values did stimulate early capitalism – debate on these matters has extended over a long period (Swedberg, 1998, Chapter 5). For the cultural critique of capitalism, Protestant values have been ambivalent. As well as being a prod to capitalist development, as Weber claimed, they were formative for the Counter-Enlightenment and cultural opposition to capitalism. Authors such as Hamann and Herder, who were in the midst of the German Counter-Enlightenment, were born and raised within Pietism and its call for individual spiritual growth. Protestant values, which accentuated the religious and secular cultivation of the free individual, could underscore cultural thought and were among the factors driving Romantic anti-capitalism. They might well have had a dual effect, promoting both capitalism and the resistance to it, but this implies a picture more complex than Weber's.

A different strand of idealism has looked at how governments plan economic reform or activist policies. Karl Polanyi's writings on the establishment of a capitalist economy are a good example (Polanyi, 1944; Block and Somers, 1984). Although a socialist himself, Polanyi criticised Marxian materialism and sought an alternative giving autonomous influence to ideas and culture (Litvan, 1991; Block, 2003). He argued that the spread of markets in the capitalist era was not spontaneous (as suggested by orthodox economics) or the result of material and technological forces (as in Marxian economic determinism) but had been instituted by the State. Markets, which were already present in pre-capitalist societies, could expand into employment and finance only when previous institutions had been dismantled or transformed. The changes were achieved by a systematic programme of public reform rationalised by classical economic theory. A capitalist economy was attainable only through a governmental effort to create and preserve the conditions necessary for market trade. The theoretical scheme took no account of ongoing social relations, as if markets could be disembedded from their social context; for Polanyi this was unfeasible and the neglect of social relations was always going to bring difficulties. By the twentieth century the harsher features of capitalism had been mollified through social policies and the welfare state. Polanyi noted the irony that free-market capitalism had been instituted on programmatic lines, but socially planned welfare measures had emerged haphazardly ('laissez-faire was planned, social planning was unplanned'). The nub of his work was the belief that ideas, concepts and plans exert an independent effect on economic affairs – his views are often seen as the reverse of the Marxian concentration on the material forces of production.

Another idealist was John Maynard Keynes, who throughout his career showed faith in wise public policy. As the son of a Cambridge professor and a pupil of Alfred Marshall, he belonged to a liberal intellectual elite that esteemed ideas, philosophical discourse and practical understanding. For much of his life he had the good fortune to be a government advisor with a realistic chance of influencing economic policies. This background led him to query laissez-faire and support intervention, not through Utopian social planning but in the practical sense of solving problems and attaining limited aims (Keynes, 1931 [1972]). He never aligned himself overtly with cultural thought, but in his political philosophy he was an admirer of Edmund Burke, a major figure in the cultural tradition (Skidelsky, 1983, Chapter 6; Fitzgibbons, 1988, Chapter 4). Burke had been vehemently opposed to the Utopian, programmatic French Revolution, yet he had an idealist political philosophy that advocated policy intervention on a gradual, piecemeal basis. For Burke, public policy should keep away from crude universal principles and be sensitive to local conditions; this tallied with Keynes's opinions on intelligent, case-by-case problem solving and active involvement of ideas in public life. Keynes consistently valued practical rationality and state intervention – his theoretical work on probability, monetary theory and macroeconomics fits this pattern, as does his commentary on the Treaty of Versailles, the Gold Standard and the inter-war depression. He was conscious that ideas from erroneous theorising could impede economic policy, as is clear from the much-quoted final paragraph of the *General Theory* (Keynes, 1936, Chapter 24, Part V). Problems like chronic unemployment, once they have been properly understood, should in Keynes's view be soluble by adopting the right policy measures. The idealism can be criticised for its naivety in underestimating the power of business interests in a capitalist economy: Kalecki, for example, concurred with Keynes's macroeconomic theories but was less optimistic about governments having the political will to remove unemployment (Kalecki, 1943; Sawyer, 1985, Chapter 7). Keynes's idealist policy activism is far more sanguine than Polanyi's story of programmatic laissez-faire policies coupled with fragmentary welfare measures to paper over the cracks.

A final example of idealism within economics is the work of Joseph Schumpeter, which has a more individualistic tone. Schumpeter, unhappy with orthodox economics, offered as an alternative a dynamic and historical theory built around entrepreneurship (Schumpeter, 1934). For him, change is kindled by the creative thought of the individual entrepreneur who introduces the technical innovations underlying economic development. Entrepreneurs innovate so as to have a temporary monopoly from discovering new techniques and products not yet exploited by rivals. Whereas neoclassical doctrines saw monopoly profits as abnormal and inefficient, Schumpeter argued that they are integral to capitalism and essential for economic growth. Eventually the next wave of entrepreneurship destroys the market power of the previous wave and replaces it with a new temporary monopoly: the upshot is a continuous process of creative destruction. The entrepreneur becomes a hero, and anything that harms entrepreneurship must threaten economic prosperity. In his later writings, Schumpeter worried that the new corporatism would smother the creative function of the entrepreneur and cause the stagnation and eclipse of capitalism (Schumpeter, 1942). His individualism discouraged him from acknowledging that collective and institutionalised activities can also be creative. Similar views on entrepreneurship have been taken up by the neo-Austrian school, with differences over the role of equilibrium and institutions (Kirzner, 1973, 1999; Boettke and Coyne, 2003). Markets in neo-Austrian economics are still largely portrayed as natural, spontaneous processes that permit entrepreneurship to flow – the creativity of the entrepreneur has no cultural origins and acts through a universal concept of the market.

The variants of causal idealism considered above arose independently and never mounted a united challenge to economic orthodoxy. They differ among themselves in how they locate the origin of ideas, as Figure 8.1 illustrates. Each type of idealism corresponds to a different level in Figure 8.1. For Weber and Tawney the relevant ideas begin at a collective level, in a generalised spirit or climate that informs both the institutional structure of society and the behaviour of decision-making individuals. In Keynes and Polanyi, the collective spirit receives less attention and analysis focuses on governments and businesses who borrow ideas from external sources, often economists. Schumpeter and the neo-Austrians idolise the entrepreneur and see ideas as arising from creative, energetic and gifted people. All three views have to incorporate human agency at some stage, but the first two are more at ease with culture and social structure. None of them meshes with economic orthodoxy, and they have been categorised as heterodox or non-economic. Most economists have distrusted idealism and either been materialist or stayed silent on the idealism/materialism issue.

## 8.2  MATERIALISM IN ECONOMICS

The tacit materialism of economic orthodoxy is an adjunct of its desire for naturalistic explanations. From the outset, classical and neoclassical economics have depicted a laissez-faire capitalist economy as if it were natural and spontaneous. Ideas and conscious planning have been played down in favour of natural forces, hence the popularity of natural prices,

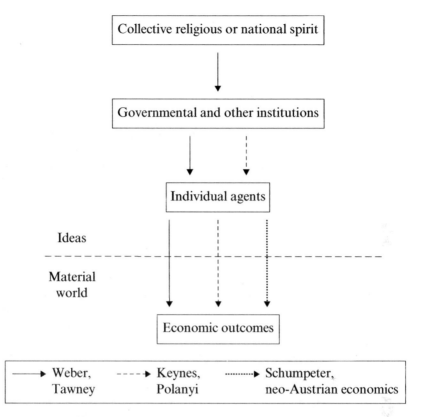

*Figure 8.1    Varieties of idealist thought in economics*

natural interest rates, natural unemployment and so forth. Neoclassical assumptions about fixed individual preferences have also fostered materialism. Little is said about how preferences can change and how such changes can influence the economy; ideas and beliefs are left to other academic disciplines. If culture becomes perceived as non-economic and beyond economic discussion, then alternatives to materialism are exiled. Increasing disciplinary specialisation has led orthodox economics further into a materialist cul-de-sac. Orthodox economic analysis lacks the theoretical apparatus for idealist explanation and, by default, finds itself confined to materialism. The word 'materialism' rarely appears in orthodox discourse, but a materialist outlook has been taken for granted in classical and neoclassical theory.

The clearest example of overt materialism lies outside orthodox economics, in the writings of Karl Marx. By contrast with the implicit, half-hidden materialism of orthodox economics, Marx made historical materialism the bedrock of his analysis. Having been trained in German idealist philosophy, he found it remote from the real world and rebelled against it by switching to materialism. His approach was, all the same, historical and modelled on Hegel's idealism. Hegel saw the dialectical opposition of ideas as the cause of historical change; Marx transposed the dialectic to a material domain with conflicts among material interests and economic classes. In historical materialism, large economic and social changes require tensions between new forces of production and older institutions better suited to earlier production methods. Ultimately material interests prevail, and existing institutions are swept away by new ones that harmonise with the material production base. Culture and ideology too fall into line with material interests, so as to justify them. Material production is the motor of history and an understanding of economic development must begin with conflicts and tensions among material interests.

Marx's writings about historical materialism were sometimes ambiguous and inconsistent, leading to different interpretations (Rigby, 1998). Disputes have arisen over what is meant by material forces (the 'economic base'). A narrow interpretation restricts the economic base to the physical means of production, so that it refers to technology alone; a broader interpretation extends it to the social relations of production, which incorporate the institutions and personal relations surrounding the workplace. Figure 8.2 shows these alternative views. Case (a) gives the narrow interpretation in which the economic base is the material forces of production: all else falls within the institutional and ideological superstructure. Case (b) widens the economic base to take in social relations that bear upon production, productivity and the intensity of work. Both cases can claim support from Marx: case (a) corresponds to the brief but well-known account of historical materialism in the preface to *A Contribution to the Critique of Political Economy* (Marx, 1859 [1971]); case (b) is closer to the more expansive but vaguer account in *The German Ideology* (Marx and Engels, 1846 [1970]). In each case the economic base has a decisive causal influence on the superstructure: the main direction of causality in Figure 8.2 is upwards, as shown by the solid arrows. Cautious exponents of historical materialism, including Marx himself, have eluded technological determinism by permitting reverse influences of ideas upon the material world, as shown by the dotted arrows.

Case (a) limits the economic base to material production and classifies productive institutions as being superstructural. This yields a stringent materialism with none of case (b)'s compromise but with a tendency to undervalue the social organisation of production and assert technological determinism. It remains unsaid how and why material forces have lordship

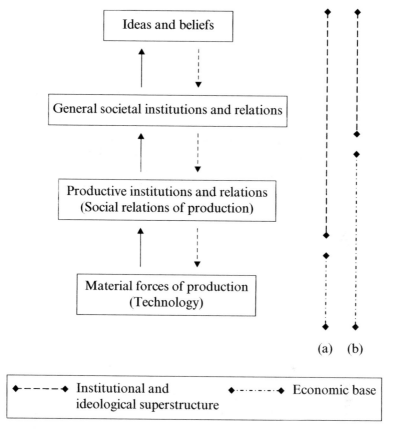

*Figure 8.2    Versions of historical materialism*

over institutions, ideas and beliefs. New technologies do not spring up out of nowhere and must be introduced by conscious decisions and actions of producers. Causality seems to go in the opposite direction, with ideas guiding technology, so how do material factors mould ideas and institutions? In answering this question, materialists generally turn to functional explanation – ideas and institutions survive and prosper if they are functional for the material mode of production, otherwise they wither away and die. Often the functionalism is implicit, though it is made explicit in some Marxian analysis (Cohen, 1978; Callinicos, 1987, Chapter 2). The causal mechanism, seldom described, is presumably natural selection in which the most productive technologies win out over the less productive and engender matching institutions and ideologies. While Marx's writings allude to natural selection, his theorising was never formally Darwinian

(Hodgson, 1993a, Chapter 5). The strict materialism of case (a), in tracing all fundamental change back to material factors, suffers from vagueness about causality.

Case (b) has the advantage of recognising the social aspects of technology, the labour process and the organisation of work. Since new production methods must have a social setting, it would be arbitrary to bind technology to tools, machines and buildings. Alongside the material means of production, productivity depends on work intensity, working hours, working conditions, managerial practices, worker–employer relations, monitoring of work, skill levels and worker morale. Allowing for these introduces a social element into production which cannot be disentangled from material elements – to try to do so would give a thin, mechanical view of technology. Marxian theory can represent how production is organised through the labour process and social relations of production (Lazonick, 1990). In case (b) the social relations are part of the economic base and thereby have causal influence over the superstructure (ideology and non-economic institutions). From a materialist angle, case (b) is problematic because it puts non-material items into the economic base. Economic change can be instigated by reform of productive relationships, as against new tools or machines, and so the materialism is diluted: the reforms originate at the economic base but have an idealist taint. Defining the economic base too widely could wreck Marxism's materialist vessel.

Institutionalism is the other chief example of overtly materialist economics. Thorstein Veblen was well versed in Marxian economics and a friendly critic of Marx (Veblen, 1906, 1907). He agreed with the materialism and argued that institutions and non-material culture adapt to technological changes only after a cultural lag (Brinkman and Brinkman, 1997). Pleased with the thrust of Marxism, he had reservations about its theoretical details and rejected some of them (O'Hara, 1997; Hodgson, 2004, Chapter 6). For Veblen, historical materialism was a teleology that depicted economic development as following preordained stages but did not explain the causal process: the remedy should be to aim for a true evolutionary theory on Darwinian principles. Within Veblen's theoretical framework, habits link individual behaviour to institutions and explain how behaviour persists. He criticised the labour theory of value which in his opinion was superfluous to evolutionary theory and merely added random assumptions and value judgements. In effect, he accused Marx of not being materialist enough: the teleology and neglect of natural selection meant that Marx's causal materialism was unconvincing. The chinks in Marxian theory had to be filled by reconstructing economics as a Darwinian evolutionary science. Veblen was never to finish this task, and his evolutionary economics remains incomplete.

Though Veblen knew the importance of culture and avoided reduction-ism, his materialism has been disfigured by oversimplified, determinist interpretations. Problems have arisen with the 'Veblenian dichotomy' between habits and factual knowledge as sources of behaviour (Waller, 1994). Veblen's economic analysis (in *The Theory of the Leisure Class*, for instance) distinguishes between ceremonial and technological behaviour: the former is habitual and has symbolic or institutional functions in pre-serving social structures; the latter is factually based and fulfils practical functions in organising production. When superimposed on materialism, the ceremonial/technological distinction implies that the technological or material level governs productive activities. Technology plays an active role as the fount of economic change; institutions play a passive role in resisting or adapting to change. As he did with his evolutionary economics, Veblen left the ceremonial/technological distinction vague and incomplete (Waller, 1982). Later institutionalists (notably Clarence Ayres) went on to derive a technology/institutions dualism that gave technology pre-eminence in the absolute, instrumental valuation of eco-nomic behaviour. Such lopsidedness can be criticised for its reductionism and downgrading of culture (Mayhew, 1987; Jennings and Waller 1995). Unless it is handled gingerly, the Veblenian dichotomy can overemphasise technology; it can even become an 'institutional' theory that denigrates institutions and leaves them with subordinate status. Dogmatic mate-rialism was not Veblen's intention, and other strands of institutionalist thought have been less enamoured with technology: John Commons put greater emphasis on collective action, purposeful behaviour and the legal foundations of the economy (Rutherford, 1983; Biddle, 1990; Ramstad, 1990). Institutionalism does not have to be causally materialist, but the incompleteness of Veblen's programme has made it vulnerable to deter-minist 'completion'.

Problems over causality are endemic to materialism in both orthodox and heterodox economics. Materialists cannot appeal to supernatural forces, guiding spirits or natural wills, nor can they base their theories on the ideas and beliefs of human agents. The causal void encourages func-tional arguments where economic and social arrangements have material benefits that explain their existence. An example from orthodox econom-ics is the invisible hand – markets are presumed to come about spontane-ously and have desirable efficiency properties summarised in the theorems of welfare economics. Beyond this general presumption, little is volun-teered about how markets appear and spread, how they operate, and how the efficient equilibrium outcome is reached. Functional arguments may sometimes have merit (and are hard to erase), but they are widely admon-ished for failing to offer causal explanations (Vromen, 1995, Chapter 5;

Jackson, 2002). If materialism is to be causally persuasive, then it requires a fuller account of economic evolution.

## 8.3 CULTURAL MATERIALISM

In the stand-off between idealism and materialism, culture is usually situated on the idealist side. Under causal idealism culture can influence the material world, which becomes a malleable resource to be used and exploited for cultural ends. Yet cultures would not exist without material nature. A culture can be created and reproduced only by material production: human beings must subsist, and culture must be spread and preserved through education, communication and recording of information. Equating culture with ideas and beliefs excludes these activities, but they fit in with culture defined as a process, way of life or the arts. How, then, can cultural thought reintegrate itself with the material world? Orthodox economics is of little relevance here, as it excludes culture. Marxian historical materialism has been apt to slide into technological determinism, but its humanist variants are more astute and find ways of reconciling culture with materialism. On a wider front, the case for a cultural materialism has been made in anthropology, literary theory and cultural studies (Jackson, 1996). The anthropological and literary versions of cultural materialism are similar but not identical, and both are useful in demonstrating how economics can relate to culture.

Anthropology has a long tradition of materialist argument, which began with the evolutionary theories of the nineteenth century. The case for materialism was revisited in the 1960s by Marvin Harris, who sought to reformulate anthropology through what he termed 'cultural materialism' (Harris, 1968, 1979). For Harris, all cultures must be adapted to their material environment, and this must be the starting point in explaining them. Even when cultures vary, having no single development path, their evolution is guided by the opportunities and problems posed by the material world. Anthropology should be temporally and spatially relativist but only within an explicit materialism. Harris was eager to distance his materialism from that of evolutionary and Marxian anthropology – while sharing their materialist propensities, he rejected the belief that human societies pass through a series of stages or epochs heading towards higher levels of civilisation. He queried the Marxian dialectical method that sees economic and social development as being propelled by tensions between ideas/institutions and material forces of production. In his view, human behaviour always matches its material environment and adjusts continuously without dialectical conflicts and sudden revolutionary changes. By disengaging materialism from dialectical and programmatic theories of evolution, he was fashioning a purer materialist anthropology. Research methods were to be empirical, on the grounds that a solid empirical knowledge of the material foundations of a society was the prelude to understanding its institutions and beliefs.

Critics of Harris's cultural materialism have felt that it overdoes material causality and ends up being reductionist. Other anthropologists have been more respectful of the autonomy of culture, admitting that a system of ideas can be self-sustaining even if beliefs are false and ill matched to their material context; anthropologists should thus be prepared to use interpretative methods as well as empirical investigation of material circumstances (Geertz, 1973; Sahlins, 1976). Marxian critics have argued that abandoning dialectic removes the tensions and mismatches necessary to generate change – a theory in which ideas and material conditions are in perpetual harmony carries a static, conservative message (Bloch, 1983, Chapter 5). Harris denied the charge of reductionism and claimed to have allowed for ideas influencing material conditions and being mismatched with them in a non-dialectical way (Harris, 1979, Chapter 3). Material factors do nevertheless have great causal weight within his theory, which suggests a causal materialism less subtle than that of Marxian dialectics. Exclusively empirical methods may be in thrall to the concrete, material and observable at the expense of ideas and beliefs. Despite Harris's statements to the contrary, his cultural materialism has not offered a satisfactory, non-reductionist means of connecting culture with its material setting.

The term 'cultural materialism' has also been deployed in literary and cultural studies in a version that resembles the anthropological one but has some differences – the two arose separately and their usage does not overlap. In its literary version, cultural materialism comes from New Left writers like Raymond Williams and E.P. Thompson, who stressed the pervasiveness of culture and its relevance to everyday life. The materialism of the New Left reflected their Marxian leanings, together with their belief in the 'ordinariness' of culture (Williams, 1958b). A formal concept of cultural materialism was put forward by Raymond Williams as a theoretical background for his previous work on culture (Williams, 1977, 1980, 1981a). It has two components: all human behaviour is cultural, so that cultural/non-cultural divisions are spurious; and culture has to be grounded in material production, so that cultural commentators must attend to material concerns. The effect is to close the fissures between culture, society and nature by realising that everything social is cultural and that all culture depends on material production. Unlike conventional Marxian schemes, culture no longer lies within a separate superstructure and impinges on the economy. Williams's cultural materialism, ubiquitous in cultural studies, has barely been noticed in orthodox (or heterodox) economics.

Compared with the anthropological version, the literary version of cultural materialism is more reticent in assigning causality to material forces and gives no endorsement for an empiricist method. This exempts it from many criticisms directed at the anthropological version, although it may then be attacked for being too vague and general to have analytical substance. Traditional Marxists see cultural materialism as mislaying Marxian dialectics and understating the causal heft of material production, but the fluid account of causality could be a bonus (Eagleton, 1989). If one wishes to stay at arm's length from causal materialism and still nest culture in the material world, then a framework such as that of Williams will ensue. It is at a general and abstract level but goes far enough to breach the economics/culture divide.

The two versions of cultural materialism have much in common, especially their all-pervasive view of culture and their desire to blend it with the material world. They diverge over causality: the anthropological version endows material factors with a causal power absent from the literary version. In philosophical language, the cultural materialism of Raymond Williams is primarily ontological, devoted to the underlying reality, whereas that of Marvin Harris is both causal and ontological. Choice between them hangs on whether one wants a materialist account of history. Causal materialism has trouble in tying down causal processes, hence its frequent dalliances with functional explanation. If one aims only for a closer connection between culture and the economy, then one does not have to go down the causal materialist route – one can just adopt an ontological materialism that does not explain history by material causes. The milder, literary version of cultural materialism is non-reductionist and lets ideas have independent causal effects on the material world.

Within the philosophical and scientific literatures, arguments for non-reductionist materialism are expressed through the concepts of emergence, emergent properties and emergent powers (Hodgson, 2004, Chapter 5). Emergence implies a stratified reality composed of levels or layers: the higher levels depend on lower ones for their existence but may possess emergent powers irreducible to lower levels. Non-reductionist materialism places material nature at the lowest level and human institutions/culture at a higher level: institutions and culture rely on material factors without being wholly explicable in material terms. They may have emergent properties that rule out causal materialism.

The notion of emergence was introduced in the 1870s by the British journalist/philosopher George Henry Lewes, who intended it to bridge the gap between materialism and idealism (Lewes, 1879). Having studied in Germany, Lewes was acquainted with German idealist philosophy and interested in how it related to materialist natural science. Human consciousness, if viewed as an emergent property, could be located in the material world but still have emergent powers irreducible to the material level – emergence could unify two apparently contradictory views. Lewes provided a rare point of contact between cultural and scientific traditions. Emergent properties were taken seriously in biology but never quite entered the mainstream of natural science. In the late nineteenth and early twentieth centuries, emergence was championed by various scientists and philosophers (notably Conwy Lloyd Morgan and Alfred North Whitehead) as a vehicle for holistic and non-reductionist methods. The early twentieth century was, however, the zenith of positivism and nadir of cultural thought – in such a hostile atmosphere, arguments for emergence did not prosper and eventually faded away, to reappear only when cultural thought was revived towards the end of the twentieth century.

In its stronger, anthropological version, cultural materialism cuts across emergence as it makes material forces sovereign over institutions, ideas and values. In its milder, literary version, it is equivalent to an ontological materialism that grants emergent powers to ideas and institutions. When relating culture to the economy, causal materialism goes beyond what is strictly necessary and opens up new avenues of criticism. The better option is ontological materialism, which rests content with having causality that emerges from material nature but may not be reducible to it. Theoretical analysis can then give due credit to ideas and culture without appealing to anything supernatural or disembodied from nature. Cultural materialism of this kind comes close to a scientific realism modified for social sciences (Bhaskar, 1979; Sayer, 1992). A realist and ontologically materialist social science yields a 'critical naturalism' that sees natural and social sciences as having the same goal in investigating a complex, layered reality but recognises the differences between them and the need for different methods (Jackson, 1995). Anti-naturalism can be avoided, and foundations can be laid for a closer relationship between economics and culture. With reductionism dispelled, it becomes possible to argue for an intricate, two-way causal link between ideas and material conditions.

A benefit of ontological materialism is that, by putting economic activity within a material setting, it raises questions about the natural environment. Both orthodox and Marxian traditions, belying their materialism, have been slow to delve deeper and ask how the economy affects the natural world (Norgaard, 1992; Atkinson, 1991). They have stopped with technological change or the invisible hand, implicitly assuming problem-free exploitation of natural resources. The 'materialist' theories are only half-engaged with material nature and poorly equipped to register the environmental implications of material production. During the nineteenth century and later, some authors outside orthodox and Marxian economics tried to place economics in its natural context – their views, far from uniform, amounted to an ecological critique (Martinez-Alier, 1987). More recently, Marxians have argued that historical materialism is broad and versatile enough to accommodate ecology and the environment (O'Connor, 1998; Burkett, 1999; Foster, 2000; Hughes, 2000). Most writers on ecology have had backgrounds in natural science and have not participated in cultural criticism. Two exceptions were John Ruskin and William Morris, who combined a cultural stance with a love of the natural, pre-industrial environment. Ruskin, in particular, had keen feelings for nature and has been acknowledged as a forerunner of ecological thought – his studies of geology, climate, plants and wildlife gave his work a materialist dimension (Wilmer, 1996). Cultural materialism can help to overcome the idealism/materialism split that keeps culture and ecology apart – it has greater depth than the materialism of orthodox economics and is compatible with a layering that digs beneath material production to consider the environmental consequences of economic activity.

## 8.4   IDEOLOGY

Within idealism or emergent-powers materialism, ideas are free to have causal effects on the economy. Among the relevant ideas are economic doctrines which, if acted upon, have a bearing on events. In this respect, economic theory becomes part of its own subject matter. The difficulties are especially acute for heterodox economists, whose ideas differ from the ones that prevail in the economics profession. An orthodox economist believes that orthodox theory is an accurate portrait of economic behaviour and a trustworthy guide for policy – the concord between theory, reality and policy reduces the independence of ideas. A heterodox economist, on the other hand, is disenchanted with orthodox theory, thinks that it misrepresents the economy, and denies its value as a policy guide. The object of study is distorted by erroneous ideas that inform economic behaviour. Economics may be fulfilling an ideological function, and any critical approach must confront this.

Ideology has never had a single, absolute definition. In most uses, it denotes a system of ideas and beliefs that permeates a society or social group and influences behaviour. Several variant meanings are possible (Geuss, 1981, Chapter 1; Williams, 1988; Eagleton, 1991, Chapter 1). Sources of disagreement include whether ideology encompasses a whole society or applies to smaller groups, whether it articulates the beliefs of an elite, whether it legitimises the interests of certain classes, whether it can be true or necessarily entails falsehood, and whether it can be independent of material production. Different answers to these questions yield a huge array of alternative views within the literature on ideology.

The term 'ideology' originated in the late 1700s with the French Enlightenment – it was coined by the philosopher Destutt de Tracy and referred to the scientific study of ideas (McLellan, 1995, Chapter 1; Decker, 2004, Chapter 2). Aiming to explain where ideas come from, it was materialist and saw ideas as being causally dependent on the material world. Although it was dedicated to examining ideas, it opposed idealism and insisted that ideas were determined by material forces. Ideology failed to establish itself as a science and was not destined to join the academic disciplines founded during the nineteenth century. The meaning of ideology was to shift, until it no longer referred to the study of ideas but to the ideas themselves – as in modern usage, an ideology became a prevalent set of ideas and beliefs (Williams, 1988). The materialist beginnings were remembered, however, and ideologies have mostly been viewed as having material causes and justifying material interests. Concepts of ideology can still be idealist, given the importance they attach to ideas, but have grown from materialist arguments.

Materialist accounts of ideology are best illustrated by the Marxian tradition. For Marx, an ideology was the panoply of ideas, beliefs and values that suffuses a society and sustains current economic and social arrangements – located within the superstructure, it ultimately depends on the economic base. At times in Marx's writings, the bond between ideology and material interests seems closer that at others (McLellan, 1995, Chapter 2). In *The German Ideology*, the bond is loose and the formation of an ideology requires conscious deliberation by the dominant economic class; in *Capital*, commodity fetishism predicates a tight bond between capitalist production and its wider perception in ideas and beliefs (Marx and Engels, 1846 [1970]; Marx, 1867 [1976], Chapter 1). Generally speaking, Marx's materialism became stronger in his later work, a tendency reinforced by interpretations from Engels and Second International Marxism. The twentieth century witnessed a reaction against this apparent determinism, in the humanist Marxism of Lukács, Gramsci and the Frankfurt School (Lukács, 1923; Mannheim, 1936; Marcuse, 1964; Gramsci, 1971). Also critical of deterministic materialism was the structuralist Marxism of Althusser, where the superstructure has relative autonomy from the economic base and is determined by material forces only 'in the last instance' (Althusser, 1969, 1984). Despite their many differences, humanist and structuralist Marxism agreed on giving more credence to the causal influence of ideas and ideology. Some Marxian approaches have had a greater hint of idealism than others, but they all must bow to a materialist view of history.

Writers in the cultural tradition rarely alluded to ideology, distrusting its associations with materialism. Early cultural critics of capitalism took it as self-evident that classical economic theory peddled ideas apologetic to the new market arrangements. Orthodox economists were making a supposedly scientific case for laissez-faire, which depicted self-interested commercial behaviour as having desirable social consequences through the invisible hand. To criticise orthodox economics was to criticise capitalism, and the two forms of criticism proceeded in tandem without the need to distinguish them. Cultural critics were keenly aware of how economic theory rationalised the economic transformations occurring in the nineteenth century. Unlike materialists, the idealist cultural thinkers ascribed causality to ideas: this should, if anything, enhance the significance of ideology defined as a system of ideas. When discussing ideology, one can be neutral about idealism versus materialism.

Orthodox economics finds little space for ideas and beliefs: it does not envisage a layered reality in which ideas exist as a distinct level and have causal effects on the material world. Economic theory is assumed to be a lifelike image of material reality, so that theoretical ideas about reality are much the same as reality itself. Theories are conflated with their subject matter, and economics serves to elucidate things, as against presenting a perhaps false picture that legitimises a given social order. Orthodox economics lacks the conceptual depth to cope with ideology and unwittingly fulfils ideological functions. Marxian and other critics have always pointed out the ideological streaks within orthodox economics – from their perspective, the orthodox reluctance to discuss ideology is only to be expected. Neoclassical economics purports to be a positive, value-free science, yet it praises competitive markets for being allocatively efficient and treats inefficiencies such as unemployment as the result of market imperfections (Milgate and Eatwell, 1983). With perfect competition as the benchmark and ideal, the case for activist public policy is relegated to an imperfectionist mode and must deal with tricky 'second-best' special cases and correction of market failures. Because the underlying model is sympathetic to laissez-faire, any other policy arguments must be conducted on unfavourable terrain and exposed to easy criticism from libertarians. Neoclassical theory is a belief system that gives a naturalistic justification for laissez-faire, regardless of whether individual economists personally back such policies.

A critical economics has to fall somewhere in the middle ground between two extreme positions on ideology. At one extreme, exemplified by neoclassical economic theory, lie approaches that do not mention ideology, play down ideas, and proceed as if theory coincides with reality and never moulds or distorts our perceptions. Theorists are then unable to raise ideological matters and liable to forget how academic work contributes to ideology. There is no distance between economists' ideas, the belief system of orthodoxy, and the economic reality being studied; any viewpoint beyond orthodoxy is omitted. The tendency to equate economics with neoclassicism and define heterodox theories as non-economic confirms the deafness of orthodoxy towards genuine criticism. At the other extreme, exemplified by structuralist Marxism and post-structuralism, lies the view that ideology is everywhere and drenches the whole of our lives: language, thoughts, institutions and social relationships are all imbued with ideology and perpetuate the power of the dominant social classes. Nobody can evade ideology, even if they try, and all discourse is unavoidably ideological. This extreme is the opposite of the first but also stymies effective criticism – if all discussion is saturated with ideology, then external assessment is impossible. Critical academic study requires an intermediate position in which ideology is recognised and addressed but not seen as filling every corner of thought. It then becomes feasible for academics to distance themselves from the current ideology, be critical, and aim to correct erroneous assumptions and theories.

# 9. Agency and structure

Culture, defined as a process, betokens how people are cultivated within society: they are human agents who decide their own actions, but their capabilities are honed by the social context and would not take the same form elsewhere. Human agency depends on its institutional surroundings and cannot be fully understood in isolation. Cultural thought has cherished human creativity, while regarding it as being at least partly a product of culture and society. In a process of culture, human agency is entwined with social structures.

Once social sciences had begun to develop, culture was redefined as a state rather than a process and the connections between agency and structure were obscured. The new economic and social theories modelled human agency and social structure as separate entities and often favoured one over the other. Neoclassical economics went down the individualistic road and constructed its theory around the rational agent; social theory in the Durkheim tradition went down the structural road and adopted social structure as its core concept. The separation brought dualism, which divided agency from structure, and reductionism, which cast explanations wholly in terms of one or the other.

Although orthodox social science has been dualistic and reductionist, agency–structure interaction has increasingly been remarked and discussed. Since the 1960s and the revival of cultural thought, social theorists have searched for non-dualistic social theory that allows agency and structure to be mutually dependent. The search is by no means straightforward, as reductionism can easily resurface, but efforts are being made to overcome the problems of existing theories. Dualism and reductionism have been challenged and lost their erstwhile dominance – nowadays few social theorists are happy to approve them. This has made scant impression on orthodox economics, which has ignored wider movements in social science and the humanities. Individualistic reductionism remains entrenched as the foundation of orthodox theorising and the 'economic way of thinking'. Recent social theory is, nevertheless, relevant to all social sciences and shows us how economic theory could be reformulated. The present chapter starts by considering reductionism in orthodox economics, before looking at the case for non-reductionist theories.

## 9.1 AGENCY AND STRUCTURE IN ORTHODOX ECONOMICS

In its earliest, Ricardian form, orthodox economics was not individualistic and had no rule about the primacy of the human agent. Things changed when orthodoxy switched to neoclassicism and economics was reformulated from individualistic first principles. Rational economic man became the touchstone of orthodox theory. Under neoclassical assumptions, economic behaviour is instrumentally rational and any explanations and models should be thus expressed. Market-clearing equilibria are spontaneous and institution-free, emanating from the preferences of traders. The competitive ideal leads to consumer sovereignty, whereby consumers ordain what is produced and how it is allocated. Social structure receives little emphasis: individuals play no social roles and markets emerge from trading opportunities with no basis in institutions or social structures. An accent on the individual, with a neglect of social structure, gives priority to human agency. Yet the neoclassical treatment of agency is open to query; problems arise with how it is defined and how it relates to determinism and free will.

Enlightenment philosophy has been mostly deterministic and materialist, aiming to find a naturalistic causal explanation for all phenomena, including human behaviour. Thoughts and motives are insufficient to explain behaviour, and social sciences must reveal the causal laws behind human actions. Reasons cannot be causes: the grounds proffered by individuals for their actions are invalid as a causal explanation. Arguments for free will (and against determinism) were widespread in medieval philosophy and, post-Enlightenment, have been allied with Romanticism and idealism. From this perspective, human free will is an uncaused cause that cannot be dissected and broken down to causal laws – attempts to do so are doomed to failure. It follows that reasons can be causes, and the motives behind human behaviour have explanatory force. Determinism and free will may seem incompatible, but some philosophers have sought to reconcile them on the assumption that human actions are determined by internal mental processes that represent an inner cause and give the illusion of free will. These 'compatibilist' arguments have not been universally accepted, as they may swing the balance towards determinism, and the nature and significance of free will remains an ongoing debate (O'Connor, 2000; Kane, 2002; Watson, 2003). It is widely acknowledged, however, that human beings can behave as if they possess free will, whether or not this is illusory and subject to deeper causal laws.

Neoclassical economics stands squarely in the Enlightenment tradition by having a deterministic account of individual behaviour: human agents are instrumentally rational, in a means–ends framework, and choose the optimum means to attain a given end. In consumer theory, the end is utility, the means is the consumption of goods and services, and the two are linked through a preference function. Behaviour can be modelled mathematically as utility maximisation with a budget constraint and any other relevant restrictions. Early cardinal versions of neoclassicism saw utility as a measurable quantity of satisfaction or usefulness; later ordinal versions dismissed the psychological interpretation as superfluous and had a purely formal concept of utility (Davis, 2003, Chapter 2; Screpanti and Zamagni, 2005, Chapter 6). In both cases the determinism leaves no slack for individuals to exercise free will and act otherwise: once preferences are fixed, individuals have no option but to behave in accordance with them (anything else would be irrational). Knowing a person's preferences would permit his or her behaviour to be predicted and manipulated like a tool or machine. Neoclassical economics has a mechanistic outlook that models rationality as a bunch of programmed responses and denies purposeful reasoning or free will (Shackle, 1969; Loasby, 1976; De Uriarte, 1990; Hodgson, 1993a, Chapter 14). Individuals are bound to their preference functions and unable to escape into expressive rationality with conscious deliberation about preferences and objectives (Hargreaves Heap, 1989, Chapter 8, 2001). The model of behaviour comes nearer to the predictable, instrumental patterns found among animals or programmed machines than the willed and purposeful actions of a free agent (Ackoff and Emery, 1972). Notwithstanding the stress on individual choice, orthodox economics whittles human agency down to an individualistic determinism.

Neoclassical theory has little truck with social structure. All individuals have self-contained preferences that are unexplained but not apparently contingent on social context or relationships with others. Rational individuals derive their optimum behaviour without procedures, routines, norms or pre-existing roles. Personal relations have no effect on the attitudes or behaviour of the individual agent, whose actions are atomistic. Theorising starts at the bottom with the rational agent, and the need for higher, structural levels goes unnoticed. When neoclassical theory is applied to actual economic behaviour it has to operate at an institutional level above the individual, as when dealing with governments, firms or trade unions. Methodological individualism requires that activities at higher levels should be reducible to individual behaviour: if any institution is not given an individualistic explanation, then it becomes an anomaly and an impediment to explanatory theorising. Exogenous institutions outside the individualistic scheme constrain rational behaviour and prevent market-clearing equilibria. Neoclassical economics has an implicit dualism of agency and structure that debars interaction between them.

The theorems of welfare economics juxtapose perfect competition with Pareto efficiency and social structures with inefficiency. In perfect competition, rational self-interested behaviour among atomistic agents yields optimality: structural relations are undesirable because they upset the efficient equilibrium. Social structures acquire a negative aura and, since perfect competition is the benchmark for neoclassical theory, this spreads across the whole of orthodox economics. Theorists wanting plausible models have to add institutional imperfections and rigidities. Any such model becomes a special case beside the general case of perfect competition and has a 'second-best' label, given that removing imperfections would restore the competitive 'first-best'. Under these circumstances, social structures and institutions are alien intrusions upon the competitive ideal to be avoided wherever possible. The pejorative view of social structures discourages structural arguments within neoclassicism.

Agency–structure interaction is poorly defined in orthodox economics, which has a bias towards individual agency but models it in a way that precludes free will. The bluster about choice, liberty and consumer sovereignty falls short of allowing proper agency, and economic rationality consists in little more than obeying fixed, pre-programmed preference functions. Social structures likewise have only a flimsy existence as imperfections and rigidities. These attenuated accounts of agency and structure are unsuitable for comprehending the agency–structure problem.

## 9.2    STRUCTURAL SOCIAL THEORY

The word 'structure' (like 'culture') was originally a noun of process that referred to the act of building, not the end product (Williams, 1988). In its historical usage, structure signified impermanence and transformation: both Platonic idealism and medieval Christian philosophy regarded unstructured entities as being perfect, timeless and permanent, whereas the structured, man-made world was imperfect, transient and temporary. This original meaning of structure was lost during the nineteenth century when structure came to be understood as a state rather than a process – it began to denote the outcome of building. The shift in meaning was similar to the one that redefined the word 'culture' and occurred over the same period. If anything, the meaning of structure changed more dramatically than that of culture: while it once indicated variability, it now indicated fixity. The change happened simultaneously with the emergence of social sciences and had important consequences for social theory.

Social structure, defined as a process, would refer to the way in which a society was constructed from the behaviour of its members. Such a definition would allow for societies being restructured and could envisage the evolution and remaking of a society. Structure as a process never quite made it into social theory: by the time that social structure blossomed as an academic concept, structure had turned static. Social theorists have disagreed on the definition of social structure, and the term has been used in various ways (Porpora, 1989; Hays, 1994; López and Scott, 2000). The commonest has been the role-based view of Durkheim and Parsons. In the quest for a scientific sociology, Durkheim rejected neoclassical individualism and theorised at the social level (Durkheim, 1895 [1982], Chapter 5). Structural theories gained ground during the early twentieth century, assisted by their claims to scientific status, and reached their peak from the 1940s to the 1960s. Parsons had a role-based model as the foundation of his systemic social theory, which became the orthodoxy for mid-twentieth century sociology (Parsons, 1951). In Parsonian theory a social structure is a set of pre-existing, interrelated roles played by individual actors: structural relations are among roles, not actors, and continue to exist even if the entire cast of role occupants is changed. The theory is timeless and static, so that social structures persist regardless of the agents involved. Each social structure has a function, by analogy with a living organism whose interrelated parts contribute to the organism's survival. Social structures are separated from individual agency, in a dualistic relationship, and have the final say on individual and social behaviour.

Structural theories in sociology could never match the hegemony of neoclassical theory in orthodox economics. Sociology was more pluralistic than economics and found space for alternatives, especially the Weberian interpretative tradition. The reductionism in social theory was less strident: it stemmed from formal theories but was not axiomatic. Mathematical and quantitative methods were less prominent, and the structural slant came about through the practice of theorising rather than programmatic design. By the 1960s, structural theories were being upbraided for their timelessness, inadequate treatment of human agency, functional explanation, and political conservatism (Mills, 1959, Chapter 2; Wrong, 1961; Homans, 1964; Gouldner, 1970). The critique was contemporaneous with the revival of cultural thought and shared the same sources. As new ideas have developed and expanded, social theorising has spawned a multitude of theories that differ in the weight they give to social structure. Within this pluralism, social structure remains a core concept, and a role-based view is still the one most frequently encountered.

A role-based view means that social structures may conflict with individual agency. In the resulting dualism, agency and structures exist apart, have little mutual dependence, and interact chiefly through tensions, frictions and constraints. Sociologists have given precedence to structure within the dualism. A social structure is reproduced because most people perform their allotted roles and do not act otherwise – conformity and normalised behaviour are the order of the day. Social structures serve as guidelines for individual behaviour, supplying everyone with a template for personal interaction. The roles are essentially a script or blueprint that must be followed if the society is to survive and function successfully. Individual agents have little space to act independently and, if they did, society would be destabilised and cease to exist in its current form. Social structures hold agency in check, so as to prevent the chaos of untrammelled individual behaviour. In this respect an agency–structure conflict, with structures ultimately in control, becomes a feature of all stable societies.

Agency–structure dualism is seldom even-handed and often brings reductionist theorising in which either agency or structure predominates. The dualism of orthodox economics, with atomistic models and sparse social structures, gives an individualistic reductionism. The dualism of much social theory goes to the opposite pole and gives a structural reductionism, where human behaviour can be understood only through social structures. Individual agents are separate from structures but passively follow structural roles. Agency loses its potential for initiating change and is locked into a fixed structural framework defining an unchanging, continuously repeated pattern of social relations. Structural reductionism has been less doctrinaire than its individualistic equivalent but has similar consequences in directing attention towards only one side of the agency–structure dualism. In principle, dualism does not have to be reductionist, but the agency–structure tensions are apt to produce asymmetry as one side 'wins' the battle. Orthodox economics has favoured individual agency (in a weak, deterministic form), sociology has favoured social structure. Disciplinary divisions have affirmed the contrast and dispelled attempts to overcome dualism. Each discipline has its own theories, and 'individualistic' economics has been demarcated from 'structural' sociology.

## 9.3   NON-REDUCTIONIST SOCIAL THEORY

In responding to structural reductionism, some social theorists opted for smaller-scale methods that relaxed structural constraints on behaviour and looked towards agency, personal interactions and subjective states of mind: examples were symbolic interactionism, ethnomethodology and phenomenological sociology, all of which had earlier sources but attracted renewed interest in the late twentieth century (Craib, 1992, Chapters 5 and 6; Outhwaite, 2005; Layder, 2006, Part 2). Piecemeal, bottom-up social theorising replaced grand system building. A micro orientation was teamed with interpretative methods, though the focus was on the individual rather than the cultural context. The new theories and methods were an antidote to structural excesses and helped reinstate agency but were liable to overreact and give it priority over structure. A perennial problem for social theory has been the difficulty of incorporating agency and structure without letting one subdue the other. Recent social theory has met the problem explicitly by acknowledging agency–structure interaction and searching for a non-dualistic perspective. This endeavour touches all social sciences, including economics.

The salient issue is how to make agency and structure interdependent without dissolving their distinct identities or granting either of them precedence. Agency–structure dualism preserves their distinctness but says little about how they are related and suffers from individualistic or structural biases. In seeking alternatives, social theorists have highlighted the interdependence of agency and structure while resisting a merger and upholding their separate existence. One alternative is to have agency–structure duality instead of dualism, so that agency and structure are conceptually distinct but thoroughly intertwined and dependent on each other for their existence (Bhaskar, 1979; Giddens, 1976, Chapter 3, 1984). In agency–structure duality, social structures can be reproduced only by continuous human agency and individual agents acquire their abilities only after being moulded by the structural environment. Agency and structure cannot exist in isolation, neither is pre-eminent, and each can influence the other (Jackson, 1999). Duality-based social theory should offset the tendencies in agency–structure dualism to set up a contest between two sides, with one side as the winner. The idea of duality is now familiar in social theorising but has not yielded a unified theory – Bhaskar and Giddens differ, for example, in their definitions of social structure (Bhaskar, 1983). Many social theorists have made arguments akin to duality and emphasised agency–structure interdependencies but have devised their own conceptual language and schemes (Bourdieu, 1977; Alexander, 1985; Munch and Smelser, 1987; Turner, 1988; Archer, 1995, 1996; Mouzelis, 1995). While these theories have many differences, they suggest a loose consensus on the need to bring agency and structure closer together and make them interdependent.

Duality-based social theory has an affinity with cultural thought. Formation of individual agents within a structured social context is a modern theoretical restatement of culture as a process. Culture is the bond between agency and structure, a fact long known in cultural thought but only lately rediscovered by social theorists. Cultural processes had been obscured in the social theorising of the early twentieth century, when

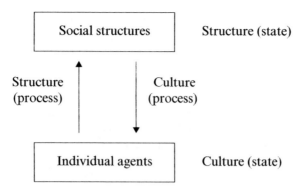

*Figure 9.1    Duality of agency and structure*

culture became frozen as a state and structure too became static and rigid. To have social structures formed and reproduced through individual agency squares with the definition of structure as a process. Giddens uses the term 'structuration' to cover the formation of structures, but this forgets that structure can be a process: using a new term ratifies the later notion of structure as a state. Agency–structure duality fits neatly into cultural thought, as Figure 9.1 shows.

Culture as a process describes how individuals are formed and shaped within society; structure as a process describes how social structures are created and reproduced through individual agency. The end products of culture and structure are cultivated individuals with given ways of living and acting (culture as a state) and structured social relationships (structure as a state). A duality-based social theory invokes the former notions of culture and structure as processes in order to glue together their later, static definitions and calm the dualistic tensions between them.

Alongside duality, another alternative to agency–structure dualism has been to argue for new concepts of social structure founded on personal relations rather than impersonal roles. In figurational sociology, human agents are related not through role playing but through chains of personal interaction varying in their intensity and durability (Elias, 1978, 1991). These personal relations or 'figurations' take in both agency and structure: they are a vehicle for human agency, enabling agents to do things otherwise unfeasible, and a social framework that continually reproduces society. A stark agency–structure dualism becomes redundant, as each is encapsulated within figurations. Weak, informal personal relations are closer to agency and strong, formal ones closer to structure; in a figurational method neither agency nor structure exists in a pure form and figurations encompass them both. Other sociologists have made similar arguments in different conceptual terms. An 'interaction order' based on personal relations can, for example, be contrasted with an 'institutional order' based on impersonal relations (Goffman, 1983). Unlike figurations, the interaction order coexists with the institutional order: role-based social structures are retained but augmented by personal social structures that bridge the dualistic agency–structure gap. The interaction order is an outlet for individual agency within society: it enriches social theory without losing the possibility of binding, impersonal roles. Personal relations in social theory can end the dualism of agency and structure by either melding them into a figurational whole or adding a personal level – the interaction order – to stand beside the institutional order of impersonal roles. The first alternative redraws the map of social theory by transcending agency and structure, but the second keeps them and theorises about the middle ground of personal relations.

Personal social structures are compatible with agency–structure duality. Any personal relationship must have the active involvement of the agents concerned and would cease to exist if either agent withdrew. Human agency is essential if personal social structures are to persist and thrive. As with impersonal roles, personal relations influence behaviour and mould human agency. Isolated individuals would not be able to act or think as normal – their identity depends on their social context, without which they would be different people. Many human capabilities rely on the support and cooperation of others known to us. Agency and personal social structures are interlaced in a duality resembling that between agency and impersonal roles; the agency–structure link is often stronger with personal social structures. This opens up the prospect of combining the two novel strands in social theory by allowing for both agency–structure duality and a layering of social structures.

Once personal social structures are added to impersonal ones, social structure has the form shown in Figure 9.2. Impersonal roles remain important for social structure, but a personal element now intrudes. No social role or contract can ever be so complete as to cover every facet of the role occupant's or contractor's behaviour; loopholes are inevitable. Gaps in formal arrangements are filled by informal relations among people who find their own ways of working. Roles are performed differently by different role-occupants, so social structures have a personal as well as impersonal side. Some roles are tighter than others, leaving less space for personal ways of working, but no roles can ever dictate exactly how a person must behave – the real world is too complex for that. Social structure consists of impersonal roles that exist independently of role occupants, along with personal relations among the current role players. To neglect either the personal or impersonal element would give an incomplete understanding;

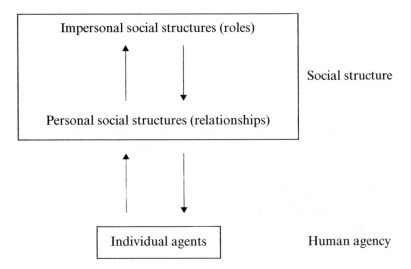

*Figure 9.2    An augmented account of social structure*

both elements are yoked to human agency through agency–structure duality. Personal social structures have sometimes been seen as an agency–structure hybrid (as in figurational sociology), but here they are integrated into a layered social structure while coexisting with a separate concept of agency.

Critics of duality-based and figurational social theory have accused them of obfuscating the agency–structure distinction, to the detriment of social structure, and explaining behaviour in terms of agency (Callinicos, 1985; Layder, 1987, 2006; Mouzelis, 1989; Archer, 1990; Outhwaite, 1990). Attempts to pull agency and structure closer together may mix them and give the upper hand to one or the other. Since many social theorists have been reacting against structural functionalism, the danger is that playing down structure leads to overcompensation and an undue preoccupation with agency. The theories of Giddens, who has his own weakened definition of social structure, and Elias, who replaces social structure with figurations, are easy targets for such criticisms. If role-based social structures are retained, then a careful duality need not blur the contributions of agency and structure. Some authors have proposed holding on to dualism, perhaps in combination with duality, so as to remind ourselves about agency–structure tensions (Mouzelis, 1995; Layder, 2006). On an individual level, certain agents may feel fettered by social structures and uncomfortable with them, while others may feel empowered and pleased to conform to them – the first case seems nearer to dualism, the second to duality. To capture both cases, one might let dualism coexist with duality, portraying different degrees of agency–structure tension (Mouzelis, 1995, Chapter 6). There is no consensus on the combined usage, and duality has normally been an alternative to dualism: agents who reproduce social structures unwillingly are then viewed as being in a constrained duality relation rather than a dualism. Agreement on agency–structure interaction has not generated unanimity on how the interaction should be theorised. When employing duality, one should recall the likelihood of agency–structure conflicts and not assume that interaction is always harmonious.

## 9.4　THE CASE FOR NON-REDUCTIONIST ECONOMIC THEORY

Recent social theorising has sprouted mainly from the sociological literature, motivated by an urge to break free from structural reductionism. This is not an issue in orthodox economics, where social structure hardly registers and individualism reigns supreme. One might then wonder whether the sociological arguments pertain to economics. They do have generality, as they criticise all reductionist theories, not just those with a structural bias. When applied to orthodox economic theory, the thrust of the critical message is reversed: the argument is no longer to buttress agency but to give due allowance for structure and stop individualistic reductionism. Once agency becomes interdependent with structure it loses its primacy and blends into a broader picture of social activity; theory can accommodate culture as a process and renounce claims about universal, timeless behaviour.

Disavowal of reductionism sanctions the independent existence and causal influence of institutions and social structures, which can be defined formally, recognised, and licensed to exist without being reduced to individual behaviour. The desire for 'microfoundations', so pervasive in neoclassical theory, is superfluous, and explanations can be micro or macro according to the behaviour being investigated. All economic activities may have individualistic and structural aspects, with no presumption of an even balance between them – at times the structural aspect might dominate, at other times the individualistic. The dictum that rational individual agency governs economic behaviour is lifted, and economic theory is free to examine culture and social structure.

As a substitute for reductionism comes a stratified perspective in which several distinct layers coexist and interact. Individual agency and social structures (personal and impersonal) are layers amid a larger scheme that has other layers at higher and lower levels. Instead of following a prescribed programme of reductionist explanation, theorists can afford to be open-minded. If institutions guide economic activities, then this can be admitted and tolerated in explanatory analysis. A stratified perspective allows higher levels to possess powers emergent from lower levels but not wholly reducible to them. Higher levels can exert a downward causal influence on lower levels, so that the parts cannot be understood without the whole (Lawson, 1997, Part III; Hodgson, 2002, 2003; Davis, 2004). While institutions rely on human agency for their existence, they have causal effects above and beyond agency. Since agents are shaped by their social environment, structure and agency are inextricably bound together in a duality. This goes for all behaviour, including economic activities.

One area that could benefit from stratification is the theoretical modelling of markets. Despite their omnipresence in economic theory, markets are seldom clearly defined and often equated with any sort of trading (Hodgson, 1988, Chapter 8; Sayer, 1995, Chapter 4, 2003; Rosenbaum, 2000). For neoclassical economists the ideal, perfectly competitive market has anonymous trade, no market power, and price-taking behaviour by all traders. Neoclassical theory is taciturn about the social and institutional context, as if markets could somehow appear from nowhere whenever trading opportunities occur. Perfect competition does not happen in practice, and actual markets display market power, price-setting behaviour and interactions among traders known to each other. To define a market by the features of perfect competition would exclude nearly all trading activity described as a market in common language. From a heterodox angle, market trading depends on institutional context and should not be modelled as spontaneous and disembedded from social relations (Granovetter, 1985). Traders make personal contacts and undertake relational exchange with known and trusted trading partners (Goldberg, 1976, 1980; Macneil, 1981). Markets typically have a degree of personal trading: it is most obvious in labour markets, which turn on the cultural background to employer–employee relations (Austen, 2000). Observed trading behaviour is miles away from perfect competition, yet orthodoxy still covets this as the ideal. A fuller theoretical account of markets should assess the institutions that define property rights, regulate transfers of property, and create the roles of seller and buyer (Fourie, 1991; Swedberg, 2003, Chapter 5). Structural approaches of this kind are consonant with traditional social theory but have a weakness in their omission of relational exchange. In a layered structural framework, relational exchange can be included at the level of personal social structures coexisting and interacting with the impersonal, role-based level (Jackson, 2007b). A single framework can then embrace the formal and informal relations among traders, as well as the differing engagement of individual traders with these social structures.

Markets are no longer handcuffed to an abstract case of perfection and can be defined more accurately and realistically.

Layered structural thinking also has relevance for theories depicting firms and other organisations. In a role-based theory, the internal composition of a firm is a set of pre-existing roles and positions, independent of the role occupants and related through a hierarchy. Within actual firms, formal roles and positions are never fully specified. Employment contracts are incomplete and job descriptions do not cover every eventuality or say exactly how an employee should interact with colleagues. Role occupants, while meeting the formal requirements of their post, can find personal ways of working in the loopholes left by contracts. Each role occupant has unique attributes and interacts differently with managers and co-workers. The spaces within roles open up the slackness by which a given social structure can weather the complexities and uncertainties surrounding events. Personal relations and networking have been highlighted in recent commentary on information technology, post-Fordism and postmodernity (Amin, 1994; Nielsen, 1994; Castells, 2000). All economies have large informal components, especially in the domestic sector, that make a major contribution to production but are omitted from national accounts and overlooked in most economic analysis (Wheelock, 1992; Wheelock and Oughton, 1996; Elson, 1998). A layered, non-reductionist theory can set personal relations within a larger agency–structure framework. The personal element adds flexibility to social structures and helps to explain how they adapt to external pressures and challenges (Jackson, 2007a). Any durable institutions have internal slackness that leaves room for variable, personalised ways of working to cope with unforeseen circumstances. Institutionalists have been awake to the complex, layered quality of institutions and avoided tying them to a single analytical level (Neale, 1987; Searle, 2005; Hodgson, 2006b). Layered social structures can represent this stratified quality in theoretical terms.

Structural arguments have found it easier to explain stability than change. If social structures are layered, then variability among roles and personal relations creates openings for transformation. In a stable society, one would expect personal relations to conform to pre-existing roles (but not match them exactly), with few tensions or pressures for change. Small variations in personal ways of working bring flexibility and suppleness that protects the overall social system. At a time of change, personal relations become estranged from current roles and positions, and an adjustment in one or the other may ensue: roles may be reformed to fit new behaviour, or behaviour may adapt to fit new roles. Economic development is then marked by a series of matches and mismatches between personal and impersonal social structures. The conflictive, dialectical vision resembles heterodox theories of social and economic change: examples are regulation theory and related accounts of long waves in economic development (Tylecote, 1991; Freeman and Louçã, 2001; Boyer and Saillard, 2002) and the institutionalist theories that appeal to tensions between institutions, technology and socio-cultural values (Bush, 1987; Dolfsma, 2004, Chapter 3; Dolfsma and Verburg, 2008). By the materialism of regulation theory, changes start at the level of productive activities (the accumulation regime) and cause a mismatch with an institutional context (the mode of regulation) better suited to earlier production methods. The mismatch blocks economic progress, and sustained growth becomes possible only when institutions are reformed and rematched with the new production methods. Materialism says that changes must start at the bottom with new ways of working that clash with prevailing institutions until formal roles and positions are revised accordingly. But a layered structural theory is not confined to causal materialism and can also include the alternative, idealist standpoint (Jackson, 2003). Social changes may be implemented top down through the replanning of formal roles and positions – this arises when managers in business or government redesign their organisations from a prior theoretical scheme. A recent example on a large scale has been the administrative reforms to create internal markets and new working practices within public services such as health care (McMaster, 2001). Here the formal roles and positions change first, and employees must adapt their ways of working to fit the new roles. A layered, non-reductionist theory carries no presupposition that social change starts in one particular layer.

Besides enhancing social structure, a layered theory strengthens individual agency. Social structures never influence individual behaviour so thoroughly as to erase the ability to do otherwise. Even if structures sometimes constrain human agency, they also amplify it through learning and personal development. Realisation of human capabilities depends not only on individual and material factors but on institutions and personal relations (Jackson, 2005; van Staveren, 2008)). As cultural thinkers have long argued, creativity and the potential to act must be cultivated within a supportive social setting. Social structures are vital for an individual's sense of identity. Human behaviour has a self-referent or reflexive quality in the tendency to form and uphold an identity based on self-images or imagined images in the eyes of others (Goffman, 1971; Rosenberg, 1979; Gecas, 1982). These images, which feed on the social and cultural context, are central to the formation of the self within modern societies. People express themselves by selecting among existing cultural images and internalising the images into personal identity. Choices among consumer goods are a way of communicating values, delivering messages, propping up self-esteem and declaring membership of social groups (Douglas and Isherwood, 1980; Campbell, 1987; Coşgel, 1997, 2008; Dolfsma, 2002, 2004). Reflexivity has a big impact on consumer spending and is thoroughly exploited by advertisers, but gets limited attention from economists and has been discussed chiefly in consumer research and other non-economic literatures (Sirgy, 1982; Belk, 1988; Leslie, 1997). Economic behaviour can be grasped only by studying social structures and asking how they carve an individual's identity and self-perception. Paradoxically, more detailed study of social structures would improve our knowledge of the individual agent.

Another feature of human agency is intersubjectivity. This implies that agents do not exist in isolation and cannot be modelled adequately by an individualistic theory: interactions between agents may change their beliefs and preferences, rendering atomism untenable (Fullbrook, 2002; Beckert, 2003; Davis, 2003, Chapter 6). Intersubjectivity takes many forms. The simplest and most direct is when agents imitate each other to yield normalised behaviour patterns. Long-standing norms may acquire permanence through being codified and taking an impersonal form unconnected with any particular agents. More complex interactions occur if agents consciously reassess their identity and values by drawing comparisons with other people. Social interactions are then reflexive, with individuals defining themselves in relation to others, and give rise to expressive rather than instrumental rationality. In economics, intersubjective behaviour appears wherever consumers copy each other, follow fashions, or use consumption to assert their social status. Theories of such behaviour have been around for a long time: examples are Veblen's notion of conspicuous consumption, Duesenberry's relative income hypothesis, Katona's psychological approach to economic behaviour, and Hirsch's arguments about positional goods (Veblen, 1899; Duesenberry, 1949; Katona, 1951, 1975; Hirsch, 1977). None has entered the economic mainstream, yet the emptiness of neoclassical consumer theory and the prevalence of conspicuous consumption suggests that these and similar ideas will persist (Ackerman, 1997; Rosenbaum, 1999; Trigg, 2001; Mayhew, 2002; Mason, 2002; Lavoie, 2004). Much culturally sensitive research on consumer behaviour has been done outside mainstream economics in the separate field of economic psychology (Earl and Kemp, 1999; Earl, 2005). Intersubjectivity may also propel speculative behaviour, as in Keynes's account of how investors anticipate the decisions of others (Keynes, 1936, Chapter 12; 1937). The resort to imitation when confronted with uncertainty means that investors are afraid to make subjective individual judgements and fall in line with mass opinion (Dupuy, 2002). Any theory that calls upon interactions among agents cannot be purely individualistic and needs other levels of analysis for personal relations and social conventions.

Most theories of human agency have assumed that agents formulate intentions only as individuals. If agents formulate collective intentions as well, then there are further links between agency and structure (Davis, 2002, 2003, Chapter 7). This idea, bypassed in orthodox economics, has been considered by philosophers and social theorists (Bratman, 1999; Searle, 1990, 1995; Tuomela, 1995). If collective intentions exist, then a human agent can have intentions defined through self-interest (I-intentions) and through the reciprocal, mutually reinforcing attitudes of a social group (we-intentions). The latter require a belief that other group members share the same values, whether or not this is actually the case. To argue for we-intentions is not to argue for a group mind or collective will – agency still resides at the individual level but identifies with a higher, group level. Collective intentionality can clarify the theoretical status of firms and other organisations. Orthodox economics models firms as rational, profit-maximising agents, treating their internal composition as a black box, and prefers not to dwell on multiple objectives. Since firms cannot think or act for themselves, their modelling as agents is problematic (Thompson, 1982; Douglas, 1987; Khalil, 1997). Social theories with collective intentionality permit layered firms and organisations: at the institutional level a firm has a legal identity and comprises formal roles and positions, from chief executive downwards; at the relational level it comprises the ongoing personal relations among owners, managers and employees; at the individual level it comprises the human agency of everyone involved, not only through self-interested I-intentions but through collective we-intentions. Collective intentionality is strong in a cohesive, harmonious organisation but weak in a fragmented one with alienated, disengaged staff. We-intentions flesh out the complex agency–structure relations in a non-dualistic theory and introduce group identities internalised within the individual.

Releasing economics from reductionism would evaporate the claims to a unique economic method founded on individualism and instrumental rationality. Economics could be reintegrated with social theorising and defined by subject matter, not method. Non-reductionist social theory provides a framework within which more specific research can take place: it is broad enough to be a safeguard against partial and lopsided views. The original notions of culture and structure as processes are consistent with the framework, and any particular economic theories would be special cases of a general social theory attuned to cultural thought.

# 10.  Interpretative methods

Cultural thought has always advocated interpretative methods. All cultures depend on how people think and behave in particular historical circumstances. Theory and empirical research cannot tap into human motivation, given that thoughts are unique, not directly observable and only patchily and selectively recorded. As an alternative to rationalism and empiricism, the Counter-Enlightenment argued for interpretative methods. Scholars can try to comprehend and reconstruct why people acted in a certain way – interpretation plugs the holes in social studies and provides the means for an understanding of human behaviour.

The case for interpretation has never been readily accepted by social scientists. According to strict empiricism, thoughts are outside our sensory range and any attempt to reconstruct them is speculative. In the study of human motives, natural scientists have balked at going further than introspection, the internal observation of one's own thoughts. Anyone else's thoughts are out of bounds to introspective empiricism and unsuitable as an object of scientific study. Although introspection was tolerated in early psychology, positivism and behaviourism replaced introspective methods with experimental ones. Under the later, less tolerant regime, natural sciences could study observable human activity and the physiology of the brain but not human thought. Immediate investigation of thinking and ideas, whether interpretative or introspective, was excluded.

Interpretative methods have had few proponents, least of all in economics. Most social sciences grew up during the first half of the twentieth century, a time when positivism was rampant and the desire to copy natural sciences overwhelming. Hermeneutics – the formal practice of interpretation – was narrowly defined and peripheral. Orthodox economics, under the thumb of neoclassicism, has been impervious to interpretative methods, which have been sidelined to economic history or heterodox schools. By the late twentieth century, the revival of cultural thought brought renewed interest in hermeneutics (Winch, 1958; Berger and Luckmann, 1967; Giddens, 1976, Chapter 1; Ricoeur, 1976, 1981; Taylor, 1979b; Bleicher, 1980; Outhwaite, 1986). Many academic disciplines now take interpretation seriously, but economics remains an exception: orthodoxy carries on as if interpretative problems do not exist. This is complacent and unwise, as interpretation is fundamental to all social studies.

# 10.1  HERMENEUTICS AND INTERPRETATION

While a case for interpretative methods can be found in eighteenth-century writers like Vico and Herder, hermeneutics as a subject dates back to the early nineteenth century. In its original sense it referred to the study of historical texts – usually from classical antiquity or biblical sources – and the recovery of their meaning. These texts, with their cultural and linguistic distance from the present, were not self-explanatory and required a special interpretative effort. A better understanding of texts was attainable only if a sensitive scholar could imaginatively return to the time and place of writing and empathise with the author. Interpretation had an empirical starting point in the written, observable text but went on to penetrate thoughts, beliefs and feelings. The goal was scientific: to reveal the truth and acquire disinterested knowledge by exposing the real meaning of historical documents.

The textual focus of hermeneutics eventually broadened out into a general method for social sciences. During the nineteenth century Friedrich Schleiermacher and Wilhelm Dilthey elaborated and formalised hermeneutics, making a contrast with natural sciences. Schleiermacher combined cultural/linguistic analysis and reconstruction of authorial intent, with the aim of putting individual creativity within a cultural context (Schleiermacher, 1838). Knowing the author became paramount and tended to overshadow linguistic issues. Dilthey regarded hermeneutics as the defining method of the human sciences, applicable in textual exegesis but reaching beyond that to any social research (Dilthey, 1910 [1976]; Rickman, 1961). Understanding (*Verstehen*) could be gained by extending interpretation to all ideas and beliefs. Study of texts became a subset of the study of human societies, which diverged from the methods of natural sciences.

The concentration on authorial meaning and subjective re-enactment in early hermeneutics left it with an individualistic slant. To interpret only the thoughts of an author risks overlooking the context within which the author is located. A preoccupation with the individual was at odds with the cultural tradition, which had given equal billing to historical circumstances. As hermeneutics developed into a specialised sphere of authorial interpretation, it moved away from cultural or social matters towards the individual agent. It hoped to unveil the motives behind personal behaviour and explain objectively why people acted as they did. Such reasoning led Dilthey and Weber to correlate hermeneutics with a variety of methodological individualism. This differs from the axiomatic individualism of neoclassical economics, but it rests all explanation upon interpretations of individual behaviour. Culture and society play no independent part and become subordinate to individual meanings and intentions.

Later hermeneutical thinking has avoided individualism and placed greater weight on social context. An impetus in this direction came from the philosophy of Edmund Husserl and Martin Heidegger, who saw hermeneutics as dealing not with internal thought but with the individual's existence and relationship with the world. Interest shifted away from epistemology and the understanding of the individual to the ontology of a person's being and consciousness. Husserl was concerned with the 'life-world' (*Lebenswelt*) or lived environment that frames our consciousness and determines the meaning of objects but eludes the usual methods of scientific explanation (Husserl, 1913 [1931]). Heidegger, dissatisfied with discussion of the individual self alone, examined the larger notions of self-in-the-world or self-in-time, which entailed the inseparability of consciousness from its spatial and temporal setting (Heidegger, 1927 [1962]). His arguments were taken up and extended in Hans-Georg Gadamer's philosophical reformulation of hermeneutics (Gadamer, 1975, 1976; Bleicher, 1980, Part II). For Gadamer, interpretative understanding is possible only if context is acknowledged – it puts the object of study within a cultural context and sets that context against the one that prevails here and now. To understand human behaviour we need to locate it within the way of life from which it emerged, and appreciate how this way of life differs from our own. Hermeneutics is historically specific, so that a single, definitive interpretation no longer beckons. Understanding ensues from a discourse between two traditions, one containing the investigator, the other the object of study. In Gadamer's eyes, hermeneutics is crucial for any scholarly enquiry, natural or social, and unifies the sciences into a non-positivistic whole.

Modern hermeneutics has scrutinised how language generates meaning. This had been latent in hermeneutics from the start but was obscured when interest diverted to the thoughts of individual authors. A shared language permits communication between individuals who may not be living in the same time and place. Understanding texts or actions at a historical or geographical remove demands a common element in language and its use, so that the analyst can jump the cultural defile and re-express meaning to make it intelligible to current readers. Linguistics has been prominent in twentieth-century philosophy and social sciences, as in structuralism and Wittgenstein's language-games. Structuralism has looked for absolute language structures, a possibility at variance with the cultural specificity of hermeneutics. Wittgenstein's language-games have a semantic relativism that meshes with hermeneutics, yet he said little about the interpretative problems of transcending language barriers. From a hermeneutical viewpoint, a specific way of life can be utterly different from ours but still leave space for understanding by investigators willing to mediate. Comprehension of behaviour and texts comes from a cultural dialogue as against a straight interpretation of someone's thoughts. Any interpretative method has to heed cultural context.

A thorny issue with hermeneutics is whether it can supply objective knowledge or is confined to subjective and contestable accounts. In its earliest versions, it was presented as a specialised technique that yields objective scientific results. This can be seen in Schleiermacher's formalised hermeneutics, although subjectivity when interpreting behaviour remained a problem. Later versions were less formal, and the fervour for objectivity seemed to diminish. Hermeneutics stood on the non-scientific side of the anti-naturalistic wall between sciences and humanities. Knowledge from interpretation, while appropriate to the humanities, was viewed as being different in kind from the objective findings of natural sciences. Pushed further, hermeneutics raised doubts about natural-scientific research, in Gadamer's argument that all human activities (including natural sciences) must rely upon interpretative understanding. This divulges the interpretative flaws in natural sciences but may undermine critical study by making everything subjective. The relativism jars with earlier hermeneutics, which hankered after objectivity, and amounts to a pyrrhic victory: hermeneutics may be truly general, spanning all natural and social sciences, but nowhere does it disperse the fog of subjectivity.

Various attempts have been made in recent social theory to honour and practise hermeneutics without dissolving into a subjectivism that casts doubt on academic work. Salient here is the critical theory of the Frankfurt School and related authors (Held, 1980; Geuss, 1981; Kellner, 1989; Craib, 1992, Part IV). Humanistic and anti-positivist, the Frankfurt School was sympathetic to hermeneutics; at the same time, abiding by its Marxian origins, it avoided extreme subjectivism and relativism in order to have a critical position from which to analyse capitalism. Hermeneutics, though relevant for all scholarship, had to be supplemented with empirical and theoretical methods. The social theory of Jürgen Habermas, who inherited the Frankfurt School tradition, is a prime example of such reasoning (Habermas, 1979, 1984, 1987). He prefers not to abandon the Enlightenment hopes for objective knowledge but disowns positivism and searches for a critical theory with some interpretative zest. The centrepiece of his social theory is communicative action based on shared understandings. Unlike the instrumental behaviour portrayed in orthodox economics, communicative action cannot be atomistic and happens only when individuals find common ground by linguistic or other means. The accent on communication and interpretative understanding gives hermeneutics a leading role. It does not exhaust social investigation, however, and constitutes just one component of Habermas's larger scheme – it is necessary but not sufficient in social theorising.

Critical realist social science has a similar attitude towards hermeneutics (Bhaskar, 1979; Outhwaite, 1987, Chapter 4; Sayer, 1992, Chapter 1). For critical realists, social science must be grounded in realist ontology, otherwise scientific goals would have no secure foundation and criticism would be impossible. Arguments that hermeneutics governs all social studies could convey an implicit realism that grants interpretative methods exclusive access to reality. A hermeneutic hegemony would pre-commit social studies to hermeneutics and deny the existence of a social reality defined separately from interpretation. To prevent this, ontology should be distinct from any methods chosen and non-reductionist about agency and structure. Hermeneutics could then be recognised, but interpretative understanding would not be the only legitimate method or sole arbiter of realism – empirical or theoretical methods could be used when appropriate. Critical realists have been generous in supporting interpretation but unwilling to allow hermeneutics a monopoly of scientific method. Instead, they want pluralism that includes hermeneutics.

The complex and slippery nature of hermeneutics has provoked lively debate. There is no official hermeneutic methodology, nor is one ever likely to emerge. Rather than fixed procedures, hermeneutics offers ideas about social investigation and what distinguishes it from natural science. The ideas alone cannot confer success in social science, but if neglected they leave things partial and incomplete. When cultural thought was rejuvenated in the late twentieth century, social theorists realised the pervasiveness of hermeneutic questions and incorporated them into social theory. The rest of the chapter discusses what interpretative methods imply for social theorising in general and economic theory in particular.

## 10.2   PRE-INTERPRETED SOCIAL REALITY

Modern hermeneutics has highlighted the difficulties of interpreting human behaviour. The chief obstacle is pre-interpretation: our prior beliefs distort our understanding. In textual study we cannot recover an author's thoughts, and claims to have done so are open to challenge. Nor can we recreate and re-experience a text's reception within its own period. Interpretation must mediate between one context and another. We have no external place, untainted by presuppositions, from which we can undertake social study. As we never escape pre-interpretation, it is healthy to respect this and not minimise interpretative difficulties or brush them aside. Problems of pre-interpretation mean that social studies are daunting and recondite, but not impossible, and need interpretative skills from the researcher.

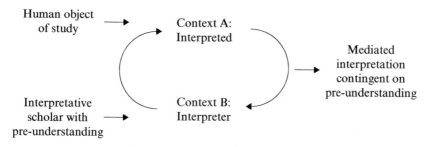

*Figure 10.1    The hermeneutic circle*

These problems are often summarised by the hermeneutic circle. Circularity comes from the interplay between the different contextual worlds of interpreter and interpreted, which can never be merged but can be brought closer together. An interpreter is unable to relive an agent's thoughts and feelings or re-enter the agent's cultural environment, but can nevertheless have a critical understanding from his or her own cultural milieu. Interpretation becomes a two-way process in which one contextual form of behaviour can be studied only from the perspective of another, producing an outcome contingent on both, as in Figure 10.1.

A scholar in Context B has no other vantage point and must study with pre-interpretations from the prevailing culture and language. If this is appreciated, then the scholar can seek a mediated interpretative appraisal of behaviour in Context A. Comparisons between contexts may show how they differ and enable the scholar to understand actions in Context A from a perspective in Context B. Facets of behaviour may be common to both contexts, especially if one believes that some human motives are universal and invariant. Interpretations are context-specific, and so a scholar in Context C would obtain results different from those obtained in Context B. Context-dependent results seem to imply relativism or subjectivity that denies the possibility of social science. The hermeneutic circle does indeed hint at the huge puzzles and perplexities faced by social scientists, but it does not invalidate social study – the relativity, spatial or temporal, stops short of ontological relativism.

The quandaries raised by the hermeneutic circle vary with the object of study. Generally speaking, the further apart in time and space are Contexts A and B, the greater are the hurdles to interpretation. Interpretative understanding of a society thousands of years in the past, organised on wholly different principles from the modern world, is harder than understanding of contemporary societies. Wherever Contexts A and B have broad similarities, the chances for effective interpretation are improved.

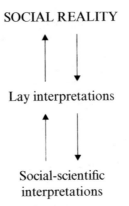

*Figure 10.2    The double hermeneutic*

This is not to say that interpretative study is ever straightforward. Even if interpreter and interpreted share the same cultural/linguistic setting, Contexts A and B are not identical and perfect understanding remains elusive. Consider, for example, the interpretative hitches among academics. Since they are working within a common profession and should have well rehearsed interpretative skills, academics might be expected to understand each other. Yet interpretative problems frequently beset academic work and misunderstandings of authorial intent are legion. If they cannot be expunged from the academic community, then they must be widespread in everyday life. At first glance natural sciences might seem safe from interpretative troubles because their objects of study, generally inanimate and non-human, lack intentional behaviour to be interpreted. Natural science does, all the same, rely on mutual understanding among scientists. While academic disciplines differ in their hermeneutic content, all involve hermeneutics to some degree.

Recent social theory has taken up and embodied interpretation. Traditional hermeneutics was done by the scholar, but ordinary people are also immersed in interpretation – they too are trying to understand each other and make sense of the world in which they live. The informal, lay interpretations of social reality coexist with social-scientific interpretations and may interact with them. This yields a 'double hermeneutic' whereby scholarly interpretations stand alongside informal ones that influence beliefs, values, behaviour and social relations (Giddens, 1976, Chapter 2). Figure 10.2 shows the resulting interdependencies.

Social scientists aim to understand social reality, which exists as a real object of study. Their access to it is indirect and passes through human agents who themselves interpret it in a less formal way. Many of the lay interpretations will be casual, imitative and taken from a selective acquaintance with scientific research. Social science has to be aware that it can affect its own object of study. When lay interpretations mimic social-scientific ones, probably in a simplified form, the danger exists that social sciences become partly self-fulfilling: they appear to be corroborated by observed behaviour merely because agents base their actions on prevailing beliefs. Critical social science should remember this and not be led astray by correspondence between lay and social-scientific views, both of which could be wrong. In a double hermeneutic, the standard hermeneutic circle applies to both lay and social-scientific interpretations but is compounded by the interactions between them.

Economics has always had a double hermeneutic because it has informed economic agents and policy-makers. Governments, advised by economists, pursue policies derived from academic economics (usually orthodox). Financiers and industrialists have a less direct link to economic theory but still subscribe to the competitive logic of neoclassicism and borrow their world view from economics. The main economic agents – firms and governments – may see the economy through the lens of economic theory and act accordingly. Rational economic man, for instance, has become a prescriptive ideal: people may behave with self-interested 'rationality' in the belief that this is the route to commercial success. Any social scientist interpreting such behaviour is confronted by agents whose lay interpretations of economic reality are a rehash of economic doctrines. Theory can transform the economy for better or worse, and mistakes made by earlier generations of economists may come back to haunt later ones.

Despite the many interpretative questions surrounding economics, orthodox economists have shown little appetite for hermeneutics. Their ahistorical and individualistic theories have shut out the hermeneutic circle and skewed attention away from interpretative methods. Neoclassicism supposedly captures the essence of economic behaviour and paints an accurate picture of the economy. If people are influenced by the theory, then this just reinforces how they would have behaved in any case. Interpretative efforts are redundant: orthodox theorists already know all about economic behaviour and have no need for further interpretations. Where people interact, the universal rationality and strong informational assumptions make hermeneutics unnecessary. In modern orthodox economics, conscious interaction is often depicted using game theory: everyone knows the game and behaves with instrumental rationality that decides their relations with others. Interpretative problems surface (implicitly) only under uncertainty when information is incomplete and expectations have to be modelled. The theory of rational expectations asks how agents perceive the world but nullifies this by assuming that they know the 'correct' neoclassical model (Wible, 1985; Giddens, 1987; Hodgson, 1988, Chapter 10). Commitment to a single, global theory has made economic orthodoxy blind to hermeneutics. Misunderstandings within the discipline are allegedly minimal, as orthodoxy claims to be a consensus in which economists agree on basic principles and speak the same theoretical language.

Heterodox economics, by its nature, diverges from orthodoxy and interprets the economy differently. For heterodoxy, economic thought has not ascended towards a modern mainstream consensus but follows a pluralistic pattern with unresolved arguments about fundamentals. It is therefore imperative to examine economic methodology and study the history of economics in order to understand the origin and rationale of economic theories, along with their relationship to the social and cultural environment. Curiosity about past economic debates brings hermeneutics to the fore. Heterodox economists must live within the kingdom of orthodox economic theory: the beliefs of economic agents are marred by the false doctrines of orthodox economics. The heterodox economist must not only criticise orthodox doctrines but know how they influence economic behaviour and contribute to a climate of opinion. Interpretation lies at the hub of a critical economics, and heterodox economists would benefit from being earnest about it (Berger, 1989; Lavoie, 1990; Gerrard, 1993; Prychitko, 1995). Opening up economics to hermeneutics does not impose a nihilistic relativism and can be made consistent with realism (Hargreaves Heap, 2002). Hermeneutics has arisen spasmodically in heterodox economics, without being fully acknowledged or discussed. Two heterodox schools with significant hermeneutic content are Post Keynesian and Austrian economics.

Post Keynesianism emphasises how fundamental uncertainty affects investors and other economic agents (Lawson, 1988; Davidson, 1994, Chapter 6). With no perfect foresight or probabilistic information about the future, they cannot maximise expected values in the manner of neoclassical theory (Shackle, 1955; Davidson, 1982). Behaviour takes a different form, and economists need to understand people's motives. Since investment is the most volatile component of aggregate demand and the prime mover of economic fluctuations, Post Keynesianism focuses on the attitudes of entrepreneurs, investors and financiers – they are macro-actors whose economic status gives them power over national income, employment and other aggregate variables. For Keynes, investors cannot decide by expected values (as neoclassical theory would suggest) and use other methods. Long-term investment decisions rely not on mathematical probabilities but on confidence about future prosperity. Confidence is socially determined and not just informational, as new information may at times upset existing beliefs and reduce confidence. Investors and speculators anticipate the average views among all investors rather than estimate the genuine returns to an asset, and so expectations become vulnerable to lurches when investors chase conventions and fashions (Keynes, 1937). Economists must understand the behaviour of agents who are themselves struggling to understand the behaviour of other agents: two or more levels of interpretation are involved. Keynes's suspicion of positivism, mathematical methods and ahistorical abstraction led him to ponder interpretative issues. He saw economics as a moral science imbued with value judgements and allowing 'unscientific' introspection and common sense (Carabelli, 1988; O'Donnell, 1989; Davis, 1991; Coates, 1996). His writings about uncertainty, probability and economic method inspired later work in the Post Keynesian and institutionalist traditions (Levine, 1997; Dequech, 1999; Wilson, 2007). The subjectivism of George Shackle revolved around fundamental uncertainty and its consequences for the individual, whereas economists writing in a realist vein have looked towards the structural context behind beliefs and expectations (Shackle, 1972, 1974; Lawson, 1985b, 1994; Runde, 1990, 1991; Hargreaves Heap, 2000). All this literature appreciates how uncertainty causes interpretative problems within economics. In most cases the hermeneutics has remained implicit, and few connections have been made with the wider social-scientific or philosophical literatures.

Austrian economics (in its revived, neo-Austrian form) rejects neoclassical theory, together with equilibrium analysis and formal empirical testing (von Mises, 1949, 1957; Hayek, 1948, 1952; Kirzner, 1976; Lachmann, 1986). The Austrian alternative, developed by von Mises and Hayek, is subjectivist and sees economic agents as having free will and a capacity for purposeful, self-determined action. An economic agent must interpret the world in order to decide how to act; academics must likewise interpret individual acts if they are to understand and explain economic behaviour. Austrian economics has an interpretative quality, as is clear from the overt appeals to hermeneutics and *Verstehen* (Ebeling, 1986; Lachmann, 1990; Prychitko, 1995). The hermeneutics in Austrian economics has been flanked by methodological individualism: interpretation is devoted to individual intentions, with little allowance for social context. Von Mises set out a 'praxeology' or theory of human action that put purposeful behaviour at the individual level and justified methodological individualism on a priori grounds (von Mises, 1949, 1978). Austrians have favoured the individualistic hermeneutics in Dilthey and Weber and in the phenomenological social theory of Alfred Schutz (Prendergast, 1986; Pietrykowski, 1996). The individualism and subjectivism misses the breadth of hermeneutic discussion. From its beginnings, hermeneutics has gone beyond the individual and given due credit to culture and the social environment. Recent hermeneutical thought has moved away from individualism towards social context. Some Austrian writers have spotted the larger implications of hermeneutics, but membership of the Austrian school dictates a stress on subjective individual experiences (Lavoie, 1994; Quinn and Green, 1998; Prychitko and Storr, 2007). To chain interpretative methods to individualism squanders their ability to embrace culture. The Austrian case for hermeneutics, though welcome as far as it goes, has been partial and subservient to the programme of methodological individualism.

All social science has several levels of interpretation with complex interactions among them. Economists must ask how economic agents interpret the world and how their interpretations depend on each other. Interpretation becomes even more pervasive if one considers the meaning of signs and symbols, as examined in semiotics. This is another area neglected by economists and merits some discussion.

## 10.3  SEMIOTICS AND STRUCTURAL LEVELS OF MEANING

Semiotics (or semiology) interprets signs and symbols – it has become a specialised academic field, mostly within linguistics, but its ramifications for social science are much wider (Noth, 1995; Sebeok, 2001; Johansen and Larsen, 2002; Hawkes, 2003). Hermeneutics and semiotics differ in their objects of interest. Most hermeneutic studies have interpreted the thoughts and behaviour of human agents and treated the understanding of signs and symbols as a means to this end. In semiotics, signs and symbols are interpreted in their own right; their meaning is irreducible to the intentions of particular people. Semiotics assesses sign systems, symbols and language and how they affect social and individual behaviour. Hermeneutics has sometimes been defined as a special case of semiotics covering situations where authorial intent is present, but it can also claim greater generality as it is not confined to signs and symbols. To say that hermeneutics deals with agency and semiotics with structure would be oversimplified and misleading: in a non-reductionist social theory, agency and structure are intertwined. Hermeneutics and semiotics should be complementary, and many interpretative problems have both a hermeneutic and semiotic side.

As a formal branch of study, semiotics is traceable back to the linguistic theorist Ferdinand de Saussure and the pragmatist philosopher Charles Sanders Peirce (Saussure, 1916 [1983]; Peirce, 1893–1910 [1955]). Saussure argued that a language can be broken down to its component parts and the relationships among them. What determines meaning is not individual speech acts or words but how these combine into a system. Language provides the structure or rules upon which individuals draw when they communicate with each other. The structural method led to Saussure being called the founder of structural linguistics and of structuralism in the broader sense. For him, we can discover the finite number of linguistic rules, even if communication based on these rules may be infinitely diverse. Every element in a linguistic structure is a sign whose meaning comes from its relation to other signs. Peirce's work was similar but on a larger canvas: he formulated a theory of signs as a bridge to a general theory of meaning and communication. In his scheme, signs take three main forms: icons, which portray their referent through physical resemblance; indices, which are causally connected with their referent; and symbols, which designate their referent by convention. A symbol may have no physical or material link with its referent and can exist simply within a logical system or structure. Words are symbols, and so Peirce's theory pertains to language, but symbols do not have to be linguistic – physical objects may also be symbolic. Study of signification includes verbal language along with all other modes of communication.

Semiotics distinguishes between what a sign refers to and what it signifies. Many signs have an obvious physical referent, but this alone does not give the sign's meaning, which depends on how it fits into a sign system. A sign is not a mere shadow of its referent and may carry its own message. In semiotic analysis the referent may be semi-detached from the sign system that conveys the sign's true significance. One can show this through the semiotic triangle, as in Figure 10.3.

The signifier is the material element (such as a printed text, photograph or physical object) and the signified is its meaning within a sign system: together, the signifier and signified constitute the sign. As part of a language, a sign should have meaning for the person who originated it and for other participants in the discourse. Semiotics permits layering among sign systems, so that a sign from one semiotic triangle may be a signifier in another. The referent is there in the semiotic triangle but may have only marginal relevance. If the sign is an icon or index, then it has a material relation with its referent from resemblance or causality, although the relation may shed little light on its true meaning; if the sign is a symbol, then it has only a conventional tie with its referent. The sign–referent connection, seen as straightforward in positivistic science, becomes arbitrary and unreliable. Since meanings are no longer unambiguous, academic study must examine the intricate relations among referent, signifier and signified.

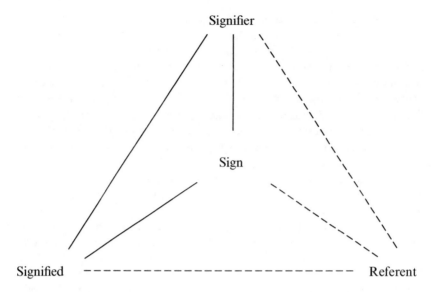

*Figure 10.3    The semiotic triangle*

Semiotics evaluates sign systems and how they affect human behaviour. The bond with social studies is strong, but semiotics and structuralism have copied natural sciences in bidding to be ahistorical and universal. Unlike hermeneutics, which was always in the social and cultural half of anti-naturalism, semiotics has had a foot in both camps. Much of structuralist linguistics has been a quest for absolute units of language applicable everywhere and culturally invariant. Conventional meanings are local, however, and cannot be wholly explained through the general properties of language. To interpret sign systems, one should ideally be sensitive to local and historical context and avoid a reductionist programme of boiling everything down to universal principles. As structuralism has developed into post-structuralism, it has been relativised; interest has switched from universal language to how sign systems have been socially constructed. The stress on social construction brings semiotics closer to cultural thought and hermeneutics.

Economic orthodoxy has kept away from signs or symbolism. In orthodox economics, a theoretical term has an uncomplicated relation with its referent, and the two are interchangeable. Goods, money, prices, wages and so forth are assumed to be well described by economic theory and have plain meanings; they are not symbolic. Supply and demand supposedly gauge the preferences of the rational individual agents upon whom the theory rests. There are no doubts about whether consumption has symbolic value, whether the declared reasons for production and consumption are the real reasons, or whether economic theory itself may be a sign system. Theory is fused with its referent and stands in for actual economic behaviour and the economy at large. Occasionally, ideas with a semiotic flavour have appeared on the edges of orthodox economics. An example is the screening hypothesis, which argues that education may not have an investment function (as in human capital theory) and acts as a screening or signalling device that indicates natural abilities or social background: the role of education as a signal supplants its role as a real economic variable (Riley, 2001). These ideas could go further and be a gateway for semiotics to enter economics, but their influence has been limited. The core of orthodox economics remains undisturbed by signs or symbolism.

Heterodox economics has shown greater aptitude for semiotic thinking. Peirce was a founder of semiotics and also a progenitor of American institutionalism (Mirowski, 1987; Liebhafsky, 1993). His writings on signs and symbols were allied to his pragmatist philosophy in which truth becomes a product of habit or convention. Habitual truths must depend on context and absolute, context-free knowledge is unattainable, a view consonant with hermeneutics and semiotics (Baert, 2003). Pragmatism could lead to an anti-realist deadlock (see Chapter 7), but its relativism need not be ontological and Peirce never denied metaphysics or the possibility of science – his pragmatism retained an allegiance to realism (Hoover, 1994). For Peirce, a sign system is conventional and may exist independently of external referents, which is not the same as pronouncing that an external reality does not exist. Entire bodies of thought or ways of life, including economic theory and economic activities as a whole, may be assembled through sign systems. Semiotics thereby has relevance for economics as a discipline and for the behaviour and motivation of economic agents.

Economists can all too easily create a private language or sign system severed from external reality. In the semiotic triangle signified and referent are distinct, and so academic theories can be based nominally on everyday things but have almost no purchase on the real world. Theorising can be self-justifying and self-absorbed, until it loses the capacity to adapt or accommodate diversity. Orthodox economics is a potential example. Neoclassical theory has grown from tentative abstractions about rational economic man into a complete, axiomatic system. All the elements are related and promote smooth discourse within the orthodox economic community – they have been taught to generations of students as the language of a trained economist. While internally logical and apparently grounded in reality, orthodox theory may nonetheless be far away from its referents. A reality check is said to come from formal empirical testing, but the numerous difficulties ensure that tests are inconclusive and theories can always be rescued if desired (as the Duhem–Quine thesis attests). The core beliefs of neoclassical economics are insulated from falsification and define the discipline – the sign system has usurped the real object of study. Orthodox theory has become conventional and gains its significance primarily as an emblem of expert status and membership card for the economics profession. To prevent this, the usual remedy is to advocate pluralism of theory and method. Peirce argued against exclusively deductive or inductive empiricism and defended 'abduction', the creative formation of theories and hypotheses. Academics should be prepared to explore new theories unencumbered by current conventions and sign systems.

Institutionalists working in the pragmatist tradition have been attuned to the symbolism of economic activity. Consumption may be motivated not by needs but by social pressures. Higher income groups may use conspicuous consumption to underline their social status, form a cohesive social class and distinguish themselves from the rest of society (Veblen, 1899). The symbolic value of a good exceeds its practical value, and the case for efficiency and cost minimisation vanishes – extravagant expense signifies status. Any consumer behaviour impelled by social trends is likely to be symbolic and part of a sign system. Examples abound in advertising and fashion, where sign systems have little to do with physical consumption but have a big impact on consumer behaviour (Williamson, 1978; Barthes, 1985). Advertisers and marketers know all about symbolic value and exploit it in their selling. Their aim is to create habits and conventions that lead people to consume certain goods regardless of whether the good delivers a benefit beyond its symbolic value. Most academic studies of this topic have been outside economics, in consumer research, advertising and marketing (Mick, 1986; Zakia and Nadin, 1987; Beasley and Danesi, 2002; McFall, 2004). The findings contradict economic orthodoxy but chime with the habitual and socialised behaviour in heterodox economics.

Semiotics becomes more relevant for economic behaviour as the economy grows and productivity increases. During early phases of capitalist development, most goods fulfil material needs and have a physical justification unrelated to social status or group membership. During later phases, consumption expands away from necessities towards discretionary items for which tastes have to be created and demand sustained through social pressures. Cultivation of wants was noted in the mid-nineteenth century by Ruskin (1862 [1985]) and went a lot further in the twentieth (Galbraith, 1969, Chapter 11, 1972, Chapter 18). Much consumption now rests upon symbolic value, and the marketing strategies of producers and retailers take advantage of this. Postmodernist discussion, generalising these tendencies, has talked about signs and symbolic exchange dominating and redrawing the whole economy (Baudrillard, 1988, 1993; Lash and Urry, 1994; Bauman, 2000, Chapter 2, 2001). Economic activity now seems energised not by subsistence but by the maintenance of a lifestyle defined through consumption and other status symbols. Complete satisfaction is never attained because lifestyle goals are revised upwards and fashions are in constant flux, a state of affairs encouraged by advertisers. Consumption can be hived off from any material benefits and valued solely for symbolism, as when consumers are allured by the badge, label or name attached to a good rather than its intrinsic properties. Consumer behaviour is then socially created, with wants stirred up by advertising and incapable of satisfaction – the contrast with neoclassical consumer sovereignty is total. Signs and symbols influencing consumption do not impart information but create meaning and significance directly.

Proponents of semiotics and post-structuralism have sometimes suggested that everything is now symbolic, in a virtual economy of signs and symbols (Baudrillard, 1975, 1993). Taken to a postmodernist extreme, semiotics may lead to anti-realism whereby reality has no existence beyond a socially constructed sign system. Semiotics need not imply anti-realism, though, and can accompany a realism that permits the possibility of science (Nellhaus, 1998; Fairclough et al., 2004). Nor does it imply that symbolic value resides in a self-contained realm. While symbolism does have great importance in modern economies, it cannot displace material production, distribution and consumption (Callinicos, 1989, Chapter 5; Fine and Leopold, 1993, Chapter 19). To oversell semiotics would be to forget the material basis of the economy. As cultural materialism argues, all cultural activity is rooted in material production, and so are the sign systems delineated in semiotics. The symbolism behind consumer behaviour, abetted by producers and retailers in their marketing campaigns, has an intimate connection with material production. Even if a sign system has nothing to do with its material referents, it is joined with the material world: symbolism has powerful effects in increasing demand, stimulating production and realising profits. Any fantasies about a virtual or symbolic economy obscure the place of symbolic value in production, distribution and consumption. The symbolic aspects of economic behaviour should be subsumed into a theoretical vision that can handle both the virtual and the material (Goux, 2001; Peterson, 2003). Semiotic analyses can contribute to economics, but they should not entice us into overstatements about a dematerialised world. The appropriate contribution of semiotics is as one ingredient among others within a pluralism of method.

## 10.4   MEANING AND INTERPRETATION IN ECONOMICS

Orthodox economics has been wary of interpretative methods, lest they damage the scientific credentials of economics and pull it closer to the humanities than the natural sciences. Yet interpretation is unavoidable and permeates a social science such as economics. One cannot safely ignore interpretative matters: far from being irrelevant, they enter into every corner of the economy and economic discourse. Some examples are considered below.

### Interpreting Economic Literature

Hermeneutics in its original sense – interpreting texts – arises when we study past economic literature. Most writings can have alternative interpretations; in this respect economics is no different from any other discipline. Many famous economists left classic interpretative riddles: Adam Smith generated much debate over the apparent contradiction between his economic and moral writings (Brown, 1994a, 1997; Tribe, 1999); David Ricardo was never a paragon of clarity and underwent a major rereading by Sraffa and the neo-Ricardians (O'Brien, 1981; Peach, 1993); Marx has experienced countless reinterpretations, as in the contrasts between early and late Marx (Bottomore, 1984; Reuten, 2003); Keynes's economics has sparked much debate on how it should be interpreted and whether it can be synthesised with neoclassicism (Coddington, 1983; Littleboy, 1990; Gerrard, 1991). None of these are minor technical details and all have repercussions for the nature of economics. Continuous reappraisal of existing theories is the lifeblood of a critical approach. For orthodoxy, though, neoclassical theory enshrines universal economic behaviour: it is pointless to look for alternatives or return to earlier doctrines. Consensus allegedly exists on core assumptions that are axiomatic and immune to misunderstanding. The mathematical rigour and completeness is achieved only through a simplified, abstract framework with many cracks. Key terms in neoclassical economics (such as utility, production, exchange, markets and consumption) are poorly defined and unclear in their relation to actual economic activity. Interpretative matters are dodged by the mathematical theorising but remain latent; any effort to decipher neoclassicism and connect it to the real world has to be interpretative.

### Conduct of Economic Debate

As well as interpreting current and historical texts, economists need to understand and participate in academic debates. Scientific method has tried to remove ambiguity and find a yardstick of truth that would resolve disagreements – logical positivism was such an attempt. More recent philosophy of science, in the growth-of-knowledge tradition, has challenged positivism and asserted the role of argument, debate and persuasion. Scientific progress is cultural, as a sequence of paradigms is formulated, diffused through the profession, and eventually replaced with new ones. The process depends on discourse and mutual interpretation. Theories create their own languages, and orthodox economic language differs from heterodox (Neale, 1982; Fritz and Fritz, 1985; Samuels, 1990, 2001; Brown, 1994b). With no universal arbiter of truth, judgements of fact may be subjective. Economics is laden with value judgements, so that interpreters of academic work may have to tease out values not openly declared by the author. Orthodox economics plays down interpretation and aspires to be value free, but any critical economics must be interpretative and normative.

**Understanding Micro Agents**

Economists frequently study ordinary workers or consumers, who are micro agents with no personal influence on the economy but whose behaviour in aggregate determines how it functions. Orthodox economics assigns instrumental rationality to these agents and models them as utility maximisers with given, well-defined preferences. Originally this assumption was due to the interpretative abstractions of J.S. Mill in trying to understanding typical economic behaviour (Blaug, 1992, Chapter 3; Persky, 1995). The interpretative background has long faded from memory, and instrumental rationality has hardened into a universal axiom of orthodoxy. Economists, if they are to understand economic behaviour, should not be reliant on a single past interpretation now embalmed in theory. Neither pure theory nor formal empirical work can grasp individual motivation, and interpretative methods are needed instead. Scholars should be free to interpret and re-interpret motives that may not be instrumentally rational.

**Understanding Macro Agents**

Some people, by dint of their high status in governmental or business hierarchies, are macro agents whose decisions have far greater consequences than those of the average citizen. If a few individuals decide economic events, then it becomes vital to understand their motives. As with micro agents, economic orthodoxy resorts to instrumental rationality and overlooks interpretation. Macro agency is distinctive as there is little aggregation and just a few actions may be crucial. Attention falls upon the immediate circle of the most powerful agents, as against the social and cultural forces affecting everybody. When macro agents deliberate about their decisions, they interpret the economy and may be beholden to prevailing economic doctrines. Orthodox models, universal and unqualified, are influential among policy-makers but not well suited to all local circumstances (Gudeman, 1986, 2001; Katzner, 2002). Economic research requires interpretative sensitivity from the economist, especially if macro agents are thought to have erroneous beliefs. Most orthodox economists either ignore these issues or evade them by assuming that agents have beliefs founded on a single, correct economic model. Heterodox economists cannot be so offhand about interpretation: they face the twin task of understanding macro behaviour and criticising the doctrines on which it is based.

## Knowledge and Information

Orthodox economic theory has often abstracted from information and assumed that agents have full knowledge of past, present and future; it only ever relaxes its informational assumptions slightly, by allowing probabilistic information and letting agents collate information subject to a search cost. Information must be quantitative in order to preserve neoclassical optimising behaviour. In practice, fundamental uncertainty may thwart numerical calculations, so that the informational shortfall is not estimable. Acquiring knowledge may be more than just an exercise in accumulating information units, and much knowledge extends beyond the codified form envisaged in orthodox economic theory (Boulding, 1956; Polanyi, 1967; Lundvall and Johnson, 1994; Ancori et al., 2000; Dolfsma, 2001). Studying and learning give rise to alternative interpretations of the world based on prior beliefs, values and social context. Economists, like any other social scientists, should be alert to subjective knowledge and how it affects behaviour. Informational issues are another instance of multiple hermeneutics: economic agents are hoping to secure enough knowledge to inform their activities; economists seek knowledge on a wider scale, which includes understanding the behaviour of partially informed agents. These complexities have no simple resolution, but a familiarity with interpretative methods would be a beginning.

## Signs and Symbolism

Economics has customarily aligned itself with materialism and positivism. In doing so, it has left little space for signs and symbols – they are felt to be irrelevant. Casual inspection of economic behaviour leads one to doubt such a view, and symbolism is rife. Prime examples occur in consumption, as many goods have symbolic value only loosely linked to their practical function but tightly linked to fashion and social status. The literature on consumer culture theory clearly demonstrates this (Arnould and Thompson, 2005). Symbolism is not limited to consumption, and enters the production and monetary spheres. Firms and other economic organisations have corporate cultures that use symbols in maintaining a group identity and external image (Deal and Kennedy, 1982; Smircich, 1983; Alvesson and Berg, 1992; Alvesson, 2002). Within firms, production is organised hierarchically with elaborate symbolism of rank and status, including job titles, remuneration, perks and working environment. Management has its own jargon, fashions and catch phrases which amount to a private language unrelated to everyday working practices but with real consequences for how firms are governed. Another area of signification and symbolism is money and the social relations underlying it (Dyer, 1989; Horwitz, 1992; Anjos, 1999; Goux, 1999, 2001; Ingham, 1999, 2004; Gilbert, 2005). The emergence of credit money during economic development means that money takes on a dematerialised form that exists as a sign system without being commodity-based. Money is not a representation of material reality in a simple sign–referent connection (as orthodox theory implies), but derives from social relations among borrowers and lenders, providing the language of modern capitalism.

**Social Construction and Ideology**

A theme of recent interpretative study has been the way that our experiences are socially constructed: ideas and values are interwoven with language, structured by power relations and serve the interests of dominant groups (Hodge and Kress, 1993; Potter, 1996; Gergen, 1999). The arguments have a kinship with earlier views of ideology, though they are idealist and say less about material forces. By this reckoning, economic arrangements are a social artefact justified ideologically as something natural and inevitable. Orthodox economists have been compliant and helped promote a purportedly timeless, unqualified case for competitive markets. Heterodox economists have been less compliant but may flounder to release themselves from ideology: post-structuralism has queried the ability of academics to cut through ideology and find objective accounts of reality. Yet ideology need not be so pervasive, and ceases to have meaning when everything is seen as ideological (Eagleton, 1991, Chapter 1). An augmented realism can recognise postmodernist worries but still uphold an independent and critical study of reality (Manicas, 1987, Chapter 13;

Bhaskar, 1989; Layder, 1990). Economists should be self-aware about the ideological setting of their theories and then pose broader questions about how ideology creeps into economic affairs. Any attempt to come to terms with ideology has to use interpretative methods.

The foregoing examples show that both the subject matter and practice of economics are replete with interpretative issues and that interpretation is unavoidable, like it or not. Economists who follow positivistic methods are making implicit interpretations, adopting those made by others, and reacting to sign systems and symbolism. Suppressing these issues dulls one's sensitivity to individual motivation and social context. The interpretations offered in orthodox economics are unacknowledged and have curdled into an artificial reality of universal economic behaviour where meanings are obvious and understanding is direct. Orthodoxy has built a socially constructed world from which social construction is absent. Interpretative methods are the best defence against such outcomes and form an indispensable part of social or economic investigation. In a mature and well-rounded economics, they should be accepted and given a place alongside theory and empirical study.

# 11.   Social and economic evolution

Ideas of culture and cultivation have usually entertained the likelihood of gradual social change. A culture is replicated only if succeeding generations are cultivated in the same way of life, and small variations can accumulate and transform society. Possibilities for social evolution are inherent in culture when it is viewed as a process: it provides continuity with the past by reproducing beliefs, values and practices, but leaves openings for novelty.

Accounts of social evolution were in vogue during the Enlightenment, prompted by the benefits of the new scientific methods. As knowledge piled up and was applied within society, the result would be steady improvement. Evolution was linear and predictable, based on knowledge that had universal value and offered the same rewards for all societies. Few doubts were expressed about the certainty of progress or reliability of scientific methods. Such unbounded confidence was challenged by the cultural thinkers of the Counter-Enlightenment and Romanticism. Their pluralism disclaimed a single evolutionary route towards omniscience and found virtues in historical societies and primitive peoples. In their view, development branches out into greater diversity and alternative paths to self-fulfilment, rather than following a unique, optimal path. Scepticism about scientific progress has resurfaced with the revival of cultural thought since the 1960s. Postmodernism has forsaken grand Enlightenment narratives and replaced them with relativism and diversity.

In modern academic discourse, evolution is associated with Darwinism and its offshoots. Darwinian thought extended evolution to the natural realm and brought new ideas of natural selection that dug down to the biological substratum of human behaviour. While raising the profile of evolution, Darwinism complicated things by adding a biological layer to the existing social layer and introducing different causality. Human behaviour could now be explained through biological factors, and the bonds between biology and culture became troublesome. Darwin's materialism was hard to reconcile with the idealism of cultural thought and led to conflicts, notwithstanding a common interest in evolution. The impulse behind evolutionary economics has been the desire to learn from Darwin and craft a Darwinian theory of economic evolution. The present chapter looks at how cultural and biological evolution are related and examines the implications for economic theorising.

## 11.1    CULTURAL THOUGHT AND SOCIAL EVOLUTION

The word 'evolution', derived from the Latin *evolvere*, refers to an unfolding or unrolling over time (Williams, 1988). To speak of evolution is to suggest gradual, forward moving historical development, as distinct from abrupt or discrete changes. Beyond this, evolution is loosely defined and the precise nature of the unfolding remains fluid: it could be predictable or unpredictable, aimless or destined for a final end point, occurring in stages or a smooth continuous flow. Theorists who invoke evolution disagree on how it happens and where it may be heading. Assumptions of progress have been standard in Enlightenment philosophy but queried by cultural thought and the Counter-Enlightenment.

Traditional views of the natural world regarded it as fixed and God-given; likewise, the early Enlightenment appealed to constant, unchanging natural laws. In the social realm, the Enlightenment expected a continuous bounty as science dispelled superstitions and yielded knowledge and economic benefits (Trigger, 1998, Chapter 3). Evolutionary history and social theory began to emerge during the eighteenth century and flourished in the nineteenth. Writers of the Scottish Enlightenment such as Millar and Ferguson penned schemes of social evolution; Whig history (epitomised by Macaulay) was eternally optimistic. In the French Enlightenment, Turgot and Condorcet foresaw regular social and scientific advances converging on a perfect ideal. Evolutionary thought spread far and wide during the nineteenth century: examples are Comte's positive philosophy, the dialectical evolution of Hegel and Marx, and the evolutionary anthropology of Morgan and Tylor. These pre-Darwinian theories had many differences but shared a belief that social evolution proceeds through stages towards a destination that scientific scholarship can identify (Sanderson, 1990; Sztompka, 1992, Chapter 7; Burke, 2005, Chapter 5). Little was said about natural selection, and evolution was understood in its original sense as an unfolding of history. Even the theories dubbed Social Darwinism were not based firmly on Darwin and relied on earlier authors (Rogers, 1972; Jones, 1980; Hodgson, 1993a, Chapter 6; Paul, 2003). One should be careful to note the larger context of evolutionary thought that inspired Darwin but differed from his own ideas.

The evolutionary doctrines of the Enlightenment were reflected in classical economics, with its study of the wealth of nations accumulated through laissez-faire capitalism. Adam Smith's invisible hand followed in line from Bernard Mandeville's *Fable of the Bees*: self-interested actions by individuals conjure up a natural order without the need for design. The mood is sanguine, as the natural order is superior to anything achievable by global planning or control. As long as the economy evolves spontaneously, it should reach a steady state in which order comes from apparent chaos. Nobody has to apply knowledge at the aggregate level, and each person merely acts in his or her own interests. This differs from Utopianism, where accumulated knowledge allows better social planning. Classical economics saw increasing specialisation as a means to enhance productivity without central control. Governments just had to realise the benefits of laissez-faire and step aside from guiding the economy or interfering with business decisions. The analogy was with nature, which also displays spontaneous order in Newtonian mechanics and the biology of living organisms.

Among classical economists, Enlightenment optimism was subject to limits. Malthus in particular criticised the Utopians Condorcet and Godwin, writing his essay on population as a polemic against Utopianism: his aim was to demonstrate the impossibility of a perfect society (James, 1979, Chapter 2; Avery, 1997). For Malthus, population pressure on resources meant that wages would be restricted to subsistence level and unable to grow. When the Malthusian population principle was incorporated in the Ricardian model, the same negativity entered classical economics as the 'iron law of wages'. Laissez-faire capitalism encouraged productivity and capital accumulation but could not improve the lot of the average worker. Malthus's stress on population and the battle for resources was acknowledged by Darwin as an influence on the theory of natural selection (Vorzimmer, 1969; Herbert, 1971). Classical economics was not evolutionary in the Darwinian sense, however, and rested upon a predictable passage towards a final steady state. Economic orthodoxy kept its distance from Darwin and became less evolutionary once it switched to neoclassical theories with timeless modelling, static equilibria, and fixed individual preferences.

The cultural thought of the Counter-Enlightenment was compatible with social evolution, though it toned down the optimism of the Enlightenment. Among its objectives was to introduce spatial and temporal relativism into social studies, so as to repel absolutist and anti-historical tendencies. Historical specificity implies that social change must be possible and that one set of social circumstances can be transformed into another, but it is non-committal about the pace of change, how changes are enacted, and whether they follow a well-defined path. Many historians and cultural thinkers have dealt with a single historical period (and compared it with other periods) without delving into the causality behind historical change. Cultural approaches carry no account of evolution and can coexist with various evolutionary theories. Some writers have linked culture with developmental evolution following a prescribed series of stages, whereas others have avoided linearity.

The earliest cultural thought was unhappy with simplified historical programmes and made no sweeping judgements about one period's superiority over another. A sequence of historical stages was likely but not wholly predictable. Later stages were not a terminus and earlier stages could re-emerge. Vico, for example, identified several stages of thought, conduct and social organisation (the ages of beasts, gods, heroes and men) but permitted cycles if a society reverted to earlier stages (Burke, 1985, Chapter 3). Evolution had no climax. Historical experience showed that all great civilisations, whatever their accomplishments, eventually crumbled or underwent fundamental transformations. This was a puzzle for Renaissance and Enlightenment thinkers, who were perplexed as to why the much-admired civilisations of Ancient Greece and Rome had come to an end and been superseded by something allegedly inferior. A linear evolutionary path of accumulating knowledge should not regress back to earlier stages, and the risk of regression raised doubts about the Enlightenment itself. For Vico, on the other hand, historical cycles were normal and social evolution was not a procession towards an ideal end-state.

Herder's writings were marked by their refusal to judge other periods or societies: he denied that present societies are in all respects better than earlier ones (Barnard, 1965; Berlin, 1976a; Trigger, 1998, Chapter 4). Humanity was not following the highway to progress or converging on a unique, perfect society. According to Herder, societies were apt to diverge rather than converge. Improved knowledge would open more outlets for self-expression, including behaviour that might not conform to narrow definitions of rationality. States and governments had finite lives, but cultures could live on indefinitely and branch out into ever greater diversity. Social evolution had no template or chronology; it was unpredictable and disorderly. This relativistic attitude was later taken up by Romantic anti-capitalists, who were well aware of the huge social transformation wrought by capitalism but unwilling to applaud this as unalloyed progress. Material benefits could be undone by social, environmental and aesthetic costs, so that the net outcome was far from self-evidently desirable. Pre-capitalist societies might be preferable in some respects to capitalist ones. Romantic beliefs were consistent with historical evolution but not with a single developmental scheme applicable everywhere and heading towards a final, optimum destination.

Because cultural thought has had an idealist hue, the source of social change has generally been traced to ideas. The Hegelian tradition, for example, takes a dialectical form whereby ideas come into conflict and propel society in a series of historical stages towards collective fulfilment and self-expression (Taylor, 1979a, Chapter 1; Pinkard, 1988, Chapter 8;

McCarney, 2000, Part 2). Dialectical processes, neither continuous nor wholly predictable, are too messy for smooth, regular evolution and leave space for randomness, uncertainty and historical accidents. Hegel's evolutionary stance was more restrictive than Herder's, as it had a teleology in which history was moving towards the ultimate freedom. Yet the journey to the end point was fitful, non-linear and haunted by breakdowns, pitfalls and reversals. Full knowledge was available only with hindsight, and people had only partial control over the course of history. Ideas initiated and drove social change but could not tame it – nobody could plan things perfectly. Interpretative methods meant that reasons could be causes, and understanding of behaviour stood independently in explaining history. Human agents possessed free will: it was unnecessary to reduce reasons to the material level as in natural sciences. History depended on the often conflictive interactions of purposeful human beings acting individually or through social groups.

Marxian approaches, which owe much to Hegelian dialectics, differ from most cultural thought in their materialism. Ideas can initiate short-term changes, but in the long term must be in tune with the prevailing material interests. All major changes start with the material base and then move on to institutions and ideologies: the strength of the resulting materialism has varied among Marxian theorists but remains a defining feature of Marxism. Apart from the idealism/materialism issue, Marxian views of social evolution have many similarities with cultural ones. Both are dialectical and both adopt developmental evolution either without an end or with an end that is distant and not entirely knowable in advance. Marx did have a periodic scheme of history (primitive communism – slavery – feudalism – capitalism – communism) reaching fruition in an ideal state. This mirrors Enlightenment philosophy, but Marx's evolution was Hegelian: he would not predict when, where or how communism would come about and wrote little on its nature or content. Despite his reverence for science, he ridiculed Utopian 'scientific' blueprints for ideal societies and disparaged any claims to foresight about social progress. His caginess about the future has been criticised as a weakness, but it brings him closer to cultural thought.

Evolutionary ideas were applied to human societies before they were extended to the natural world. Serious discussion of natural evolution was galvanised by the research of Lamarck and Lyell in the late-eighteenth and early-nineteenth centuries (Bowler, 2003). Evolution in the natural sciences ballooned only with Darwinism in the late nineteenth century, and the genetic foundations for evolution were discovered only in the twentieth century. The elements of Darwinism – variation, selection and inheritance – differed from earlier evolutionary arguments and represented a new theory. As Darwinian principles have spread, the initial and literal meaning of evolution has been obscured. Nowadays the unqualified term 'evolution' connotes Darwinian natural selection rather than unfolding historical development. Earlier senses of evolution are still detectable, but most scientific usage has been Darwinian. This is in some ways surprising, because Darwin was at first wary of the word 'evolution' lest it muddle his theory by suggesting a sequence of historical stages in place of blind, continuous natural selection (Bowler, 1975; Gayon, 2003). His caution was overwhelmed by general usage, and evolution is now synonymous with Darwinism. The revised meaning of evolution has diverted our gaze towards biology and away from culture: an unfortunate consequence has been to alienate cultural thought from Darwinian evolution, to the extent that they are frequently portrayed as contradictory and mutually exclusive.

## 11.2   TENSIONS BETWEEN CULTURAL THOUGHT AND DARWINISM

Since cultural thought predated Darwinism, writers in the cultural tradition drew from pre-Darwinian sources and were oblivious of natural selection. Darwin and his followers wrote mostly about animal populations and saw themselves as biologists. The distance between culture and Darwinism came from a difference of interests (and growing disciplinary specialisation) but has hardened into tensions and conflict. Culture and nature are sometimes paired in a dualism of opposites, as if culture were incompatible with evolution by natural selection. This raises questions about why the tensions have arisen and whether they can be alleviated.

   An underlying cause of tension is that cultural thought has been banded together with the humanities and Darwinian evolution with the natural sciences. In any anti-naturalistic division of humanities and sciences, cultural thought has fallen on one side and Darwinism on the other. Cultural thought has been mostly idealist, giving prominence to human creativity and the ability to act independently. People are masters of their own destinies who (unlike animals) can build and reproduce cultures. Darwinian theorising begins with the material environment. Natural selection is a universal principle, valid for both human and animal populations, which in the long term governs all physical and social development. Human beings, however creative and resourceful they may be, are subject to natural selection and at its mercy. The idealism of the humanities stands against the materialism of Darwinian biology. Any rapprochement would have to breach the anti-naturalistic wall separating humanities from sciences.

A related problem is that cultural thought has normally called upon teleology or purpose, whereas Darwinian evolution is blind and without purpose or direction. Purpose may appear in cultural thought at individual or higher levels. At the individual level, people have free will and formulate aims that are reasons for human activity and explain why people behave as they do. At the group or social level, Hegelian cultural thought allows for collective interests that drive social change: historical development results from dialectical clashes and resolutions among ideas. Because individual or group interests have causal power, teleology is traceable to ideas and beliefs. In Darwinian evolution, long-term changes are due to natural forces unguided by human or divine purpose. Living creatures survive and their behaviour persists only if they reproduce and multiply. Evolution has no teleology and never obeys a master plan; aimless Darwinism overrides purposeful human development.

Other tensions are to do with units of selection and levels of analysis. Cultural thought may have an individualistic sheen in human subjectivity and free will, but culture as a process or way of life depends on the social backdrop. Individuals realise their creative potential only by grace of the prevailing culture, so cultural methods cannot rest upon the individual level alone. Culture, which binds individual and social levels, requires a layered theory. Darwinian arguments turn on natural selection among members of a population and their offspring. The theory, built upon individual units, has no need for other analytical levels such as groups or social classes. Group behaviour may be relevant if it influences natural selection but often plays a lesser role. The ethos of Darwinism is disaggregated and competitive, not social and cooperative, though group selection and layering can be included within a Darwinian framework.

Further difficulties stem from whether individual traits are inherited at birth or acquired later. Cultural thought revolves around cultivation and learning. For individuals, culture as a process implies acquiring traits within a social environment; for societies, a way of life implies replicating values and behavioural norms in each generation. While some physical and mental capacities are inherited, they vary little among societies – most social variation is from acquired capacities. Darwinism centres on biological inheritance, such that essential qualities are present at birth. Acquired traits may have short-term significance but count for little in evolutionary terms as they cannot be passed on. In the debate over environment versus genetics, cultural and Darwinian thought find themselves on opposite sides.

Taken together, these differences suggest a dilemma with stark alternatives. To pick one is, it seems, to spurn the other. A strict culture/nature dualism is misleading, however, as it overlooks the possibilities for a non-dualistic view. Cultural thought and Darwinism both wish to understand the origin of personal or social characteristics and how these may change over time. Darwinian evolution makes the larger claims of being relevant to all periods and populations, whether plant, animal or human. Evolution proceeds always and everywhere, at different rates but never with a known destination. Cultural thought pertains to human (or anthropoid) populations which, on a geological time scale, are recent phenomena. For most of the Earth's existence the human population was zero and natural selection went ahead in the absence of humanity. Only within human history have cultures been superimposed on Darwinian processes. Culture has accelerated social and economic development through sources of change that have human origins; it supplements Darwinism with purposeful human behaviour and innovation. A cultural method has to acknowledge this and go beyond natural selection alone.

Many of the frictions in culture/nature dualism are akin to those in other dualisms such as idealism/materialism, agency/structure and relativism/realism. These contrasts, leading scholars to oversimplify and distort matters, are avoidable through more elaborate and sensitive theorising (Dow, 1990; Jackson, 1999). Cultural writers have not, on the whole, been at loggerheads with Darwinism. The chief antagonists of cultural thought were the absolutist, anti-historical zealots of the Enlightenment, not the later Darwinian school who were mindful of diversity and haphazard evolution. By their disaggregated 'population thinking', the Darwinians too moved away from the fixed, absolute categories of Enlightenment philosophy (Mayr, 1976, 1985). The controversies over Darwinism had more to do with religion than culture, ignited by the clash with supernatural beliefs that were foreign to cultural thought. Darwinism abolishes an external creator or designer but has no such ban on purposeful behaviour by human agents or the appearance of cultures. The tensions between cultural and Darwinian thought are not insurmountable.


## 11.3   CULTURE AND NATURAL SELECTION

Does cultural as well as natural evolution take a Darwinian form? Several features of cultural change are obviously non-Darwinian. Since human beings can think critically and self-consciously, cultural change may be planned from above without overt selection. When selection occurs it may hinge on purposeful behaviour that creates variety and makes deliberate choices; the effect is to increase diversity, speed up evolution and add causal powers missing from plant and animal populations. Culture has often been partnered with Lamarckian evolution based on inheritance of acquired attributes. Lamarck did not belong to the cultural tradition – he was a materialist of the French Enlightenment – but later writers have discerned parallels between Lamarckian and cultural evolution (Popper, 1972; Simon, 1981; Nelson and Winter, 1982; Gould, 1983). This puts cultural and natural evolution on opposite sides of the Lamarckian/Darwinian divide, even though Darwin never actually rejected Lamarckian inheritance. Subsequent biological research did reject it (the Weismann barrier) and elicited the neo-Darwinism that underlies modern theories of biological evolution. The neo-Darwinian model thus seems aloof from culture.

Universal Darwinists have nonetheless proclaimed the relevance of neo-Darwinism for the social realm. Such reasoning has become fashionable lately, with examples in sociobiology, genetic reductionism and evolutionary psychology (Wilson, 1975, 1978; Dawkins, 1983, 1989; Cosmides and Tooby, 1987; Cronin, 1991; Dennett, 1995). For Universal Darwinists any persistent and widespread human behaviour, as embodied in institutions and cultures, must have passed the test of natural selection and be open to evolutionary explanation. Culture must enable human beings to subsist and reproduce, or else it would have withered away. Recent Darwinian thought has plumped for the gene rather than the individual as the unit of selection, so that both individuals and cultures become means of ensuring genetic reproduction. Culture here is secondary in evolutionary explanations: it can be treated as either negligible (as in sociobiology) or reducible to biological needs (as in evolutionary psychology). In a Universal Darwinist scheme, culture exists because it facilitates human survival and can be explained in the same way as biological characteristics.

The denial of Darwinism in cultural evolution seems to contradict the Universal Darwinist bid for its global relevance. Yet social change is sufficiently complex that we should beware simple either/or dualisms. Darwinism remains neutral about how natural selection operates: genetics were appended only later and need not be the only inheritance mode. Nothing in the Darwinian framework dictates that it applies to biology alone or that biological evolution always predominates. A flexible interpretation of Darwinism may still fit in with cultural thought.

In order to consider this, one must look at the ingredients of Darwinism: variation, selection and inheritance. Variation poses few difficulties for cultural thought, which from its beginnings has attended to human variety and diversity. Cultural thinkers have always disliked universal, mechanistic theories depicting human behaviour as predictable and uniform. Darwinism, though allied to natural science, has a similar open-endedness and resistance to closed, stable systems. It too sets great store by variation, albeit from biological origins, and extols the diversity of nature. Introducing culture into a Darwinian framework multiplies the sources of variation as cultural sources are added to biological ones.

Cultural variety stretches across many levels, from the individual upwards. At the individual level, creative human agents cultivated within society guarantee that diverse behaviour is ever present. People may fall back on instincts and habits, but they have free will and can break away from past behaviour. Variations at a higher, social level are also important in cultural thought. Individuals are nurtured within a social context and participate in a culture or way of life; innovative behaviour yields incremental changes to the culture without wholly transforming or overturning it. Social evolution has led to great diversity over time and place, as is evident from historical and anthropological studies. In many cases differences between societies exceed differences within societies; both kinds of variation are ubiquitous. Some cultural arguments have had a collectivist or nationalist edge that values uniformity within a society or nation so as to preserve a collective identity. This seems to go against diversity, but cultural thought allows for trade-offs between diversity at individual and collective levels: greater individual diversity within groups or societies may dilute collective diversity and reduce variation among groups or societies. Though cultural arguments can be abused to foment nationalism or imperialism, their interest in collective identity was intended to honour the diversity of human societies at a group level. Interplay between individual and group levels is congruent with Darwinism, as it came into Darwin's own thinking about behaviour (Ruse, 1989). Later Darwinian writers have dwelt upon individual or genetic variation, but there is no reason to drop group or collective variation from a Darwinian framework.

The second ingredient of Darwinism – selection – is not quite so easy to reconcile with cultural methods. Selection broaches the issues of who does the selecting and what they select, both of which could be awkward. On the issue of who selects, Darwinism adheres to natural selection with no guiding hand to make choices. Selection is through differences in survival rates and reproductive success: the organisms or groups with many offspring are 'selected' to prosper. No active selection by a human or supernatural agent takes place; nature alone is the selector. In his later career, Darwin came to regret using the term 'natural selection' and preferred 'natural preservation' on the grounds that it gave no hint of active choices being made (Ruse, 1979, Chapter 8). Cultural thought, by contrast, is readier to admit human choices when explaining historical events. People may try to influence events by a non-natural selection among alternative actions. Frequently people do not control their destinies and make decisions that have unintended consequences. Even here, the outcomes are the result of indirect human choices. The importance of agency and purposeful behaviour in cultural thought seems to set it apart from Darwinian natural selection.

Attempts have been made to nest human agency within a larger evolutionary scheme. Purposeful acts by human agents have short-term effects for a given population, but the effects last in the longer term only if the population survives and reproduces itself. Agency is subsumed in natural selection, which decides the fate of human beings as well as plant and animal species. What appears a distinct form of causality is just another contributor to variety. For Darwinians, human beings are free agents thanks to previous natural selection: we think creatively because this has helped us to survive and reproduce. Human free will is subordinate to a deeper causality from the evolution of the mind. Everything has an evolutionary explanation, including human behaviour that seems to transcend natural selection. As critics have pointed out, such arguments come close to a reductionism that drags all behaviour down to human biology and minimises agency or culture (Sahlins, 1977; Rose et al., 1984; Kitcher, 1985; Gould, 2001). Biological reductionism is common within Darwinian evolutionary theory (especially sociobiology) but not inevitable: it can be evaded if one recognises emergent powers and takes a non-reductionist stance on agency and human biology (Hodgson, 1993a, Chapter 15; Vromen, 2001). Emergence gives space for human agency that is rooted in biology but not wholly reducible to it. This affords independence to human agency and warrants cultural thought within a wider Darwinian outlook.

Selection also requires assumptions about what is being selected. Darwinism means population thinking, and the units making up a population must be specified. For Darwin the unit was the organism, and natural selection was among individuals. But even if characteristics are at the level of the organism, their durability depends on interaction with other organisms in the same or different species. Individuals can survive only when their species survives, and so individual preservation mingles with species preservation. The species becomes a vehicle for the organism, and to select organisms is to select the species as well. Neo-Darwinism, informed by the genetic discoveries of the twentieth century, has pushed the selection units lower, to the level of the gene (Dawkins, 1989). As inheritance operates through genes, reproducing genes is paramount for natural selection. Evolutionary success follows when individual organisms pass on their genes, irrespective of any other aspect of their physical functioning. Variation happens through random errors and mutations in the transmission of genetic information. Organisms or species may still be germane, but the unit of selection is the gene. Whenever selection seems to occur at higher levels, the evolutionary theorist just has to delve deeper and see things in genetic terms.

It remains difficult, nevertheless, to tie selection down to one level alone. Many potential units of selection are correlated. Selection of genes implies selection of the organisms carrying those genes, along with the species to which the organism belongs and any groups by which the species is organised. To select at one level is to select at all levels, and it is arbitrary to seize upon one level as dominant: evolution takes place within a stratified world that has many interconnected layers. Darwinism has no formal need for the gene as a unit of selection, as is clear from Darwin's ignorance about genes. Focusing on one level flirts with reductionism and neglects levels above or below the one being emphasised. Social scientists have a contingent interest in human biology, if it bears upon the behaviour being studied, but are concerned primarily with higher, social levels of analysis. Evolutionary social theorists should not cast aside units of selection above the genetic level.

The biological literature has discussed group selection at length without generating agreement. Believers in gene-based neo-Darwinism have discarded group selection in favour of the gene or individual as a selection unit (Maynard Smith, 1976; Williams, 1986). While group selection remains theoretically possible, its practical consequences are viewed as being weak and overwhelmed by lower selection levels. Groups are unlikely to cohere because group interests are ill-defined and altruism can be exploited by self-interested group members. Critics of genetic reductionism have argued for selection at group or societal levels (Sober, 1981; Wilson, 1983; Sober and Wilson, 1994; Field, 2001, 2006). They rate group selection as being no less legitimate than individual selection – an organism is a collective of genes, a group is a collective of individuals, and in both cases collective organisation may boost the chances of survival. Multiple analytical levels are avoidable only if collective organisation is dismissed as irrelevant, but to do this would banish much biological and social theorising. An alternative strategy is to have group selection beside individual and other levels of selection, assuming importance whenever it influences evolution. In evolutionary terms, a group exists if its members have shared interests and stand or fall together in their interactions with other groups (Sober, 1981). Social organisation offers various means of enforcing group membership, including education in common values and beliefs, instilment of duty, establishment of rules and norms, and penalties for breaking rules. Clashes between individual and group interests need not be resolved to benefit the individual, and behaviour has a mixture of motives.

Group selection brings Darwinian evolution closer to cultural thought and traditional social theory. Concepts of culture and society must have a collective level and perish under individualistic assumptions. With group selection, culture can be defined at the group level and regarded as protecting the group's collective evolutionary interests. Social structure in the standard sociological sense becomes possible and all the issues surrounding structure and agency enter the scene. Culture can play its usual role in connecting the individual with society and showing how individual and social reproduction are entwined. Locating this interdependence within a multilevel evolutionary theory allows cultural thought to live with Darwinism. When group selection is outlawed, social structures no longer delineate a group or collective and either disappear or serve individual interests. Culture likewise forfeits its collectiveness and has to be shrivelled to an individual level. Evolutionary theories without group selection can accommodate culture only in a paltry way fixated on the individual dimensions of culture. If cultural thought is to be comfortable with Darwinism, then multilevel selection and stratification are essential.

The final ingredient of Darwinism – inheritance – brings further difficulties. As human beings do not inherit a culture at birth, the inheritance mechanism for biological evolution cannot be transferred to cultural evolution. Unlike living things, cultural artefacts such as historical documents, books, artworks and buildings have no biological lifespan and may last for many generations. The permanence of these items assists cultural survival, but it does not reproduce a culture. Information in books or other written records has little cultural value unless the current human population can read and understand it. A culture can be kept alive only if each succeeding generation has the knowledge and ability to digest available information and use it actively in a way of life. Each generation acquires characteristics that will in turn be passed on to future generations. The prominence of acquired characteristics has led to culture being separated from Darwinism, at least in its neo-Darwinian form, but the distance becomes narrower if Darwinism is adapted for non-genetic inheritance.

Theories of cultural evolution, unable to rely on genetics, have to find another inheritance mode. Dual inheritance models retain a Darwinian framework but have cultural as well as biological inheritance (Cavalli-Sforza and Feldman, 1981; Boyd and Richerson, 1985; Durham, 1991; Richerson and Boyd, 2005; Chase, 2006). Habits, routines, ideas and cultural codes can all fuel cultural inheritance, for they socialise people in a given way of life – the more people who acquire a habit or follow a routine, the greater the spread and endurance of the culture. Failure to transmit habits and routines to the next generation will condemn a culture to die, regardless of any intrinsic merit it may have. By choosing them as the inheritance mode, population thinking can be extended to cultural evolution, and evolutionary methods from biology can be translated to social research. Dual inheritance models trace the distribution of habits and routines across generations in the way that biological models trace the distribution of genes. A close analogy between biological and cultural evolution seems possible, and Darwinism carries over to cultural problems. Caution is still advisable, because a culture cannot be described by individual traits alone. To portray a culture as an aggregate of individual traits may neglect the collective and social levels that are crucial to cultural thought.

Efforts to draw evolutionary analogies for cultural change have reanimated the debates on whether inheritance is Lamarckian, that is to say, whether acquired characteristics can be inherited. Lamarckism, disproved at the genetic level, might still hold true in evolutionary theories with habits or routines as the inheritance mode. A Lamarckian element arises once behaviour is adapted to the current environment and the adaptations are passed on to succeeding generations. Purposeful behaviour may lie behind this, a feature that Lamarckism shares with cultural thought. It is feasible for acquired behaviour to be passed on by learning and imitation: acquired traits can then be preserved and inherited. This confirms the impression that cultural evolution can be Lamarckian, but it does not jettison Darwinism; instead, Lamarckian cases may be embedded within a Darwinian framework (Hodgson, 2001b; Knudsen, 2001; Hodgson and Knudsen, 2006a). The Lamarck/Darwin contrast has been heightened by neo-Darwinism in biology but has less force in the cultural domain. Inheritance termed Lamarckian has been in keeping with Darwinian arguments as well, and there is no dichotomy. Lamarckian inheritance expands the range of inheritance modes without escaping the ambit of Darwinism.

From the foregoing discussion, it seems that culture can be reconciled with natural selection and that a strict culture/nature dualism is mistaken. Extending Darwinian models to culture is difficult, though, and many ambiguities occur over units of selection and modes of inheritance. The resulting theories often seem unwieldy and contrived, and it may be doubted whether they add much to cultural discussion (Fracchia and Lewontin, 1999). Evolutionary economists should be circumspect about Darwinian models and analogies, in view of the many differences between biological and cultural evolution (Witt, 2004; Buenstorf, 2006; Cordes, 2006). A formal Darwinism may dally with oversimplification and reductionism through the tendencies to break culture down into units, overlook social structures, and give biology priority over culture. The tendencies can be resisted if theorists allow properly for emergent powers and stratification, but many writers on evolution have not done so. Among the implications of emergence is that economic and social matters are irreducible to biological foundations and can be discussed separately. This has been the (usually implicit) position of cultural thought and liberates social studies from biology, especially if long-term evolutionary modelling has little relevance to the topic at hand. It would be unwise to force all cultural discussion into an evolutionary mould.

## 11.4 ECONOMIC EVOLUTION

Evolutionary ideas have long accompanied economic thought, but the meaning of economic evolution is still vague and inconsistent (Hodgson, 1999a, Chapter 6). Some economists have been Darwinians who equate evolution with natural selection; others have taken a pre-Darwinian view and seen evolution as an unfolding historical development punctuated by stages or eras (Backhaus, 2003). When discussing evolution, economists have made different assumptions about methodological individualism, competition, biological analogies and final destinations. Variable usage has created uncertainty over how evolutionary economics should proceed.

Institutionalism in the tradition of Veblen has been eager to introduce social and cultural evolution into economics (Brinkman, 1992). Veblen's project was to blend economics with Darwinism, build an evolutionary economic theory without teleology, and move away from the mechanistic equilibria of neoclassical economics. He was never to complete the project and failed to rewrite economic theory (Mayhew, 1998; Rutherford, 1998; Hodgson, 2004, Part III). The lack of theoretical foundations was a problem for American institutionalism and contributed to its decline and the rise of neoclassical orthodoxy (Rutherford, 2001; Hodgson, 2004, Chapter 18). Another problem was the legacy of Social Darwinism, which had begun with Herbert Spencer and became popular in the late nineteenth century (Bannister, 1979; Jones, 1980; Bellomy, 1984). Belying its name, it was not Darwinian and had a developmental theory that asserted the increasing complexity of advanced societies and their competitive advantage over primitive ones. The faith in competition was only loosely tethered to Darwin's work, and the predictability of evolution was alien to Darwin (Bowler, 1988; Hodgson, 1993a, Chapter 6). With its tendentious message, Social Darwinism could easily be an ideological prop, and its extreme advocates used it to justify imperialist expansion by industrial nations. Always provocative, this strain of thought was discredited after the world wars of the early twentieth century. Darwinian evolution became a taboo subject in social theory, and evolutionary arguments were received with suspicion and hostility. The resistance has broken down in recent years, but the taint of Social Darwinism remains.

Only since the 1980s have evolutionary ideas in social science been rehabilitated; economists are once again seeking an evolutionary economic theory (Boulding, 1981; Nelson and Winter, 1982; Hodgson, 1988; Andersen, 1994). Much of the recent literature has discussed industrial and technical change, with the firm as the fulcrum – competition among firms, leading to differential survival rates, provides the evolutionary analogy. Although firms and industries are central, evolution fans out across the whole economy and its supporting institutions. Darwinism is seen as being necessary but insufficient to explain economic behaviour (Hodgson and Knudsen, 2006b). The ultimate goal, not yet attained, is to fill the gaps left by Veblen and furnish evolutionary economics with a solid theoretical basis.

Other strands within institutionalism and heterodox economics have been less enthusiastic about Darwinism. Veblen's work is broad enough for alternative interpretations that minimise links with biology and instead emphasise culture and hermeneutics (Jennings and Waller, 1994, 1998; Dyer, 2000). The institutionalism of John Commons has generally been construed as downgrading natural selection in economics and highlighting artificial selection and the conscious design of institutions (Ramstad, 1994; Bazzoli, 2000; Hodgson, 2004, Chapter 13). Radical institutionalists have made overtures to Marxism and explained evolution through structural changes stimulated by conflicts among classes and other social groups (Dugger and Sherman, 1994, 1997, 2000; Sherman, 2005). Non-Darwinian, developmental evolution is endemic to heterodox economics. Further examples are regulation theory and the social structures of accumulation approach, which see economic evolution as passing through a series of stages and propelled by frictions between institutions and technology (Tylecote, 1991; O'Hara, 2000; Freeman and Louçã, 2001). Also developmental are theories that aim to capture endogenous structural changes and transformational growth (Pasinetti, 1993; Nell, 1992, Part III, 1998). Many heterodox economists, unsure that Darwinism is helpful, have treated evolution in a manner closer to Marx than to Darwin. Their qualms are not about biological reductionism, which is avoided in non-reductionist Darwinian arguments, but about whether a formal Darwinian model is a misleading analogy with biological evolution.

Alongside Veblen, the other founding father of evolutionary economics was Joseph Schumpeter, who seems to be the dominant influence in the recent literature (Fagerberg, 2003). Throughout his career, Schumpeter did empirical research on economic growth and theorised about capitalist development (Schumpeter, 1934, 1939, 1942). His core idea was creative destruction, whereby growth occurs through successive waves of entrepreneurship, each wave undermining the temporary market power of the previous one. The discontinuous changes, which never settle into a permanent equilibrium, can be viewed as evolutionary. Schumpeter made few detailed references to Darwin and did not base his theories on Darwinian principles (Hodgson, 1993a, Chapter 10, 1997). His concept of evolution came nearer to the dialectics of Hegel and Marx than the population thinking of Darwin. The entrepreneur as Schumpeter's hero resembles Hegel's great leaders who call forth the hidden collective spirit of the times and enact historical change (Prendergast, 2006). Both Hegel and Schumpeter saw evolution as periodic and developmental, only vaguely predictable, subject to randomness, and stoked by human agents but not wholly under anyone's control. Though idealist rather than materialist and sympathetic to capitalism, Schumpeter's outlook was not unlike Marx's – it was dialectical, with tensions among conflicting interests, and gave rise to a loose, long-term developmental scheme open to short-term and local variations (Elliott, 1980; Catephores, 1994; Rosenberg, 1994). Capitalist economies evolved through internal pressures and contradictions in a non-Darwinian, dialectical fashion. The newly revived evolutionary economics has been ambivalent in so far that its formal models and language are Darwinian but it refers primarily to Schumpeter as its guiding star. Developmental and Darwinian ideas have coexisted uneasily without being fully synthesised.

A further example of revived evolutionary thought comes with Friedrich Hayek, who made explicit allusions to culture. He went beyond neo-Austrian economics to seek a comprehensive evolutionary theory of economic and social development (Caldwell, 2000, 2002; Gamble, 2006; Gaus, 2006; Steele, 2007). Pivotal for Hayek was spontaneous order, such that institutions emerge from uncoordinated actions by individual agents – no government or other planning body ever has enough information to plan an economy or society, and attempts to do so would be detrimental (Hayek, 1948). His later writings generalised his beliefs into a universal vista of social and institutional change, unplanned but propitious (Hayek, 1982, 1988). Discounting biological reductionism and noting the importance of institutions, he saw evolution as bringing forth the rules and institutions that underpin liberal, market-based societies. His evolutionary theory was never spelled out but was apparently non-Darwinian and embraced higher, group levels of analysis. Critics have pointed out the inconsistency between collective evolution and methodological individualism: the evolutionary argument rests upon group selection that falls outside the neo-Austrian orbit (Vanberg, 1986, 1994; Hodgson, 1991). Austrian purism would insist that Hayek should abandon group selection, but others without the Austrian affiliation would abandon methodological individualism. Hayek's thinking was swayed by his libertarian, pro-market creed: he subscribed to a programme by which evolution can be consummated only in laissez-faire capitalism.

Recent evolutionary economics has been mostly heterodox, but several orthodox economists have also intervened (Hirshleifer, 1977; Tullock, 1979; Robson, 2002). Admirers of sociobiology and evolutionary psychology, they have tried to explain instrumental rationality through Darwinian evolution: typical economic behaviour, as in neoclassical theory, must have fulfilled an evolutionary function and assisted human prosperity, otherwise it would never have evolved and been reproduced. Sociobiology can back up economic orthodoxy by suggesting that instrumental rationality is general and natural, so that other social sciences should turn to neoclassical methods. These arguments suffer from the drawbacks of sociobiology, notably its neglect of culture and its proclivity to make everything biological. Heterodox economists dispute self-interested rational behaviour even within economics but, if it does prevail in any particular circumstances, view it as a cultural construct. Preference formation should be a cultural question, as against a biological one. In heterodox evolutionary economics, culture has an accredited place; to play down culture and mention only biological influences on behaviour is to pursue biological reductionism. Neoclassical economics and sociobiology are well matched in their lax attitudes to culture.

The revival of evolutionary arguments has been contemporary with the revival of cultural thought: evolutionary economics has burgeoned since the 1980s, as have cultural studies and postmodernism. Are the trends related, or is this just a coincidence? Evolutionary and cultural thought have both reacted against positivism and mechanistic theorising. Both are attuned to diversity and deny a single, predictable route towards scientific or social progress; they are frank about the difficulties of foretelling the future and shun grand narratives of history. In some cases culture and evolution relate directly, as when evolutionary models are adapted for cultural applications. The common features signal a wider intellectual movement against an oversimplified, mechanical and monolithic science. Cultural and evolutionary thought are, however, expressed in separate literatures, through different academic disciplines, and have substantial disparities in content and style.

One way of looking at the issue is to see them as approaching the same subject matter from different levels. Darwinian evolutionary thought addresses social existence from below, starting with biological evolution of plant and animal species and then extending it to human behaviour; cultural thought addresses social existence from above, starting with ideas and beliefs and then fitting them in with the material and biological world. Any full account of economic and social behaviour should ideally be exploring the middle terrain that brings biology and culture together and gives neither of them supremacy over the other. This is a complicated task,

*Table 11.1    A stratified view of evolution*

| Level of analysis | Object of study | Type of evolution | Cultural methods appropriate? |
|---|---|---|---|
| Conceptual | Ideas/Texts | Cultural | Yes |
| Social | Institutions/Social relations | Cultural/ Biological | Yes |
| Individual | Individual human beings | Cultural/ Biological | Yes |
| Genetic | Genes | Biological | No |
| Atomic | Atoms | None | No |

clogged by disciplinary boundaries as well as by its inherent difficulty, but it should be practicable as long as one takes a broad enough perspective.

The key to integrating culture with evolution is to have a stratified view, composed of many interacting layers, and allow for emergence, such that causal powers at one layer need not be reducible to any other layer. Cultural thought can then be housed within a Darwinian evolutionary framework. What might seem to be inconsistencies between cultural thought and Darwinism can be rationalised as different methods being used, as appropriate, at different levels of the same conceptual scheme. Darwinism pertains at the lower, biological levels and cultural thought at the higher, social levels. Many social and economic topics can be handled while abstracting from the Darwinian context. Economists should be free to appeal to Darwinian evolution when this seems apposite but not feel compelled to speak a Darwinian language. Table 11.1 shows an example of stratification.

The rows in Table 11.1 correspond to levels of analysis often found in academic work. Moving upwards, the drift is from material to immaterial, natural to social, static to historical, and universal to particular. Higher levels depend on lower ones for their existence but cannot be explained in terms of lower levels alone. Any reductionism is arbitrary, as one can always delve into lower levels – individualistic reductionism is outdone by genetic reductionism, which is outdone by atomic reductionism (with further subdivisions through subatomic levels). To explain everything at a single, decisive level is unduly restrictive: the levels are interdependent and causal powers may reside in several of them. In Table 11.1 the higher levels can evolve more easily and rapidly than the lower ones. Nothing much happens at the atomic level, since the atomic elements are the building blocks of matter and stay the same however matter is reconstituted. Genes evolve on neo-Darwinian lines, but the pace is slow and human genetics can be assumed constant in social studies. At individual and social levels, biological factors are joined by cultural processes, that is, the formation of individuals within society. Recorded human history gives plenty of evidence for the gradual but thoroughgoing transformation of cultures and human behaviour. The conceptual realm of ideas, which originates in human thought, is unconstrained by the material world (one can imagine and describe things with no physical existence) and capable of infinite variety and transformation – the speed of change is the most rapid. Evolution, understood in its widest sense, is faster at the upper levels in Table 11.1 and further away from neo-Darwinism.

At the genetic level, biological evolution has relevance for all organisms, including human beings, over a vast time horizon. In economics, the time frame is too short for significant genetic change. Previous human evolution has yielded instincts that affect behaviour, but they are fixed and cannot explain economic development, which must be based on factors other than purely biological ones. Increased knowledge of genetic inheritance in the late nineteenth and early twentieth centuries raised the possibility of eugenics: human beings could accelerate genetic change and steer it in benign directions by non-natural selection. Eugenic policies were initially seen as progressive and advocated by many scientists, social reformers and economists (Freeden, 1979; Paul, 1984; Toye, 2000, Chapter 4; Leonard, 2005). Since the Second World War, abuse of eugenics by the Nazis has led to its being ostracised on ethical grounds and falling beyond the pale of respectable academic discussion. Recent advances in genetic engineering have brought similar ethical difficulties about what is acceptable (Reiss and Straughan, 1996; Habermas, 2003; Sandel, 2007). Eugenics and genetic engineering remind us that the higher levels in Table 11.1, while ontologically dependent on lower levels, can have a downward causal influence. Our moral judgements have minimised this influence by discouraging non-natural selection and manipulation of genetic material, especially for human beings.

Above the genetic level in Table 11.1, cultural evolution begins to appear. Acquired characteristics and interpersonal relations shape behaviour and foster social change. At the highest, conceptual level, information is recorded and transmitted by non-genetic means and becomes activated as knowledge only with the engagement of human agents. Greater complexity in the upper levels of Table 11.1 means that a solely biological standpoint is inadequate and cultural methods are needed. Human agents often behave with purpose and their motives cannot be reduced to biology – in understanding human behaviour, academic study takes on an interpretative quality and must be alert to social context. Any Darwinism in the social and economic sphere should allow for purposeful and habitual behaviour, group selection and Lamarckian inheritance. Without these, a collapse into genetic or individualistic reductionism is likely.

From a Darwinian perspective, economic evolution has no plan and neither supernatural nor human purposes guide observed events. While this might encapsulate the waywardness of capitalist development, it is only a partial picture of economic behaviour. Many business and governmental organisations allot centralised power to macro agents who decide economic and social outcomes. Darwinism has little purchase here – there is no variation, selection or inheritance – and the suitable methods are those of cultural thought and the humanities. It might be argued that in the longer term, selection must prevail and that decisions made by macro agents will bite only if they pass the evolutionary test. Even the largest business and military empires are impermanent and less durable than they appear. Yet most economic theorising concerns shorter periods when existing power structures are secure and macro agents wield great authority. Instead of natural selection, the causality in idealist or materialist theories of history comes to the fore, namely purposeful behaviour by macro agents, concentrated power from hierarchical social structures, and dialectical clashes among ideas or material interests. In understanding everyday economic behaviour, cultural factors outweigh Darwinian evolution.

A danger of the quest for a true evolutionary economics is that all economic and social changes are viewed through Darwinian spectacles: precommitment to Darwinism is counter-productive if it sanctions neglect of cultural methods. Economic investigators should be left to judge for themselves whether they need a Darwinian model. Competition among firms is the obvious candidate for evolutionary treatment, but even here personal relations and power structures are widespread. Cultural thought permits broader arguments about economic change – purposeful behaviour may mesh with evolution by adding further variability, but it may stand alone as an explanation if the agent has the power to implement change directly and enforce it upon others. Sensitivity to culture strengthens the group and class levels of analysis, offsetting the individualistic and reductionist tendencies of evolutionary theorising. The crux is to maintain pluralism and give cultural methods a place when studying economic evolution.

# PART IV

# Conclusion

# 12.  Towards a culturally informed economics?

Orthodox economics has followed core doctrines that exclude cultural thought. This cultural vacuum was a by-product of the desire to imitate natural sciences, rather than a deliberate disavowal of culture. Most economists were busy with increasingly specialised research and felt no need to ponder the doubts raised by cultural critics – cultural thought was nullified by being ignored. Economics has not been nakedly anti-cultural, but the gist of its theories and methods has been to debar culture. Once orthodoxy defined itself around neoclassical theory, the separation from culture became institutionalised. Heterodox economists did bring culture into economics but, as their heterodox status attests, made little impression on the mainstream. The more cultural the heterodox ideas, the more likely they were to be put aside as unscientific or non-economic.

Barriers to culture have been stronger in orthodox economics than in social sciences as a whole. While other disciplines have had their own soul searching about methodology, none has gone as far as neoclassical economics in ruling out cultural methods. The revival of cultural thought since the 1960s has been neglected by orthodox economists who, absorbed in specialised theories, were oblivious to larger intellectual trends. Some have touted an economic imperialism that aims to export neoclassical theory into other social sciences (Tullock, 1972; Becker, 1976; Hirshleifer, 1985; Radnitzky and Bernholz, 1987; Lazear, 2000). Their attitudes show scant awareness of cultural critiques of economics or the broader panorama of social theory, cultural theory and political economy (Harcourt, 1982; Burkitt and Spiers, 1983; Nicolaides, 1988; Udehn, 1992; Fine, 1999, 2000, 2002; Fine and Milonakis, 2009). Far from acknowledging doubts about neoclassicism, they want to make it universal and apply it to areas not usually viewed as economic. The distance from cultural thought could hardly be greater: economic imperialism would eliminate cultural methods from social research.

Can economics ever be at ease with culture? Intellectually this ought to be achievable, and the revival of cultural thought provides a setting. The main impediment is institutional, not intellectual, and consists in orthodox economic dogma. It remains to be seen whether the trends towards cultural thought, duly recognised in heterodox economics, will have any effects on orthodoxy. The present chapter begins by looking for traces of cultural sagacity in mainstream economics, then examines recent heterodox developments, and finally considers what would be required for a culturally informed economics.

## 12.1   DEVELOPMENTS WITHIN MAINSTREAM ECONOMICS

The economic mainstream, with its claims to universal relevance, is proud of its ability to model all economic (and latterly non-economic) subject matter. Mainstream research during the late twentieth century spawned many sub-disciplines based on neoclassicism in pure or imperfectionist forms: labour economics, industrial economics, public economics, international economics, health economics, population economics, environmental economics, transport economics, and so on. Because the new sub-disciplines have roamed away from the customary topics of economic analysis, they have moved closer to cultural and social issues. The late twentieth century also brought the revival of cultural thought as positivistic methods were challenged and postmodernism came to the fore. Did the renewed interest in culture seep through to economic orthodoxy? Is mainstream economics more sensitive towards culture than hitherto? Even though the mainstream has been deaf to cultural ideas from outside, it might conceivably give a hearing to cultural ideas from within. Some developments that might perhaps be seen in this light are the suspension of core neoclassical principles by senior orthodox researchers, the growth of new institutional economics, and the emergence of cultural economics as a sub-discipline.

Recent economic theorising shows what appears to be pluralism and a shift away from neoclassical rationality, individualism and market-clearing equilibrium (Colander, 2000b, 2005; Colander et al., 2004; Davis, 2006, 2007; Hodgson, 2007). Pure neoclassical theory reached a peak of esteem and influence in the 1970s – the heyday of general equilibrium, monetarism and the human capital research programme – but since then its flaws have been exposed (Kirman, 1989, 2006; Rizvi, 1994; Katzner, 2001). Mainstream researchers, tired with pure neoclassical theory, have found novel lines of research that still belong to the mainstream (and do not identify with heterodoxy) but part company with standard neoclassical assumptions. 'Mainstream pluralism' comprises fields such as experimental economics, behavioural economics, game theory, neuroeconomics, evolutionary economics (in its mainstream variants), and the economics of complexity – these make up a sizeable proportion of current mainstream work, especially among senior researchers in prestigious universities. Since high-ranking academics are powerful in the economics profession, their change of tack could possibly reconfigure mainstream economics (Davis, 2008). Yet the new fields do not cohere into an alternative paradigm, and neoclassical methods are as dominant as ever in economics teaching: their position relative to heterodoxy has strengthened during the supposed pluralism (Fine, 2008). After a time lag the innovations might percolate down to economics teaching, but this is by no means guaranteed. Other periods of mainstream pluralism, such as the 'years of high theory' in the 1920s and 1930s, did not overturn neoclassical orthodoxy.

Any marginal relaxing of neoclassical assumptions should create more space for cultural arguments. Mainstream pluralism admits to a malaise within the neoclassical world view and searches for remedies. Its motives are critical, but it ignores the vast reservoir of critique available in heterodox economics and the cultural tradition – it has stayed within the mainstream and pulled its punches. All the mainstream pluralists remain committed to mathematical formalisation and positivistic methodology (Lawson, 2006; Dow, 2007; Dequech, 2008). They investigate some of the black boxes and restrictive assumptions of neoclassicism, but do so by renewing efforts to theorise mathematically and undertake rigorous empirical research, often using methods that further imitate natural science. The implicit moral is that neoclassical orthodoxy has not gone far enough in applying rationalism and empiricism to economic behaviour: it has left gaps in its theoretical coverage and held back on empirical tests. Mainstream pluralism has ratcheted up the mathematical level of mainstream economics, on the premise that problems of existing theory can be solved by more elaborate techniques. This outlook jars with cultural thought, which is sceptical about imitating natural science and champions interpretative methods.

Among the major influences on mainstream economics has been computational science and information theory (Mirowski, 2002, 2007; Mount and Reiter, 2002). Advances in computing, telecommunications and information technology since the 1940s have enhanced our ability to process and disseminate information. Computational science has used the computer as a paradigm for human behaviour, aiming to unify social and natural sciences within a common analytical framework. From this angle, any natural or social reality can be represented by a simulation that distils its essence: the artificial mimics the real, gives insights into reality and produces the 'sciences of the artificial' (Simon, 1981). Complex information can be handled by breaking it down into a large but finite number of units; as computational capacities improve, then so does our capacity to manipulate such data. The lustre and glamour of computing in its early years had an impact on the mathematisation of economics, especially in general equilibrium theory and econometrics. But pure neoclassical modelling ultimately constrains computational arguments, as it does not probe the black box of individual behaviour: computational science should ideally consider how individuals process information and how they interact. Mainstream pluralism has opened the black box and portrayed human behaviour mathematically through game theory, behavioural economics and informational economics. Whatever the merits of this enterprise, it is scarcely in tune with cultural thought; it rests on analogies with machines or automatons, like the analogies of Quesnay and other Enlightenment writers (Mirowski, 2002, Chapter 1). As recounted in Part I, a mechanistic mindset was the bane of the Counter-Enlightenment.

Computational approaches may, all the same, perform a service to cultural thought through their negative results, by showing up the limits to mathematical models and the need for alternatives. A theme of Herbert Simon's work has been the impossibility of human beings acting as perfect calculators and making optimal responses to every event (Simon, 1957, 1983). Human computational skills cannot cope with the intricacy of the real world; to simplify things, people follow procedures or rules of thumb that are satisfactory but sub-optimal. This demolishes neoclassical utility maximising assumptions and points towards social and cultural norms. At the aggregate level, computational approaches give rise to notions of complexity, whereby aggregate outcomes are not wholly explicable by their deterministic components and do not converge on well-defined equilibria (Waldrop, 1992; Kauffman, 1995; Holland, 1998; Axelrod and Cohen, 1999). Complexity contradicts the orthodox belief that all economic behaviour can be reduced to microfoundations and supports the case for new ways of theorising (Lane, 1993; Rosser, 1999; Colander, 2000a; Beinhocker, 2006). The results chime with ideas of emergence and lead to a stratified perspective in which higher layers of analysis are irreducible to lower ones. Theorising has to go beyond the individual agent and add structural and cultural layers that cannot be explained by individual behaviour. The stalemate of reductionist mathematical modelling should encourage richer theorising and weaken the grip of individualism.

Another recent development has been the new institutional economics, contrasted with the old institutionalism of Veblen and Commons (Langlois, 1986; Furubotn and Richter, 1997; Williamson, 2000; Ménard and Shirley, 2005; Brousseau and Glachant, 2008). The spur for a mainstream institutionalism came from Coase's long-standing remarks about the failure of neoclassical economics to explain the existence of firms (Coase, 1937). This problem was taken seriously only in the 1970s and 1980s through Williamson's transaction-cost economics and related research (Williamson, 1975, 1985; Dietrich, 1994). The aim has been to submit the inner workings of firms and other organisations to orthodox theoretical modelling. Since most large firms are administrative hierarchies, it behoves neoclassical theory to justify why hierarchies prevail over supposedly efficient markets. Transaction-cost economics attempts to explain how firms are organised by comparing the costs of contractual, market-type interactions with the costs of equivalent administrative arrangements. Such arguments would, if successful, tell us why particular institutions and contractual forms appear under particular circumstances. Similar arguments have been applied to the whole of capitalist institutional development (North, 1981, 1990). The analysis is functionalist in so far that institutions are explained by the functions they fulfil.

The nature of the new institutional economics is revealed by its allegiance to rational-choice individualism (Hodgson, 1989, 1993b; Mayhew, 1989; Rutherford, 1989, 1994; Dugger, 1990). Its ambition is to extend neoclassical theory beyond exchange relations to the internal organisation of firms and other institutions. Although its topics stray outside traditional neoclassicism, its methods are neoclassical in spirit. If all institutions were to be explained this way, then neoclassical theory would be much expanded: the new institutional economics can be seen as an arm of economic imperialism that widens the domain of neoclassical thought. Has mainstream interest in institutions brought greater understanding of culture? On the positive side, transaction-cost economics has nudged the mainstream towards contracts, institutions and personal relations among economic agents. Long familiar to old institutionalists and social theorists outside economics (such as Durkheim, Weber and Simmel), these are now for the first time being discussed by the economic mainstream. Neoclassical distaste for institutions has met with an internal critique and is no longer tenable. On the negative side, the individualism has meant that new institutional economics must explain institutions through rational individual behaviour. Institutions receive more credit in theorising, but they remain subordinate to the individual. This detracts from culture as a process by passing over the effect of institutions and social structures upon human agency. Orthodox economists have sometimes conceded that individual behaviour may be socially determined and discussed how customs and culture influence economic development (Basu et al., 1987; North, 1994; Harrison and Huntington, 2000; Aoki, 2001; Jones, 2006). As the new institutionalism unfurls, it may come nearer to the old institutionalism (Dequech, 2002; Field, 2007; Hodgson, 2007). Deference to neoclassical methods would, nevertheless, diminish its cultural content and hamper any convergence with cultural thought.

As well as attempting to explain institutions, the new institutional economics has addressed cultural evolution and how it relates to the economy. The arguments resemble Hayek's later writings on the spontaneous emergence of culture and share the same invisible-hand logic. Social conventions are viewed as resulting not from design but from uncoordinated actions by individual agents – the job of new institutional economics is to elucidate these processes (Schotter, 1981; Langlois, 1986). Any conventions must perform a valuable function (and are in this sense 'rational') without social planning or intentional behaviour at a macro level. The ensuing evolutionary economics stays within mainstream boundaries by keeping instrumental rationality intact and using neoclassical modelling or game theory (Schotter, 1981; Axelrod, 1984; Sugden, 1986, 1989; Hargreaves Heap and Varoufakis, 1995, Chapter 7). A prior goal of reducing culture to individual interactions often motivates the new institutionalism, on the assumption of a fixed starting point with given individuals and rules (Field, 1979, 1984). While unduly restrictive, such a goal may bring out the difficulties in portraying culture individualistically – new institutionalists, as they realise the difficulties, may be tempted to move closer to old institutionalism. Their theorising may be diverted away from individualism towards a wider outlook that accepts the cultural basis of economic behaviour (Goldschmidt and Remmele, 2005). Old institutionalists have always known that culture cannot be reduced to the individual level. If new institutionalists eventually reach the same conclusion, then they will have rediscovered (in abstruse mathematical language) something already documented by heterodox economists, sociologists, anthropologists and other social scientists.

A final development within mainstream economics, and the one most immediately connected to culture, has been the founding of cultural economics as a sub-discipline. Since the 1960s, various mainstream researchers have discussed the economics of cultural institutions and the media, the role of cultural industries in the economy, and the economic status of creative artists and performers (Throsby, 1994, 2001; Towse, 1997, 2003; Heilbrun and Gray, 2001; Blaug, 2001; Ginsburgh and Throsby, 2006). This body of work is now sufficiently established to count as a specialised field within the mainstream and has its own professional structures and journal (the *Journal of Cultural Economics*). Could the birth of cultural economics herald a rapprochement between orthodox economics and cultural thought? Cultural economics tackles cultural questions and shows that they are inseparable from the economy; it thereby has some affinity with cultural materialism and helps to resist extreme idealism that separates culture from economics. Efforts to understand artistic creativity and the valuation of cultural items have induced within cultural economics a depth unusual in the mainstream – there is greater appreciation, for instance, of multiple sources of value and the collective dimensions of culture (Hutter, 1996; Throsby, 1999, 2001, Chapters 1–3). Compared with most orthodox thinking, cultural economics is a forward step. To have culture as a subject is not to espouse cultural thought, however, and in this respect the new cultural research has made little difference.

As a branch of the mainstream, cultural economics has applied neo-classical theory to cultural matters, carving out another economic sub-discipline to stand beside the others that have grown up in the late twentieth century. This strategy confers specialist status and, given the total dominance of orthodoxy, may be the only way for cultural issues to get into the mainstream literature. Using neoclassical methods has a calamitous side-effect: it alienates cultural economics from the wider tradition of cultural thought. Cultural critiques of economics are missing from the literature on cultural economics and have no discernible effect on its theories. The upshot is to have a cultural economics estranged from cultural thought and using methods antagonistic to culture. Cultural economics could be a conduit for introducing cultural ideas into economics, but not if it cleaves to neoclassicism. It would actually make things worse if it just became a tool of economic imperialism spreading orthodoxy on to cultural terrain. To follow this route would go against the cultural tradition, whose wish was to apply cultural thought to economics, not economic thought to culture.

Mainstream pluralism and institutional/cultural sub-disciplines are evidence of widespread dissatisfaction with pure neoclassical theory. Some mainstream economists – the more reflective ones – have been looking for alternatives and relaxing the assumptions made in neoclassical models. Any diversity is better than none, but mainstream pluralism is unlikely to shift orthodox economics towards cultural methods. As the name implies, it acquiesces in the ethos of the mainstream: it is highly specialised, relies heavily on mathematics, emulates the natural sciences, and has rationalist or empiricist foundations. Though critical of pure neoclassicism, it has not drawn upon the rich legacy of critique in heterodox economics and the cultural tradition. The fundamental arguments against neoclassicism were made long ago, set out meticulously and incisively by heterodox economists, and studiously ignored by the mainstream. This remains true of the mainstream pluralists, whose work contains few references to heterodox economics, even when this would be relevant and illuminating. What seems probable is that aspects of mainstream pluralism will trickle down into the orthodox teaching syllabus (in 'advanced' rather than basic courses) but that economic orthodoxy will stay intact. The mainstream identity of the new pluralists stops them from wandering too far from orthodoxy (otherwise they would risk being branded as heterodox or non-economic) and keeps them away from cultural thought. A culturally informed economics would have to be distinct from neoclassicism, and so the best prospects lie with heterodoxy.

## 12.2   DEVELOPMENTS OUTSIDE THE MAINSTREAM

Culture has often entered directly into heterodox economics, as in the old institutionalism, or indirectly through the critique of individualistic reductionism, as in Post Keynesian and radical economics. The potential for cultural thought is clear, but obstacles are still there. Like economic orthodoxy, heterodox economics has been wont to copy natural sciences and use rationalist and empiricist methods. A desire for continuity with classical economics (most obvious in neo-Ricardianism) may also be a drag on cultural thought. Classical theory can only go so far in raising the cultural content of economics, and ideas have to come from outside. The following discussion examines promising heterodox developments, namely evolutionary economics, economic sociology, critical realism, postmodernist economics, social constructionism, and cultural political economy.

Evolutionary economics has expanded rapidly within the last few decades and exists in several varieties: orthodox ones look towards the new institutional economics, heterodox ones towards the old institutionalism or Austrian economics. Institutional and evolutionary arguments have also appeared in sociology, political science and organisation theory, and they too vary in their theoretical and methodological assumptions (DiMaggio, 1998; Nielsen, 2001, 2007). A broad evolutionary economics, on Schumpeterian or Veblenian principles, should be able to accommodate culture. Heterodox authors have sought theoretical foundations for an evolutionary economics differentiated from neoclassical orthodoxy (Witt, 1993, 2003; Andersen, 1994; Potts, 2000; Nelson and Winter, 2002; Dopfer, 2005; Metcalfe, 2005). Removing the anti-cultural tenets of neoclassicism permits a more tolerant vision that can integrate culture and economic theory. Cultural methods become feasible, though an augmented evolutionary economics cannot ensure an adequate treatment of culture. The inspiration for evolutionary economics has been mostly biological rather than cultural: it opposes static and mechanistic theories in the name of Darwinism, not the cultural tradition. If Darwinian evolutionary models are to embrace culture, they have to be flexible in allowing for groups and collectives, multiple levels of selection, and Lamarckian inheritance. It is debatable whether formal Darwinian modelling has great value in depicting culture. Population thinking reminds us that cultures are borne by individuals with finite lifespans and can be preserved only if passed on to succeeding generations. This should always be remembered, but the focus of interest may be elsewhere, in the details of a particular culture, the conflicts among ideas and beliefs, the relation of ideas to material interests, and the maintenance of prevailing beliefs through institutional power. A Darwinian model will throw little light on these issues and interpretative methods are required. Heterodox versions of economic evolution can rebut the anti-cultural foundations of economic orthodoxy but cannot on their own deliver a culturally informed economics.

A different line of culturally sensitive heterodox research, which has also expanded in recent years, has been economic sociology (Granovetter, 1990; Ingham, 1996; Swedberg, 1997, 2003; Zafirovski and Levine, 1997; Zelizer, 2001; Guillén et al., 2002; Trigilia, 2002; Beckert and Zafirovski, 2005; Liagouras, 2007; Reisman, 2007). Owing to its methods and theories it gets classified as sociology, but its subject matter is economic and by that criterion it is heterodox economics. Its main goal has been to analyse the elements of a capitalist economy – markets, firms, workers/consumers, government, property rights and so forth – from the viewpoint of sociological theory. Current economic sociology builds upon Durkheim, Weber and Simmel, who discussed these themes at length. Most researchers have repudiated both neoclassical theory and Parsonian structural-functionalism, hoping to find a position somewhere between them. Economic sociology reflects the trends towards non-reductionist and non-dualistic social theory: among the key ideas has been embeddedness, such that markets and other institutions are embedded in social structures and cannot be separated from them (Granovetter, 1985, 1992, 2005). The orthodox belief that markets are a universal, socially disembedded absolute is denied by economic sociologists. Embeddedness means that one must reckon with the personal relations and social structures surrounding institutions – theory has to be historically specific and contingent on social context. Economics, no longer isolated from other social sciences, should use the same methods and theories as any other social research. The resulting perspective is compatible with culture, especially in the anthropological sense of a given way of life.

Economic sociologists have been slow to take up cultural arguments, though, and have seemed suspicious (Swedberg, 2003, Chapters 9 and 10; Convert and Heilbron, 2007). They have tended to correlate culture with Parsonian systems theorising and, reacting against this, have preferred smaller-scale models based on the local structures and networks observed in markets and other economic institutions. To stress local structures plays down the cultural background of beliefs and values, presenting a selective picture of economic behaviour (Zelizer, 1988, 2002; DiMaggio, 1994; Dequech, 2003). Formal network theories, which enumerate contacts among individuals, are helpful in mapping out and recording economic relationships but cannot portray culture and human agency (Emirbayer and Goodwin, 1994). Economic sociology has no unified doctrines and varies in its cultural awareness. Its value has been to offer theoretical alternatives to neoclassicism that show the importance of social structure and the deficiencies of an atomistic theory. It may influence heterodox economics, with which it has many affinities, but will struggle to be noticed by the economic mainstream. The label 'economic sociology' is liable to disrupt interaction with the economics discipline, since few economists read or cite sociological literature.

A case for pluralistic social sciences, including cultural methods, has emanated from critical realism. While realism goes back to the beginnings of philosophy, its recent manifestations are largely a reply to postmodernist excesses. Critical realists reaffirm the possibility of science by assuming a real but complex object of study and arguing for methodological pluralism. Social sciences, with their distinctive subject matter, have the most to gain from the pluralism recommended (Bhaskar, 1979; Sayer, 1992, 2000). Theorising and empirical research are among the appropriate methods, together with the interpretative and historical methods used in the humanities and 'soft' social sciences. Critical realism dismantles disciplinary borders and unites the sciences within a set of common goals. Interpretative methods could then come under the umbrella of science and escape being stigmatised as unscientific. Without prioritising cultural methods, critical realism welcomes them and gives them a role in social science.

Essential to critical realism are stratification and emergence. Critical realist ontology incorporates multiple layers: the higher social and cultural layers depend on lower material ones but are not reducible to them. Layering requires a social theory that avoids reductionism or conflictive agency–structure dualism; theories favoured by critical realists are Bhaskar's transformational model of social activity and Archer's morphogenetic model, which are consistent with human agents being cultivated within society but capable of instigating social change (Bhaskar, 1979, 1989; Archer, 1995). The explicit ontology guards against implicit realism derived from a particular method. In order to sharpen its critical edge, realism can take a dialectical form (Bhaskar, 1993, Chapters 2 and 3). Arguments for critical realism in economics imply that methodological pluralism, broad enough to rope in cultural methods, should extend to economic subject matter (Lawson, 1997, 2003). A drawback is the penchant of critical realists for technical and mechanistic language – they talk about 'causal mechanisms' as if reality were a machine. Their critique of orthodox economics attacks its empiricism and positivism as against its rationalist ardour for mechanical theorising (Walters and Young, 2001; Wilson, 2005). A fondness for machine analogies sits uncomfortably with cultural methods – writers in the cultural tradition deplored such language. Critical realism can indeed prepare the ground for a culturally informed economics, but as yet its progress towards this end has been modest.

The branches of heterodox economics with the strongest links to cultural thought are those that engage with postmodernism (Ruccio and Amariglio, 2003). Few mainstream economists have been alert to postmodern ideas, unless one (generously) interprets mainstream pluralism as an expression of them. Heterodox economists have been more alert, but it is still difficult to attach modern/postmodern badges with any assurance. Problems are the imprecise nature and timing of modernity and postmodernity, along with the pluralism of postmodern thought, which eludes programmatic characterisation. Often heterodox economics can be seen as either modernist or postmodernist. Consider, for example, the Post Keynesians. Keynes had personal contact with literary and artistic modernism through the Bloomsbury Group, whose values imbued his economics (Crabtree and Thirlwall, 1980; Goodwin, 2006). The postwar Keynesian/Fordist establishment of the 1940s to the 1970s seems quintessentially modernist compared with earlier and later periods. Yet Keynes's warnings about fundamental uncertainty, his scepticism about econometrics, and his dislike of mathematical abstractions have a postmodern quality (Amariglio and Ruccio, 1995; Klaes, 2006). Keynes and Post Keynesianism defy being categorised as modern or postmodern. To have a postmodern school of economic thought would be an oxymoron in view of the postmodern disdain for grand narratives and programmes, but postmodern sentiment is visible in recent heterodox discussions of economic method, which are anti-positivist and pluralistic (Caldwell, 1982; Hands, 2001; Dow, 2002). So far, the postmodern influence in economics has come from methodology; effects on theorising have been minor.

One area with a postmodern tang has been the growing interest in economic discourse and rhetoric (McCloskey, 1985, 1994; Ruccio, 1991; Klamer, 2001). This literature has examined the disparity between the official positivistic methods of orthodox economics and the actual practices of economists. Orthodoxy has not lived up to its own principles, a failure that suggests the thinness of the official methods. Economics, like any other discipline, thrives on communication, argument and persuasion. Formal economic models, despite their apparent precision, are often metaphorical or symbolic and pliable in how they are understood (Henderson, 1994). Empirical tests may seem decisive but are never beyond challenge and leave space for varied interpretations. Economists, when deciding what to believe, are cajoled by factors other than theoretical logic or empirical results: personal relations, social background, argument/rhetoric, ideology and professional status may also intrude. If economic methods are to appreciate this, then they should broaden out and tolerate the hermeneutics usually banned from natural sciences. Interpretative methods can look in detail at economic discourse and evaluate the communication and interaction within the profession (Klamer, 2007). The same issues surround the mutual understanding of all economic agents, not just economists, and interpretative methods have the widest possible relevance (Brown, 1994b). Hermeneutics should ideally be fitted within a pluralism that still includes theorising and empirical research. The case for methodological pluralism, seldom made in orthodox economics, has been thoroughly explored in the heterodox literature (Salanti and Screpanti, 1997; Sent, 2003; Dow, 2004, 2007; Van Bouwel, 2005; Garnett, 2006). All of this is consonant with postmodernism and intellectual trends outside the economics discipline.

Other heterodox reactions to postmodernism can be found within Marxian and radical economics (Milberg, 1991; Amariglio and Ruccio, 1994; Milberg and Pietrykowski, 1994; Screpanti, 2000). The theory behind postmodernism, notably the structuralism and post-structuralism of Althusser, Derrida and Foucault, had close ties with Marxian thought and remains in touch with it. Recent work in the Marxian tradition has moved towards a looser materialism that gives greater autonomy to institutions and culture. Regulation theory analyses the institutional setting of capitalist development (the mode of regulation) and recognises the importance of culture; the social structures of accumulation approach is similar and also highlights the institutional and cultural side of the economy (Kotz, 1990; O'Hara, 2000; Boyer and Saillard, 2002; McDonough, 2008). Reformulations of Marxian theory put its relational quality in the foreground, avoid reductionism, and have a theoretical slackness that liberates institutions and culture from materialist determinism (Sherman, 1995; Cullenberg, 1999, 2000; Resnick and Wolff, 2006). Efforts have also been made to offset the Marxian emphasis on production by appraising consumption, consumer culture, and the marketing and retailing of products (Fine and Leopold, 1993; Fine, 1995; Slater, 1997; Migone, 2007; Pietrykowski, 2007, 2009; Starr, 2007). More generally, radical institutionalism has studied the institutional and cultural forces behind inequalities based on class, gender, race, age and religion (Dugger, 1996, 2000). The current drift of Marxian and radical economics is to elevate culture and keep away from reductionist theorising. Whether postmodernism can add anything to Marxism is debatable, and those wanting traditional Marxian theory have been sceptical (Callinicos, 1989; Mavroudeas, 2006). Renewed interest in culture is beneficial, though, and prominent in recent Marxian literature.

Social constructionism has also mooted the importance of culture for the economy. Constructionist arguments delineate how things seen as absolute and non-cultural are, in fact, cultural products. 'Real' variables in economic analysis may thus be artefacts of the social context formed by institutions, accounting systems and economic theories. The way we perceive economic activities and the weightings we place on them in accounting procedures may promote implicit values and create social divisions and hierarchies that seem natural and inevitable. Examples of constructionist reasoning occur in feminist economics and the political economy of old age. Feminist economics has studied the social construction of gendered identities and their consequences for economic activity (Ferber and Nelson, 1993; Nelson, 1993, 1996). Gender roles are locked into a dualism of opposites that contrasts female attributes of caring, cooperation, passivity and submissiveness with male attributes of self-preservation, competition, activity and assertiveness. The male stereotype fits snugly into the competitive self-interest of capitalism, whereas the female one is consigned to supportive activities such as housework, child care or nursing, usually low paid or unpaid and with a low or zero weighting in national economic accounts. Females are crowded into the informal and caring sectors of the economy, which are vital for reproducing the economic system but get little attention in mainstream economics (Folbre, 1994, 2001; Folbre and Nelson, 2000; Stark, 2005; Bakker, 2007; Himmelweit, 2002, 2007). Gender roles and the resulting inequalities have become institutionalised and their social origins forgotten, so that they linger without being queried.

Similar constructionist arguments have been applied to the economic status of older people, leading to what has been termed the political economy of old age (Walker, 1981; Phillipson, 1982, 2005; Jackson, 1994, 1998, Chapter 4; Estes, 2001; Johnson, 2005). Even though biological ageing is beyond human control, the social experiences among older people are shaped by the institutional context. Retirement at a fixed age, payment of retirement pensions, and formal medical and social care accentuate chronological age and create a young/old dichotomy. A socially constructed life course, with thresholds at the school-leaving age and the retirement age, comes to define the lifetime of the average person (Kohli and Meyer, 1986; Hareven, 1995; Mayer, 2004). Older people are labelled as an inactive and dependent group that imposes an increasing burden on the active young as the population ages. Their contributions to the informal economy are undervalued and their exclusion from formal economic activity damages their economic and social status. In both examples mentioned here, the effects of biological characteristics (gender, age) are intensified by the prevailing culture. Social constructionist ideas span a huge range of disciplines, but mainstream economics is absent from the list (Holstein and Gubrium, 2007, Part II). Economic applications are confined to heterodox economics or other disciplines such as sociology, anthropology, psychology, management studies and social gerontology.

Cultural methods have been advocated explicitly in the manifesto for a 'cultural political economy' (Sayer, 1997b, 2001; Ray and Sayer, 1999; Jessop, 2005). The motive is to learn from the 'cultural turn' associated with postmodernism and cultural studies, integrate it into the larger tradition of political economy, and establish alternatives to current economic research. A cultural political economy would cast aside the boundaries separating the cultural from the economic and take a post-disciplinary stance that treats them as inseparable (Jessop and Sum, 2001). It would embody postmodernist insights but still investigate material production and the natural world. The result would be an institutional or evolutionary political economy that pays heed to social construction, cultural influences on economic behaviour, economic ideology, and the impact of culture on class and other identities. These can be addressed only by asking semiotic, linguistic and rhetorical questions and using interpretative methods (Jessop, 2004; Jessop and Oosterlynck, 2008). Culture would be at the heart of economics without losing sight of the material setting on which cultural reproduction depends. The arguments have much in common with regulation theory and culturally sensitive variants of Marxism (Jessop and Sum, 2006). Kindred views have emerged from cultural studies and economic geography among authors dissatisfied with orthodox economics (Du Gay and Pryke, 2002; Amin and Thrift, 2003; Gertler. 2003; Slater, 2003; Gibson and Kong, 2005; Hudson, 2005). Cultural political economy is on solid academic ground, given the dearth of cultural thought in economics, and has the potential to fill many gaps in the existing literature. In practical terms, its desire to be post-disciplinary means that it will attract resistance. Orthodoxy already has a sub-discipline of cultural economics and is not going to greet with open arms a cultural political economy that claims relevance across all economic subject matter.

On the whole, heterodox economics has been awake to recent cultural thought: many branches of heterodoxy are historically specific, interpretative, and glad to have culture as a core concept. Also evident is the disunity and disorder among heterodox schools. Often they proceed with their own research agendas and specialised literatures, showing little curiosity about other heterodox work that has obvious similarities. The same ideas are expressed in different conceptual language, which leads to overlaps and misunderstandings. Pluralism of ideas and methods is valuable, but duplicating terminology hinders the heterodox cause and reduces its ability to present cohesive alternatives to orthodoxy. A unifying feature of heterodoxy is its embrace of culture – it upholds the venerable tradition of cultural critique. Few heterodox economists have mulled over this, and opportunities for a united front against orthodoxy have been missed.

## 12.3   RECONCILING ECONOMICS WITH CULTURE

One can imagine an alternative development path for economics that, by following cultural thought, would have yielded entirely different methods and theories. The alternative path was never taken, and economists from the beginning copied natural sciences. Cultural thought, excluded from economic orthodoxy, interacted with economics mainly through the critiques discussed in Part II. Enclaves of cultural thought survived in heterodox economics and in non-economic social sciences but had little effect on orthodoxy, which formalised its anti-cultural bias when it went neoclassical. The reaction against positivism in the late twentieth century gave orthodoxy an excuse for a rethink and a move towards cultural methods; it moved the other way towards reinvigorated positivism. Heterodox economists are far more receptive to culture but have little clout in the economics profession, so the prospects for a culturally informed economics remain unrealised.

After two hundred years or more, it may seem too late for economics to be reconciled with culture. The choice of approach was made early in the history of economics and since then has become ingrained. Using positivistic techniques, an orthodox economist can have a successful career without worrying about culture, which is 'non-economic' and the remit of other disciplines. Because the economics/culture divide has been institutionalised, it will be hard to overcome – the economics profession defines itself around core principles that allow no room for culture. This state of affairs is itself a cultural construct. Orthodox economics is an anti-cultural culture founded on theories and methods that banish cultural thought. Whatever the academic arguments, institutions deter orthodox economists from taking up cultural methods. To part company with orthodoxy harms one's career and offers few benefits apart from being true to one's personal convictions. Under these circumstances the hopes for a culturally informed economics appear slim.

Would cultural research on the economy be best undertaken elsewhere? Should we accept current disciplinary boundaries and leave culture to be studied in sociology, anthropology, history, cultural studies and geography? Revived interest in culture has at least meant that significant cultural research has been done, albeit rarely by economists. Orthodox economics, notwithstanding its internal debates, seems pleased to carry on with reductionist, individualistic theories; cultural alternatives have to be published in separate literatures by heterodox economists and academics in other social sciences. Having parallel 'cultural' literatures outside the economic mainstream is better than having no research on cultural matters and keeps alive the cultural tradition. The problem is that culture can then be pigeon-holed as peripheral, specialised and heterodox, clearing the field for orthodoxy to dominate the teaching and professional institutions of economics. Orthodox economists can enjoy expert status at the discipline's nucleus, defined conveniently by orthodox methods, and sideline alternative views. For culture to have a precarious foothold on the fringes of economic thought does little to address the issues raised by cultural criticism.

What are the main barriers to cultural methods in economics? Three items spring to mind: neoclassical theory, disciplinary boundaries, and mathematical/quantitative techniques. Of these, the first is the most antipathetic to cultural thought. Neoclassical theory is ahistorical, claims universal relevance, plays down institutions, understates human creativity, has no sense of culture as a process, evades social evolution, and models economic development in terms of equilibrium or adjustment towards equilibrium. An economics built on these principles will never accommodate culture properly and epitomises the mechanistic thinking that cultural critics have abhorred. A cultural perspective does not forbid instrumental rationality but sees it as one particular, socially specific mode of behaviour among others. The self-interest of neoclassical theory has no universal relevance but may flourish within capitalist institutions; it mirrors its social and cultural setting, rather than being innate. As the theory is so culturally obtuse, economists seldom wake up to its cultural specificity and take it for granted without considering alternatives. Some mainstream researchers have made limited forays away from neoclassicism, but the basic model and quantitative techniques still permeate economics teaching. Unless orthodoxy drops its fascination with neoclassical theory and stops identifying neoclassicism with the economic way of thinking, the chances for a culturally informed economics are minimal.

A second, related barrier is the demarcation of academic disciplines and the corresponding professional structures. The economics discipline, as presently constituted, regards cultural methods as non-economic and irrelevant. In a climate of extreme specialisation, cultural arguments are beyond the purview of economics. This compartmentalising is out of step with cultural thought, which covers all human activities and pertains to all social-science disciplines. Writers in the cultural tradition have frowned upon academic specialisation, lest it loses the breadth needed for a critical relativism and humanism. Academic work has nonetheless become organised around disciplinary divisions that expel cultural methods from orthodox economics. For economics to shift towards culture it would have to accept methods linked with non-economic disciplines such as history, anthropology and sociology. This would not imply interdisciplinary research – economists would not be obliged to collaborate with other social scientists – but it would mean a widening of horizons within the economics discipline.

A third barrier to cultural thought in economics has been the mathematisation of the subject. Cultural thinkers criticised attempts to ram human behaviour into a mechanical frame, whether in theorising or in social and industrial organisation. These views bore fruit in the early nineteenth century, when Enlightenment schemes for mathematical social sciences were deemed a failure. New mathematical techniques were available in abundance, having been used extensively in natural sciences, but were not as a rule imported into social studies. Until well into the twentieth century, economists were discreet about using mathematics and did so apologetically. The restraints were finally lifted in the 1940s, and since then economics has seen an orgy of mathematical theorising and quantitative methods; instead of being obscure and suspect, they are now the proof of expert status and intellectual muscle. Earlier qualms have vanished, non-mathematical articles have become a rarity in 'core' journals, and the mathematical content of economics teaching has escalated at the expense of breadth and pluralism. Economists' post-war enthusiasm for mathematics and econometrics was somewhat anomalous, as it went against anti-positivist trends outside economics and rested upon old techniques – constrained optimisation could have been applied to economics a hundred years earlier, but the urge for mathematisation was weaker at that time. Unquestioning use of mathematics has now become institutionalised and cannot easily be reversed. Mainstream economists would probably be happier to relinquish neoclassical theory than mathematics or quantitative techniques. From a cultural perspective, mathematics may be appropriate when the social context has been constructed in quantitative terms, as with formal accounting systems. Cultural thought is not against mathematics per se but views it as culturally specific (like any other language) and limited; much economic behaviour lies beyond mathematical modelling, so that mathematical theories should not be treated as universal.

The barriers to cultural thought outlined above are sturdy enough to block any movement by economic orthodoxy towards cultural methods. After so many years of ignoring culture, it will not suddenly see the light and apologise for past errors. Nor will it be well disposed to heterodox critiques within the discipline – the orthodox/heterodox divisions are too deep. Reform of economic orthodoxy would have to be internal, gradual and oblique to the cultural tradition, rephrasing cultural topics in its own language and terminology. Of the three barriers, neoclassical theory is the most anti-cultural but the least robust. Many neoclassical economists admit the shortfalls of the perfectly competitive benchmark and wish to get away from it – they usually opt for imperfectionist variants of neoclassicism, but their embellishment of the basic model shows disquiet with neoclassical assumptions. Mainstream pluralism is a sign that orthodox economists are looking for alternatives and may end up moving nearer to cultural thought without endorsing it overtly. The other two barriers seem unassailable. Disciplinary divisions are as strong as ever, compelling academics to give themselves disciplinary tags, work within the institutions and career ladder of a single discipline, and eschew alien methods. The pressures to mathematise and quantify economics have been massive in recent years, fortified by computing and information technology. Raising doubts about this trend would sound perverse and regressive to mainstream economists. Future orthodox developments that go in a cultural direction will have to be voiced in mathematical or quantitative language if they are to acquire legitimacy within the current institutional context. This is sad, for cultural ideas cannot be mathematised, but it still permits some progress away from the cultural desert of the pure neoclassical model.

Explicit arguments for a culturally informed economics will continue to come from heterodoxy. Culture is alive and well in heterodox economics, honoured as a core concept. If economics were to be reformed along the lines proposed by heterodox economists, then it would at last begin to take culture seriously. A recent example of such reform proposals is the Post-Autistic Economics Movement (PAEM) initiated by French economics students in protest against syllabus changes towards neoclassicism. The PAEM platform tallies with cultural critiques and reiterates points made repeatedly over the years by cultural commentators and heterodox economists (Fullbrook, 2003, 2007). These sentiments are, alas, concentrated in heterodox circles and destined to be shrugged off by the orthodox establishment. Reform would be facilitated if movements such as the PAEM could win the support of younger economists, but this is far from straightforward in the face of orthodox hegemony over teaching. Collectively, all the heterodox schools of thought put together are only a small minority of the economics profession, often located outside economics departments, so they have a daunting task in transforming the discipline.

While institutionally weak, economic heterodoxy is intellectually strong and should have confidence in its demands for a cultural approach. After the revival of cultural thought in the late twentieth century, heterodoxy is now allied with academic trends that question the positivism and absolutism of orthodox economics. Within the broader intellectual scene, it is the economic mainstream that has cut itself off from extraneous ideas and rushed headlong down a theoretical and methodological tunnel. Contrary to the image of being mainstream and middle-of-the-road, economic orthodoxy is peddling an immoderate strain of monism and universality, whereas heterodoxy has been pluralistic and outward looking. Even if the heterodox schools seem small and beleaguered within the economics discipline, they belong to the bigger cultural and critical tradition in a way that would never be possible for economic orthodoxy. The orthodox majority in the economics profession, so dominant within its own realm, becomes a minority within academic work as a whole. For heterodox economists a sensible strategy would be to tighten their bonds with cultural thought and demonstrate how neoclassicism is an extreme doctrine, isolated from opinion elsewhere and ill suited for social studies. A conscious appeal to cultural thought within economic heterodoxy would clarify its differences from orthodoxy and provide coherent alternatives. Mainstream economists frustrated with neoclassicism might be more willing to change track if they were reminded about its singularity and remoteness from wider intellectual currents.

Cultural critiques of economics have frequently been ignored, but the questions they pose are crucial and will endure. While orthodox economists persist in overlooking culture, cultural criticisms will keep reappearing and making the same arguments. Heterodox economics can only gain by joining in with the cultural tradition, helping it to prosper, and reiterating the need for cultural methods as lucidly as possible. Cultural thought has never been nihilistic, as it may seem in some postmodern versions, and does not preclude social sciences – it proposes reformed social sciences that accept their intrinsic complexities and refuse to ape natural science. Reforming economics would call for maturity and resolve in not being dazzled or intimidated by displays of technical skill, readiness to select and adopt methods appropriate to the subject at hand, and denial of reductionist theorising. The outcome would be a more modest, reflective, critical, interpretative and literary economics, unadorned with mathematical gimmickry and free to contemplate culture.

# Bibliography

Ackerman, F. (1997), 'Consumed in theory: alternative perspectives on the economics of consumption', *Journal of Economic Issues*, **31**(3), 651–64.

Ackoff, R.L. and F.E. Emery (1972), *On Purposeful Systems*, London: Tavistock.

Albury, R.. G. Payne and W. Suchting (1981), 'Naturalism and the human sciences', *Economy and Society*, **10**(3), 367–79.

Alexander, J.C. (ed.) (1985), *Neo-Functionalism*, London: Sage.

Althusser, L. (1969), *For Marx*, translated by B.R. Brewster, Harmondsworth: Allen Lane.

Althusser, L. (1984), *Essays on Ideology*, London: Verso.

Althusser, L. and E. Balibar (1970), *Reading Capital*, translated by B.R. Brewster, London: New Left Books.

Alvesson, M. (2002), *Understanding Organizational Culture*, London: Sage.

Alvesson, M. and P.O. Berg (1992), *Corporate Culture and Organizational Symbolism: An Overview*, New York: De Gruyter.

Amariglio, J.L. and D.F. Ruccio (1994), 'Postmodernism, Marxism, and the critique of modern economic thought', *Rethinking Marxism*, **7**(3), 7–35.

Amariglio, J.L. and D.F. Ruccio (1995), 'Keynes, postmodernism, uncertainty', in S.C. Dow and J. Hillard (eds), *Keynes, Knowledge and Uncertainty*, Aldershot, UK and Brookfield, USA: Edward Elgar, pp. 334–56.

Amin, A. (ed.) (1994), *Post-Fordism: A Reader*, Oxford: Blackwell.

Amin, A. and N.J. Thrift (eds) (2003), *The Blackwell Cultural Economy Reader*, Oxford: Blackwell.

Ancori, B., A. Bureth and P. Cohendet (2000), 'The economics of knowledge: the debate about codification and tacit knowledge', *Industrial and Corporate Change*, **9**(2), 255–87.

Andersen, E.S. (1994), *Evolutionary Economics: Post-Schumpeterian Contributions*, London: Pinter.

Anjos, M. (1999), 'Money, trust, and culture: elements for an institutional approach to money', *Journal of Economic Issues*, **33**(3), 677–88.

Aoki, M. (2001), *Toward a Comparative Institutional Analysis*, Cambridge, MA: MIT Press.

Archer, M.S. (1990), 'Human agency and social structure: a critique of Giddens', in J. Clark, C. Modgil and S. Modgil (eds), *Anthony Giddens: Consensus and Controversy*, London: Falmer Press, pp. 73–84.

Archer, M.S. (1995), *Realist Social Theory: The Morphogenetic Approach*, Cambridge: Cambridge University Press.

Archer, M.S. (1996), *Culture and Agency: The Place of Culture in Social Theory*, revised edn, Cambridge: Cambridge University Press.

Arnold, M. (1869), *Culture and Anarchy*, reprinted 1932, Cambridge: Cambridge University Press.

Arnold, M. (1878), 'Equality', in M. Allott and R.H. Super (eds) (1986), *Matthew Arnold: A Critical Edition of the Major Works*, Oxford: Oxford University Press, pp. 432–55.

Arnould, E.J. and C.J. Thompson (2005), 'Consumer culture theory (CCT): twenty years of research', *Journal of Consumer Research*, **31**(4), 868–82.

Aspromourgos, T. (1986), 'On the origins of the term "neoclassical"', *Cambridge Journal of Economics*, **10**(3), 265–270.

Atkinson, A. (1991), *Principles of Political Ecology*, London: Belhaven Press.

Austen, S. (2000), 'Culture and the labour market', *Review of Social Economy*, **58**(4), 505–21.

Avery, J. (1997), *Progress, Poverty and Population: Re-reading Condorcet, Godwin and Malthus*, London: Cass.

Axelrod, R.M. (1984), *The Evolution of Cooperation*, New York: Basic Books.

Axelrod, R.M. and M.D. Cohen (1999), *Harnessing Complexity: Organizational Implications of a Scientific Frontier*, New York: Free Press.

Ayer, A.J. (ed.) (1959), *Logical Positivism*, New York: Free Press.

Backhaus, J.G. (ed.) (2003), *Evolutionary Economic Thought: European Contributions and Concepts*, Cheltenham, UK and Northampton, MA, USA: Edward Elgar.

Baert, P. (1996), 'Realist philosophy of the social sciences and economics: a critique', *Cambridge Journal of Economics*, **20**(5), 513–22.

Baert, P. (2003), 'Pragmatism, realism and hermeneutics', *Foundations of Science*, **8**(1), 89–106.

Baghramian, M. (2004), *Relativism*, London: Routledge.

Bakker, I. (2007), 'Social reproduction and the constitution of a gendered political economy', *New Political Economy*, **12**(4), 541–56.

Bannister, R.C. (1979), *Social Darwinism: Science and Myth in Anglo-American Social Thought*, Philadelphia, PA: Temple University Press.

Barbalet, J.M. (2008), 'Pragmatism and economics: William James' contribution', *Cambridge Journal of Economics*, **32**(5), 797–810.

Barker, C. (2007), *Cultural Studies: Theory and Practice*, 3rd edn, London: Sage.

Barnard, F.M. (1965), *Herder's Social and Political Thought*, Oxford: Clarendon Press.

Barthes, R. (1985), *The Fashion System*, translated by M. Ward and R. Howard, London: Jonathan Cape.

Basu, K., E.L. Jones and E. Schlicht (1987), 'The growth and decay of custom: the role of the new institutional economics in economic history', *Explorations in Economic History*, **24**(1), 1–21.

Batchelor, J. (2000), *John Ruskin: No Wealth but Life*, London: Chatto and Windus.

Baudrillard, J. (1975), *The Mirror of Production*, translated by M. Poster, St Louis, MO: Telos Press.

Baudrillard, J. (1988), 'For a critique of the political economy of the sign', in M. Poster (ed.), *Jean Baudrillard: Selected Writings*, Cambridge: Polity Press, pp. 57–97.

Baudrillard, J. (1993), *Symbolic Exchange and Death*, translated by I.H. Grant, London: Sage.

Bauman, Z. (2000), *Liquid Modernity*, Cambridge: Polity Press.

Bauman, Z. (2001), 'Consuming life', *Journal of Consumer Culture*, **1**(1), 9–29.

Bazzoli, L. (2000), 'Institutional economics and the specificity of social evolution: about the contribution of J.R. Commons', in F. Louçã and M. Perlman (eds), *Is Economics an Evolutionary Science?*, Cheltenham, UK and Northampton, MA, USA: Edward Elgar, pp. 64–82.

Beasley, R. and M. Danesi (2002), *Persuasive Signs: The Semiotics of Advertising*, New York: De Gruyter.

Becker, G.S. (1976), *The Economic Approach to Human Behavior*, Chicago, IL: University of Chicago Press.

Beckert, J. (2003), 'Economic sociology and embeddedness: how shall we conceptualize economic action?', *Journal of Economic Issues*, **37**(3), 769–87.

Beckert, J. and M. Zafirovski (eds) (2005), *Encyclopedia of Economic Sociology*, London: Routledge.

Beed, C. (1991), 'Philosophy of science and contemporary economics: an overview', *Journal of Post Keynesian Economics*, **13**(4), 459–94.

Beed, C. and C. Beed (2000), 'The status of economics as a naturalistic social science', *Cambridge Journal of Economics*, **24**(4), 417–35.

Beed, C. and O. Kane (1991), 'What is the critique of the mathematization of economics?', *Kyklos*, **44**(4), 581–612.

Beinhocker, E.D. (2006), *The Origin of Wealth: Evolution, Complexity, and the Radical Remaking of Economics,* Cambridge, MA: Harvard Business School Press.

Beiser, F.C. (2000), 'The Enlightenment and idealism', in K. Ameriks (ed.), *The Cambridge Companion to German Idealism*, Cambridge: Cambridge University Press, pp. 18–36.

Belk, R.W. (1988), 'Possessions and the extended self', *Journal of Consumer Research*, **15**(2), 139–68.

Bellomy, D.C. (1984), 'Social Darwinism revisited', *Perspectives in American History*, new series, **1**, 1–129.

Bennett, O. (2005), 'Beyond machinery: the cultural policies of Matthew Arnold', *History of Political Economy*, **37**(3), 455–82.

Benton, T. (1981), 'Realism and social science', *Radical Philosophy*, **27**, 13–21.

Berger, L.A. (1989), 'Economics and hermeneutics', *Economics and Philosophy*, **5**(2), 209–33.

Berger, P.L. and T. Luckmann (1967), *The Social Construction of Reality: A Treatise in the Sociology of Knowledge*, London: Allen Lane.

Berlin, I. (1976a), 'Herder and the Enlightenment', in I. Berlin, *Vico and Herder: Two Studies in the History of Ideas*, London: Hogarth Press, pp. 143–216.

Berlin, I. (1976b), 'The philosophical ideas of Giambattista Vico', in I. Berlin, *Vico and Herder: Two Studies in the History of Ideas*, London: Hogarth Press, pp. 1–142.

Berlin, I. (1979), 'The Counter-Enlightenment', in I. Berlin, *Against the Current: Essays in the History of Ideas*, London: Hogarth Press, pp. 1–24.

Berlin, I. (1991a), 'Alleged relativism in eighteenth-century European thought', in I. Berlin, *The Crooked Timber of Humanity*, London: Fontana Press, pp. 70–90.

Berlin, I. (1991b), 'The apotheosis of the Romantic will: the revolt against the myth of an ideal world', in I. Berlin, *The Crooked Timber of Humanity*, London: Fontana Press, pp. 207–37.

Berlin, I. (1999), *The Roots of Romanticism*, London: Chatto and Windus.

Berman, M. (1983), *All That is Solid Melts into Air: The Experience of Modernity*, London: Verso.

Bhaskar, R. (1975), *A Realist Theory of Science*, Leeds: Leeds Books.

Bhaskar, R. (1978), 'On the possibility of social scientific knowledge and the limits of naturalism', *Journal for the Theory of Social Behaviour*, **8**(1), 1–28.

Bhaskar, R. (1979), *The Possibility of Naturalism: A Philosophic Critique of the Contemporary Human Sciences*, Brighton: Harvester Press.

Bhaskar, R. (1983), 'Beef, structure and place: notes from a critical naturalist perspective', *Journal for tbe Theory of Social Behaviour*, **13**(1), 81–96.

Bhaskar, R. (1986), *Scientific Realism and Human Emancipation*, London: Verso.

Bhaskar, R. (1989), *Reclaiming Reality: A Critical Introduction to Contemporary Philosophy*, London: Verso.

Bhaskar, R. (1993), *Dialectic: The Pulse of Freedom*, London: Verso.

Biddle, J.E. (1990), 'Purpose and evolution in Commons's institutionalism', *History of Political Economy*, **22**(1), 19–47.

Billig, M.S. (2000), 'Institutions and culture: neo-Weberian economic anthropology', *Journal of Economic Issues*, **34**(4), 771–88.

Blaug, M. (1992), *The Methodology of Economics, or How Economists Explain*, 2nd edn, Cambridge: Cambridge University Press.

Blaug, M. (1999), 'The formalist revolution or what happened to orthodox economics after World War II?', in R.E. Backhouse and J. Creedy (eds), *From Classical Economics to the Theory of the Firm*, Cheltenham, UK and Northampton, MA, USA: Edward Elgar, pp. 257–80.

Blaug, M. (2001), 'Where are we now on cultural economics?', *Journal of Economic Surveys*, **15**(2), 123–43.

Bleicher, J. (1980), *Contemporary Hermeneutics: Hermeneutics as Method, Philosophy and Critique*, London: Routledge and Kegan Paul.

Bloch, M. (1983), *Marxism and Anthropology: The History of a Relationship*, Oxford: Clarendon Press.

Block, F. (2003), 'Karl Polanyi and the writing of *The Great Transformation*', *Theory and Society*, **32**(3), 275–306.

Block, F. and M. Somers (1984), 'Beyond the economistic fallacy: the holistic social science of Karl Polanyi', in T. Skocpol (ed.), *Vision and Method in Historical Sociology*, Cambridge: Cambridge University Press, pp. 47–84.

Boas, F. (1904), 'The history of anthropology', in G.W. Stocking (ed.) (1982), *A Franz Boas Reader*, Chicago, IL: University of Chicago Press, pp. 23–36.

Boas, F. (1940), *Race, Language and Culture*, New York: Macmillan.

Boettke, P.J. and C.J. Coyne (2003), 'Entrepreneurship and development: cause or consequence?', *Advances in Austrian Economics*, **6**, 67–87.

Bortis, H. (1997), *Institutions, Behaviour and Economic Theory: A Contribution to Classical-Keynesian Political Economy*, Cambridge: Cambridge University Press.

Bottomore, T.B. (1984), 'Marxism and sociology', in T.B. Bottomore, *Sociology and Socialism*, Brighton: Wheatsheaf, pp. 31–73.

Boulding, K.E. (1956), *The Image: Knowledge in Life and Society*, Ann Arbor, MI: University of Michigan Press.

Boulding, K.E. (1981), *Evolutionary Economics*, London: Sage.

Bourdieu, P. (1977), *Outline of a Theory of Action*, Cambridge: Cambridge University Press.

Bowler, P.J. (1975), 'The changing meaning of "evolution"', *Journal of the History of Ideas*, **36**(1), 95–114.

Bowler, P.J. (1988), *The Non-Darwinian Revolution: Reinterpreting a Historical Myth*, Baltimore, MD: Johns Hopkins University Press.

Bowler, P.J. (2003), *Evolution: The History of an Idea*, 3rd edn, Berkeley, CA: University of California Press.

Boyd, R. and P.J. Richerson (1985), *Culture and the Evolutionary Process*, Chicago, IL: University of Chicago Press.

Boyer, R. and Y. Saillard (eds) (2002), *Régulation Theory: The State of the Art*, translated by C. Shread, London: Routledge.

Boylan, T.A. and P.F. O'Gorman (1995), *Beyond Rhetoric and Realism in Economics: Towards a Reformulation of Economic Methodology*, London: Routledge.

Bratman, M. (1999), *Faces of Intention*, Cambridge: Cambridge University Press.

Braverman, H. (1974), *Labor and Monopoly Capital: The Degradation of Work in the Twentieth Century*, New York: Monthly Review Press.

Brinkman, R.L. (1992), 'Culture evolution and the process of economic evolution', *International Journal of Social Economics*, **19**(10–12), 248–67.

Brinkman, R.L. and J.E. Brinkman (1997), 'Cultural lag: conception and theory', *International Journal of Social Economics*, **24**(6), 609–27.

Bronk, R. (2009), *The Romantic Economist: Imagination in Economics*, Cambridge: Cambridge University Press.

Brousseau, E. and J.-M. Glachant (eds) (2008), *New Institutional Economics: A Guidebook*, Cambridge: Cambridge University Press.

Brown, D.B. (2001), *Romanticism*, London: Phaidon.

Brown, V. (1994a), *Adam Smith's Discourse: Canonicity, Commerce and Conscience*, London: Routledge.

Brown, V. (1994b), 'The economy as text', in R.E. Backhouse (ed.), *New Directions in Economic Methodology*, London: Routledge, pp. 368–82.

Brown, V. (1997), '"Mere inventions of the imagination": a survey of recent literature on Adam Smith', *Economics and Philosophy*, **13**(2), 281–312.

Buenstorf, G. (2006), 'How useful is generalized Darwinism as a framework to study competition and industrial evolution?', *Journal of Evolutionary Economics*, **16**(5), 511–27.

Burke, P. (1985), *Vico*, Oxford: Oxford University Press.

Burke, P. (2005), *History and Social Theory*, 2nd edn, Cambridge: Polity Press.

Burkett, P. (1999), *Marx and Nature: A Red and Green Perspective*, London: Macmillan.

Burkitt, B. (1984), *Radical Political Economy: An Introduction to the Alternative Economics*, Brighton: Wheatsheaf.

Burkitt, B. and M. Spiers (1983), 'The economic theory of politics: a reappraisal', *International Journal of Social Economics*, **10**(2), 12–21.

Bush, P.D. (1987), 'The theory of institutional change', *Journal of Economic Issues*, **21**(3), 1075–116.

Calabrese, A. and C. Sparks (eds) (2003), *Toward a Political Economy of Culture: Capitalism and Communication in the Twenty-First Century*, Lanham, MD: Rowman and Littlefield.

Caldwell, B.J. (1982), *Beyond Positivism: Economic Methodology in the Twentieth Century*, London: Unwin Hyman.

Caldwell, B.J. (2000), 'The emergence of Hayek's ideas on cultural evolution', *Review of Austrian Economics*, **13**(1), 5–22.

Caldwell, B.J. (2002), 'Hayek and cultural evolution', in U. Mäki (ed.), *Fact and Fiction in Economics: Models, Realism and Social Construction*, Cambridge: Cambridge University Press, pp. 285–303.

Callinicos, A.T. (1985), 'Anthony Giddens: a contemporary critique', *Theory and Society*, **14**(2), 133–66.

Callinicos, A.T. (1987), *Making History: Agency, Structure and Change in Social Theory*, Cambridge: Polity Press.

Callinicos, A.T. (1989), *Against Postmodernism: A Marxist Critique*, Cambridge: Polity Press.

Campbell, C. (1987), *The Romantic Ethic and the Spirit of Modern Consumerism*, Oxford: Basil Blackwell.

Campbell, R.H. and A.S. Skinner (1982), *Adam Smith*, London: Croom Helm.

Capaldi, N. (2004), *John Stuart Mill: A Biography*, Cambridge: Cambridge University Press.

Carabelli, A.M. (1988), *On Keynes's Method*, London: Macmillan.

Carlyle, T. (1829), 'Signs of the times', in A. Shelston (ed.) (1971), *Thomas Carlyle: Selected Writings*, Harmondsworth: Penguin, pp. 59–85.

Carlyle, T. (1843), *Past and Present*, reprinted 1918, Oxford: Oxford University Press.

Castells, M. (2000), *The Rise of the Network Society*, 2nd edn, Oxford: Blackwell.

Catephores, G. (1994), 'The imperious Austrian: Schumpeter as bourgeois Marxist', *New Left Review*, **205**, 3–30.

Cavalli-Sforza, L.L. and M.W. Feldman (1981), *Cultural Transmission and Evolution: A Quantitative Approach*, Princeton, NJ: Princeton University Press.

Chalmers, A.F. (1988), 'Is Bhaskar's realism realistic?', *Radical Philosophy*, **49**, 18–23.

Chase, P.G. (2006), *The Emergence of Culture: The Evolution of a Uniquely Human Way of Life*, New York: Springer.

Cirillo, R. (1984), 'Léon Walras and social justice', *American Journal of Economics and Sociology*, **43**(1), 53–60.

Coase, R.H. (1937), 'The nature of the firm', *Economica*, **4**(16), 386–405.

Coates, J. (1996), *The Claims of Common Sense: Moore, Wittgenstein, Keynes and the Social Sciences*, Cambridge: Cambridge University Press.

Coddington, A. (1983), *Keynesian Economics: The Search for First Principles*, London: George Allen and Unwin.

Cohen, G. A. (1978), *Karl Marx's Theory of History: A Defence*, Oxford: Oxford University Press.

Colander, D.C. (ed.) (2000a), *The Complexity Vision and the Teaching of Economics*, Cheltenham, UK and Northampton, MA, USA: Edward Elgar.

Colander, D.C. (2000b), 'The death of neoclassical economics', *Journal of the History of Economic Thought*, **22**(2), 127–44.

Colander, D.C. (2005), 'The future of economics: the appropriately educated in pursuit of the knowable', *Cambridge Journal of Economics*, **29**(6), 927–41.

Colander, D.C., R.P.F. Holt and J.B. Rosser (2004), 'The changing face of mainstream economics', *Review of Political Economy*, **16**(4), 485–99.

Coleridge, S.T. (1830), *On the Constitution of the Church and State*, reprinted 1972, London: Dent.

Collingwood, R.G. (1946), *The Idea of History*, Oxford: Clarendon Press.

Collini, S. (1994), *Matthew Arnold: A Critical Portrait*, Oxford: Oxford University Press.

Connell, P. (2001), *Romanticism, Economics, and the Question of 'Culture'*, Oxford: Oxford University Press.

Convert, B. and J. Heilbron (2007), 'Where did the new economic sociology come from?', *Theory and Society*, **36**(1), 31–54.

Cordes, C. (2006), 'Darwinism in economics: from analogy to continuity', *Journal of Evolutionary Economics*, **16**(5), 529–41.

Coşgel, M.M. (1997), 'Consumption institutions', *Review of Social Economy*, **55**(2), 153–71.

Coşgel, M.M. (2008), 'The socio-economics of consumption: solutions to the problems of interest, knowledge and identity', in J.B. Davis and W. Dolfsma (eds), *The Elgar Companion to Social Economics*, Cheltenham, UK and Northampton, MA, USA: Edward Elgar, pp. 121–36.

Cosmides, L. and J. Tooby (1987), 'From evolution to behavior: evolutionary psychology as the missing link', in J.A. Dupré (ed.), *The Latest on the Best: Essays on Evolution and Optimality*, Cambridge, MA: MIT Press, pp. 277–306.

Crabtree, D. and A.P. Thirlwall (eds) (1980), *Keynes and the Bloomsbury Group*, London: Macmillan.

Craib, I. (1992), *Modern Social Theory: From Parsons to Habermas*, 2nd edn, Hemel Hempstead: Harvester Wheatsheaf.

Cronin, H. (1991), *The Ant and the Peacock*, Cambridge: Cambridge University Press.

Cruickshank, J. (2004), 'A tale of two ontologies: an immanent critique of critical realism', *Sociological Review*, **52**(4), 567–85.

Cullenberg, S. (1999), 'Overdetermination, totality, and institutions: a genealogy of a Marxist institutionalist economics', *Journal of Economic Issues*, **33**(4), 801–15.

Cullenberg, S. (2000), 'New Marxism, old institutionalism', in R. Pollin (ed.), *Capitalism, Socialism, and Radical Political Economy*, Cheltenham, UK and Northampton, MA, USA: Edward Elgar, pp. 81–102.

Dalton, G. (1961), 'Economic theory and primitive society', *American Anthropologist*, **63**(1), 1–25.

Davidson, P. (1982), 'Rational expectations: a fallacious foundation for studying crucial decision-making processes', *Journal of Post Keynesian Economics*, **5**(2), 182–97.

Davidson, P. (1994), *Post Keynesian Macroeconomic Theory*, Aldershot, UK and Brookfield, USA: Edward Elgar.

Davis, J.B. (1991), 'Keynes's view of economics as a moral science', in B.W. Bateman and J.B. Davis (eds), *Keynes and Philosophy: Essays on the Origin of Keynes's Thought*, Aldershot, UK and Brookfield, USA: Edward Elgar, pp. 89–103.

Davis, J.B. (2002), 'Collective intentionality and individual behaviour', in E. Fullbrook (ed.), *Intersubjectivity in Economics: Agents and Structures*, London: Routledge, pp. 11–27.

Davis, J.B. (2003), *The Theory of the Individual in Economics: Identity and Value*, London: Routledge.

Davis, J.B. (2004), 'The agency–structure model and the embedded individual in heterodox economics', in P. Lewis (ed.) *Transforming Economics: Perspectives on the Critical Realist Project*, London: Routledge, pp. 132–51.

Davis, J.B. (2006), 'The turn in economics: neoclassical dominance to mainstream pluralism?', *Journal of Institutional Economics*, **2**(1), 1–20.

Davis, J.B. (2007), 'The turn in economics and the turn in economic methodology', *Journal of Economic Methodology*, **14**(3), 275–90.

Davis, J.B. (2008), 'The turn in recent economics and return of orthodoxy', *Cambridge Journal of Economics*, **32**(3), 349–66.

Dawkins, R. (1983), 'Universal Darwinism', in D.S. Bendall (ed.), *Evolution from Molecules to Man*, Cambridge: Cambridge University Press, pp. 403–25.

Dawkins, R. (1989), *The Selfish Gene*, 2nd edn, Oxford: Oxford University Press.

De Uriarte, B. (1990), 'On the free will of rational agents in neoclassical economics', *Journal of Post Keynesian Economics*, **12**(4), 605–17.

Deal, T.E. and A.A. Kennedy (1982), *Corporate Cultures: The Rites and Rituals of Corporate Life*, Reading, MA: Addison-Wesley.

Debreu, G. (1984), 'Economic theory in the mathematical mode', *American Economic Review*, **74**(3), 267–78.

Debreu, G. (1991), 'The mathematization of economic theory', *American Economic Review*, **81**(1), 1–7.

Decker, J.M. (2004), *Ideology*, London: Palgrave Macmillan.

Dennett, D. (1995), *Darwin's Dangerous Idea: Evolution and the Meaning of Life*, London: Allen Lane.

Dequech, D. (1999), 'Expectations and confidence under uncertainty', *Journal of Post Keynesian Economics*, **21**(3), 415–30.

Dequech, D. (2002), 'The demarcation between the "old" and the "new" institutional economics: recent complications', *Journal of Economic Issues*, **36**(2), 565–72.

Dequech, D. (2003), 'Cognitive and cultural embeddedness: combining institutional economics and economic sociology', *Journal of Economic Issues*, **37**(2), 461–70.

Dequech, D. (2008), 'Neoclassical, mainstream, orthodox, and heterodox economics', *Journal of Post Keynesian Economics*, **30**(2), 279–302.

Devitt, M. (2005), 'Scientific realism', in F. Jackson and M. Smith (eds), *The Oxford Handbook of Contemporary Philosophy*, Oxford: Oxford University Press, pp. 767–91.

Dietrich, M. (1994), *Transaction Cost Economics and Beyond: Towards a New Economics of the Firm*, London: Routledge.

Dilthey, W. (1910), 'The construction of the historical world in the human studies', in H.P. Rickman (ed.) (1976), *W. Dilthey: Selected Writings*, Cambridge: Cambridge University Press, pp. 170–245.

DiMaggio, P.J. (1994), 'Culture and economy', in N. Smelser and R. Swedberg (eds), *The Handbook of Economic Sociology*, Princeton, NJ: Princeton University Press, pp. 27–57.

DiMaggio, P.J. (1998), 'The new institutionalisms: avenues of collaboration', *Journal of Institutional and Theoretical Economics*, **154**(4), 696–705.

Dobb, M. (1973), *Theories of Value and Distribution since Adam Smith: Ideology and Economic Theory*, Cambridge: Cambridge University Press.

Dolfsma, W. (2001), 'Metaphors of knowledge in economics', *Review of Social Economy*, **59**(1), 71–91.

Dolfsma, W. (2002), 'Mediated preferences – how institutions affect consumption', *Journal of Economic Issues*, **36**(2), 449–57.

Dolfsma, W. (2004), *Institutional Economics and the Formation of Preferences: The Advent of Pop Music*, Cheltenham, UK and Northampton, MA, USA: Edward Elgar.

Dolfsma, W. and R. Verburg (2008), 'Structure, agency and the role of values in processes of institutional change', *Journal of Economic Issues*, **42**(4), 1031–54.

Donham, D.L. (1999), *History, Power, Ideology: Central Issues in Marxism and Anthropology*, Berkeley, CA: University of California Press.

Dopfer, K. (2005), 'Evolutionary economics: a theoretical framework', in K. Dopfer (ed.), *The Evolutionary Foundations of Economics*, Cambridge: Cambridge University Press, pp. 3–55.

Douglas, M. (1987), *How Institutions Think*, London: Routledge and Kegan Paul.

Douglas, M. and B. Isherwood (1980), *The World of Goods: Towards an Anthropology of Consumption*, Harmondsworth: Penguin.

Dow, S.C. (1990), 'Beyond dualism', *Cambridge Journal of Economics*, **14**(2), 143–57.

Dow, S.C. (1997), 'Mainstream economic methodology', *Cambridge Journal of Economics*, **21**(1), 73–93.

Dow, S.C. (2002), *Economic Methodology: An Inquiry*, Oxford: Oxford University Press.

Dow, S.C. (2004), 'Structured pluralism', *Journal of Economic Methodology*, **11**(3), 275–90.

Dow, S.C. (2007), 'Variety of methodological approach in economics', *Journal of Economic Surveys*, **21**(3), 447–65.

Drechsler, W. (2000), 'On the possibility of quantitative-mathematical social science, chiefly economics: some preliminary considerations', *Journal of Economic Studies*, **27**(4), 246–59.

Drechsler, W. (2004), 'Natural versus social sciences: on understanding in economics', in E.S. Reinert (ed.), *Globalization, Economic Development and Inequality: An Alternative Perspective*, Cheltenham, UK and Northampton, MA, USA: Edward Elgar, pp. 71–87.

Du Gay, P. and M. Pryke (eds) (2002), *Cultural Economy: Cultural Analysis and Commercial Life*, London: Sage.

Duesenberry, J.S. (1949), *Income, Saving and the Theory of Consumer Behavior*, Cambridge, MA: Harvard University Press.

Dugger, W.M. (1988), 'Radical institutionalism: basic concepts', *Review of Radical Political Economics*, **20**(1), 1–20.

Dugger, W.M. (1989), *Radical Institutionalism: Contemporary Voices*, Westport, CT: Greenwood Press.

Dugger, W.M. (1990), 'The new institutionalism: new but not institution-alist', *Journal of Economic Issues*, **24**(2), 423–31.

Dugger, W.M. (ed.) (1996), *Inequality: Radical Institutionalist Views on Race, Gender, Class, and Nation*, Westport, CT: Greenwood Press.

Dugger, W.M. (2000), 'Deception and inequality: the enabling myth concept', in R. Pollin (ed.), *Capitalism, Socialism, and Radical Political Economy*, Cheltenham, UK and Northampton, MA, USA: Edward Elgar, pp. 66–80.

Dugger, W.M. and H.J. Sherman (1994), 'Comparison of Marxism and institutionalism', *Journal of Economic Issues*, **28**(1), 101–27.

Dugger, W.M. and H.J. Sherman (1997), 'Institutionalist and Marxist theories of evolution', *Journal of Economic Issues*, **31**(4), 991–1009.

Dugger, W.M. and H.J. Sherman (2000), *Reclaiming Evolution: A Dialogue between Marxism and Institutionalism on Social Change*, London: Routledge.

Dugger, W.M. and W.J. Waller (1996), 'Radical institutionalism: from technological to democratic instrumentalism', *Review of Social Economy*, **54**(2), 169–89.

Dummett, M.A.E. (1978), *Truth and Other Enigmas*, London: Duckworth.

Dupuy, J.-P. (2002), 'Market, imitation and tradition: Hayek vs Keynes', in E. Fullbrook (ed.), *Intersubjectivity in Economics: Agents and Structures*, London: Routledge, pp. 139–58.

Durham, W.H. (1991), *Coevolution: Genes, Culture, and Human Diversity*, Stanford, CA: Stanford University Press.

Durkheim, É. (1895), *The Rules of Sociological Method*, translated by W.D. Halls (1982), London: Macmillan.

Dyer, A.W. (1989), 'Making semiotic sense of money as a medium of exchange', *Journal of Economic Issues*, **23**(2), 503–10.

Dyer, A.W. (2000), 'Thorstein Veblen and the political economy of the ordinary: hope and despair', in F. Louçã and M. Perlman (eds), *Is Economics an Evolutionary Science?*, Cheltenham, UK and Northampton, MA, USA: Edward Elgar, pp. 41–53.

Eagleton, T. (1989), 'Base and superstructure in Raymond Williams', in T. Eagleton (ed.), *Raymond Williams: Critical Perspectives*, Cambridge: Polity Press, pp. 165–75.

Eagleton, T. (1991), *Ideology: An Introduction*, London: Verso.

Eagleton, T. (1996), *The Illusions of Postmodernism*, Oxford: Blackwell.

Eagleton, T. (2000), *The Idea of Culture*, Oxford: Blackwell.

Eagleton, T. (2003), *After Theory*, London: Allen Lane.

Earl, P.E. (2005), 'Economics and psychology in the twenty-first century', *Cambridge Journal of Economics*, **29**(6), 909–26.

Earl, P.E. and S. Kemp (eds) (1999), *The Elgar Companion to Consumer Research and Economic Psychology*, Cheltenham, UK and Northampton, MA, USA: Edward Elgar.

Eatwell, J. (1983), 'Theories of value, output and employment', in J. Eatwell and M. Milgate (eds), *Keynes's Economics and the Theory of Value and Distribution*, London: Duckworth, pp. 93–128.

Ebeling, R.M. (1986), 'Toward a hermeneutical economics: expectations, prices and the role of interpretation in a theory of the market process', in I.M. Kirzner (ed.), *Subjectivism, Intelligibility and Economic Understanding*, London: Macmillan, pp. 39–55.

Eichner, A.S. (1983), 'Why economics is not yet a science', *Journal of Economic Issues*, **17**(2), 507–20.

Elardo, J.A. (2007), 'Marx, Marxists, and economic anthropology', *Review of Radical Political Economics*, **39**(3), 416–22.

Elias, N. (1978), *What is Sociology?*, London: Hutchinson.

Elias, N. (1991), *The Society of Individuals*, Oxford: Blackwell.

Elliot, J.E. (1980), 'Marx and Schumpeter on capitalism's creative destruction: a comparative restatement', *Quarterly Journal of Economics*, **95**(1), 45–68.

Elson, D. (1998), 'The economic, the political and the domestic: businesses, states and households in the organisation of production', *New Political Economy*, **3**(2), 189–208.

Emirbayer, M. and J. Goodwin (1994), 'Network analysis, culture, and the problem of agency', *American Journal of Sociology*, **99**(6), 1411–54.

Engels, F. (1845), *The Condition of the Working Class in England*, reprinted 1973, London: Lawrence and Wishart.

Epstein, R.J. (1987), *A History of Econometrics*, Amsterdam: North-Holland.

Eriksen, T.H. and F.S. Nielsen (2001), *A History of Anthropology*, London: Pluto Press.

Estes, C.L. (2001), *Social Policy and Aging: A Critical Perspective*, London: Sage.

Fagerberg, J. (2003), 'Schumpeter and the revival of evolutionary economics: an appraisal of the literature', *Journal of Evolutionary Economics*, **13**(2), 125–59.

Fairclough, N., B. Jessop and A. Sayer (2004), 'Critical realism and semiosis', in J. Joseph and J.M. Roberts (eds), *Realism, Discourse and Deconstruction*, London: Routledge, pp. 23–42.

Ferber, M.A. and J.A. Nelson (eds) (1993), *Beyond Economic Man: Feminist Theory and Economics*, Chicago, IL: University of Chicago Press.

Feyerabend, P.K. (1975), *Against Method: Outline of an Anarchistic Theory of Knowledge*, London: New Left Books.

Feyerabend, P.K. (1987), *Farewell to Reason*, London: Verso.

Field, A.J. (1979), 'On the explanation of rules using rational choice models', *Journal of Economic Issues*, **13**(1), 49–72.

Field, A.J. (1984), 'Microeconomics, norms and rationality', *Economic Development and Cultural Change*, **32**(4), 683–711.

Field, A.J. (2001), *Altruistically Inclined? The Behavioral Sciences, Evolutionary Theory, and the Origins of Reciprocity*, Ann Arbor, MI: University of Michigan Press.

Field, A.J. (2006), 'Group selection and behavioral economics', in M. Altman (ed.), *Foundations and Extensions of Behavioral Economics: A Handbook*, Armonk, NY: M.E. Sharpe, pp. 165–82.

Field, A.J. (2007), 'Beyond foraging: behavioral science and the future of institutional economics', *Journal of Institutional Economics*, **3**(3), 265–91.

Fine, B. (1995), 'From political economy to consumption', in D. Miller (ed.), *Acknowledging Consumption*, London: Routledge, pp. 125–62.

Fine, B. (1999), 'A question of economics: is it colonising the social sciences?', *Economy and Society*, **28**(3), 403–25.

Fine, B. (2000), 'Economics imperialism and intellectual progress: the present as history of economic thought?', *History of Economics Review*, **32**(1), 10–36.

Fine, B. (2002), '"Economic imperialism": a view from the periphery', *Review of Radical Political Economics*, **34**(2), 187–201.

Fine, B. (2004), 'Addressing the real and the critical in critical realism', in P. Lewis (ed.), *Transforming Economics: Perspectives on the Critical Realist Project*, London: Routledge, pp. 202–26.

Fine, B. (2006), 'Debating critical realism in economics', *Capital and Class*, **89**, 121–9.

220 *Economics, culture and social theory*

Fine, B. (2008), 'Vicissitudes of economics imperialism', *Review of Social Economy*, **66**(2), 235–40.
Fine, B. and E. Leopold (1993), *The World of Consumption*, London: Routledge.
Fine, B. and D. Milonakis (2009), *From Economics Imperialism to Freakonomics: The Shifting Boundaries Between Economics and Other Social Sciences*, London: Routledge.
Firth, R. (1951), *Elements of Social Organization*, London: Watts.
Fitzgibbons, A. (1988), *Keynes's Vision: A New Political Economy*, Oxford: Clarendon Press.
Fleetwood, S. (ed.) (1999), *Critical Realism in Economics: Development and Debate*, London: Routledge.
Fleetwood, S. (2001), 'Causal laws, functional relations and tendencies', *Review of Political Economy*, **13**(2), 201–20.
Fleetwood, S. (2002), 'Boylan and O'Gorman's causal holism: a critical realist evaluation', *Cambridge Journal of Economics*, **26**(1), 27–45.
Folbre, N. (1994), *Who Pays for the Kids? Gender and the Structures of Constraint*, London: Routledge.
Folbre, N. (2001), *The Invisible Heart: Economics and Family Values*, New York: New Press.
Folbre, N. and J.A. Nelson (2000), 'For love or money – or both?', *Journal of Economic Perspectives*, **14**(4), 123–40.
Foley, D.K. (2001), 'Value, distribution and capital: a review essay', *Review of Political Economy*, **13**(3), 365–81.
Foster, J.B. (2000), *Marx's Ecology: Materialism and Nature*, New York: Monthly Review Press.
Fourie, F.C.v.N. (1991), 'The nature of the market: a structural analysis', in G.M. Hodgson and E. Screpanti (eds), *Rethinking Economics: Markets, Technology and Economic Evolution*, Aldershot, UK and Brookfield, USA: Edward Elgar, pp. 40–57.
Fracchia, J. and R.C. Lewontin (1999), 'Does culture evolve?', *History and Theory*, **38**(4), 52–78.
Frazer, J.G. (1890), *The Golden Bough: A Study in Magic and Religion*, London: Macmillan.
Freeden, M. (1979), 'Eugenics and progressive thought: a study in ideological affinity', *Historical Journal*, **22**(3), 645–71.
Freeman, C. and F. Louçã (2001), *As Time Goes By: From the Industrial Revolutions to the Information Revolution*, Oxford: Oxford University Press.
Fritz, R.G. and J.M. Fritz (1985), 'Linguistic structure and economic method', *Journal of Economic Issues*, **19**(1), 75–101.
Fromm, E. (1956), *The Sane Society*, London: Routledge and Kegan Paul.

Fromm, E. (1961), *Marx's Concept of Man*, New York: Frederick Ungar.

Fullbrook, E. (ed.) (2002), *Intersubjectivity in Economics: Agents and Structures*, London: Routledge.

Fullbrook, E. (ed.) (2003), *The Crisis in Economics: The Post-Autistic Economics Movement*, London: Routledge.

Fullbrook, E. (ed.) (2007), *Real World Economics: A Post-Autistic Economics Reader*, London: Anthem Press.

Furubotn, E.G. and R. Richter (1997), *Institutions in Economic Theory: The Contribution of the New Institutional Economics*, Ann Arbor, MI: University of Michigan Press.

Gadamer, H.-G. (1975), *Truth and Method*, edited by G. Barden and J. Cumming, London: Sheed and Ward.

Gadamer, H.-G. (1976), *Philosophical Hermeneutics*, translated by D.E. Linge, Berkeley, CA: University of California Press.

Galbraith, J.K. (1969), *The Affluent Society*, 2nd edn, London: Hamish Hamilton.

Galbraith, J.K. (1972), *The New Industrial State*, 2nd edn, London: André Deutsch.

Gamble, A. (2006), 'Hayek on knowledge, economics and society', in E. Feser (ed.), *The Cambridge Companion to Hayek*, Cambridge: Cambridge University Press, pp. 111–131.

Garnett, R.F. (2006), 'Paradigms and pluralism in heterodox economics', *Review of Political Economy*, **18**(4), 521–46.

Garnham, N. (1977), 'Towards a political economy of culture', *Higher Education Quarterly*, **31**(3), 341–57.

Garnham, N. (1979), 'Contribution to a political economy of mass communication', *Media, Culture and Society*, **1**(2), 123–46.

Garnham, N. (1995), 'Political economy and cultural studies: reconciliation or divorce?', *Critical Studies in Mass Communication*, **12**(1), 62–71.

Garnham, N. (1997), 'Political economy and the practice of cultural studies', in M. Ferguson and P. Golding (eds), *Cultural Studies in Question*, London: Sage, pp. 56–73.

Garnham, N. (2000), '"Information society" as theory or ideology: a critical perspective on technology, education and employment in the information age', *Information, Communication and Society*, **3**(2), 139–52.

Garrard, G. (2006), *Counter-Enlightenments: From the Eighteenth Century to the Present*, London: Routledge.

Gaus, G.F. (2006), 'Hayek on the evolution of society and mind', in E. Feser (ed.), *The Cambridge Companion to Hayek*, Cambridge: Cambridge University Press, pp. 232–58.

Gayon, J. (2003), 'From Darwin to today in evolutionary biology', in J. Hodge and G. Radick (eds), *The Cambridge Companion to Darwin*, Cambridge: Cambridge University Press, pp. 240–64.

Gecas, V. (1982), 'The self-concept', *American Review of Sociology*, **8**, 1–33.

Geertz, C. (1973), *The Interpretation of Cultures*, New York: Basic Books.

Gellner, E. (1985), 'Relativism and universals', in E. Gellner, *Relativism in the Social Sciences*, Cambridge: Cambridge University Press, pp. 83–100.

Gergen, K.J. (1999), *An Invitation to Social Construction*, London: Sage.

Gerrard, B. (1991), 'Keynes's General Theory: interpreting the interpretations', *Economic Journal*, **101**(2), 276–87.

Gerrard, B. (1993), 'The significance of interpretation in economics', in W. Henderson, T. Dudley-Evans and R. Backhouse (eds), *Economics and Language*, London: Routledge, pp. 51–63.

Gertler, M.S. (2003), 'A cultural economic geography of production', in K. Anderson, M. Domosh, S. Pile and N.J. Thrift (eds), *Handbook of Cultural Geography*, London: Sage, pp. 131–46.

Geuss, R. (1981), *The Idea of a Critical Theory: Habermas and the Frankfurt School*, Cambridge: Cambridge University Press.

Gibson, C. and L. Kong (2005), 'Cultural economy: a critical review', *Progress in Human Geography*, **29**(5), 541–61.

Giddens, A. (1976), *New Rules of Sociological Method: A Positive Critique of Interpretative Sociologies*, London: Hutchinson.

Giddens, A. (1984), *The Constitution of Society: Outline of the Theory of Structuration*, Cambridge: Polity Press.

Giddens, A. (1987), 'Social theory and problems of macroeconomics', in A. Giddens, *Social Theory and Modern Sociology*, Cambridge: Polity Press, pp. 183–202.

Gilbert, E. (2005), 'Common cents: situating money in time and place', *Economy and Society*, **34**(3), 357–88.

Ginsburgh, V.A. and D. Throsby (eds) (2006), *Handbook of the Economics of Art and Culture*, Amsterdam: North-Holland.

Goffman, E. (1971), *The Presentation of Self in Everyday Life*, Harmondsworth: Penguin.

Goffman, E. (1983), 'The interaction order', *American Sociological Review*, **48**, 1–17.

Goldberg, V.P. (1976), 'Toward an expanded theory of contract', *Journal of Economic Issues*, **10**(1), 45–61.

Goldberg, V.P. (1980), 'Relational exchange: economics and complex contracts', *American Behavioral Scientist*, **23**(3), 337–52.

Golding, P. and G. Murdock (1991), 'Culture, communication and political economy', in J. Curran and M. Gurevitch (eds), *Mass Media and Society*, London: Edward Arnold, pp. 15–32.

Goldschmidt, N. and B. Remmele (2005), 'Anthropology as the basic science of economic theory: towards a cultural theory of economics', *Journal of Economic Methodology*, **12**(3), 455–69.

Goodwin, C.D. (2006), 'The art of an ethical life: Keynes and Bloomsbury', in R.E. Backhouse and B.W. Bateman (eds), *The Cambridge Companion to Keynes*, Cambridge: Cambridge University Press, pp. 217–36.

Gould, S.J. (1983), 'Shades of Lamarck', in S.J. Gould, *The Panda's Thumb: More Reflections in Natural History*, Harmondsworth: Penguin, pp. 65–71.

Gould, S.J. (2001), 'More things in heaven and earth', in H. Rose and S.P.R. Rose (eds), *Alas Poor Darwin: Arguments Against Evolutionary Psychology*, London: Vintage, pp. 85–105.

Gouldner, A.W. (1970), *The Coming Crisis of Western Sociology*, New York: Basic Books.

Goux, J.-J. (1999), 'Cash, check, or charge?', in M. Woodmansee and M. Osteen (eds), *The New Economic Criticism: Studies at the Intersection of Literature and Economics*, London: Routledge, pp. 114–27.

Goux, J.-J. (2001), 'Ideality, symbolicity, and reality in postmodern capitalism', in S. Cullenberg, J.L. Amariglio and D.F. Ruccio (eds), *Postmodernism, Economics and Knowledge*, London: Routledge, pp. 166–81.

Graça Moura, M. da and N. Martins (2008), 'On some criticisms of critical realism in economics', *Cambridge Journal of Economics*, **32**(2), 203–18.

Grampp, W.D. (1973), 'Classical economics and its moral critics', *History of Political Economy*, **5**(2), 359–74.

Gramsci, A. (1971), *Selections from the Prison Notebooks*, edited and translated by Q. Hoare and G. Nowell-Smith, London: Lawrence and Wishart.

Granovetter, M. (1985), 'Economic action and social structure: the problem of embeddedness', *American Journal of Sociology*, **91**(3), 481–510.

Granovetter, M. (1990), 'The old and the new economic sociology: a history and an agenda', in R. Friedland and A.F. Robertson (eds), *Beyond the Marketplace: Rethinking Economy and Society*, New York: Aldine de Gruyter, pp. 89–112.

Granovetter, M. (1992), 'Economic institutions as social constructions: a framework for analysis', *Acta Sociologica*, **35**(1), 3–11.

Granovetter, M. (2005), 'The impact of social structure on economic out-comes', *Journal of Economic Perspectives*, **19**(1), 33–50.

Grayling, A.C. (2000), *The Quarrel of the Age: The Life and Times of William Hazlitt*, London: Weidenfeld and Nicolson.

Gronow, A. (2008), 'Not by rules or choice alone: a pragmatist critique of institution theories in economics and sociology', *Journal of Institutional Economics*, **4**(3), 351–73.

Grossberg, L. (1995), 'Cultural studies versus political economy: is anyone else bored with this debate?', *Critical Studies in Mass Communication*, **12**(1), 72–81.

Gudeman, S. (1986), *Economics as Culture: Models and Metaphors of Livelihood*, London: Routledge.

Gudeman, S. (2001), *The Anthropology of Economy: Community, Market, and Culture*, Oxford: Blackwell.

Guillén, M.F., R. Collins, P. England and M. Meyer (eds) (2002), *The New Economic Sociology: Developments in an Emerging Field*, New York: Russell Sage Foundation.

Gunn, R. (1989), 'Marxism and philosophy: a critique of critical realism', *Capital and Class*, **37**, 87–116.

Gunn, S. (2006), *History and Cultural Theory*, London: Longman.

Habermas, J. (1979), *Communication and the Evolution of Society*, trans-lated by T. McCarthy, London: Heinemann.

Habermas, J. (1984), *The Theory of Communicative Action, Volume I: Reason and the Rationalization of Society*, translated by T. McCarthy, Cambridge: Polity Press.

Habermas, J. (1987), *The Theory of Communicative Action, Volume II: Lifeworld and System: A Critique of Functionalist Reason*, translated by T. McCarthy, Cambridge: Polity Press.

Habermas, J. (2003), *The Future of Human Nature*, Cambridge: Polity Press.

Haddock, B.A. (1980), *An Introduction to Historical Thought*, London: Edward Arnold.

Hall, S. (1980), 'Cultural studies: two paradigms', *Media, Culture and Society*, **2**(1), 57–72.

Hamilton, A. (2000), 'Max Weber's *Protestant Ethic and the Spirit of Capitalism*', in S. Turner (ed.), *The Cambridge Companion to Weber*, Cambridge: Cambridge University Press, pp. 151–71.

Hampson, N. (1968), *The Enlightenment: An Evaluation of its Assumptions, Attitudes and Values*, Harmondsworth: Penguin.

Hands, D.W. (1993), *Testing, Rationality and Progress: Essays on the Popperian Tradition in Economic Methodology*, Lanham, MD: Rowman and Littlefield.

Hands, D.W. (2001), *Reflection without Rules: Economic Methodology and Contemporary Science Theory*, Cambridge: Cambridge University Press.

Hanfling, O. (1981), *Logical Positivism*, Oxford: Basil Blackwell.

Harcourt, G.C. (1982), *The Social Science Imperialists*, Routledge and Kegan Paul.

Hareven, T.K. (1995), 'Changing images of ageing and the social construction of the life course', in M. Featherstone and A. Wernick (eds), *Images of Ageing: Cultural Representations of Later Life*, London: Routledge, pp. 119–34.

Hargreaves Heap, S.P. (1989), *Rationality in Economics*, Oxford: Basil Blackwell.

Hargreaves Heap, S.P. (2000), 'How far can you get with hermeneutics?', in P.E. Earl and S.F. Frowen (eds), *Economics as an Art of Thought: Essays in Memory of G.L.S. Shackle*, London: Routledge, pp. 149–72.

Hargreaves Heap, S.P. (2001), 'Expressive rationality: is self-worth just another kind of preference?', in U. Mäki (ed.), *The Economic World View*, Cambridge: Cambridge University Press, pp. 98–113.

Hargreaves Heap, S.P. (2002), 'The reality of common cultures', in U. Mäki (ed.), *Fact and Fiction in Economics: Models, Realism and Social Construction*, Cambridge: Cambridge University Press, pp. 257–68.

Hargreaves Heap, S.P. and Y. Varoufakis (1995), *Game Theory: A Critical Introduction*, London: Routledge.

Harré, R. (1970), *The Principles of Scientific Thinking*, London: Macmillan.

Harré, R. and M. Krausz (1996), *Varieties of Relativism*, Oxford: Blackwell.

Harré, R. and P. Secord (1972), *The Explanation of Social Behaviour*, Oxford: Basil Blackwell.

Harris, M. (1968), *The Rise of Anthropological Theory*, London: Routledge and Kegan Paul.

Harris, M. (1979), *Cultural Materialism: The Struggle for a Science of Culture*, New York: Random House.

Harrison, L.E. and S.P. Huntington (eds) (2000), *Culture Matters: How Values Shape Human Progress*, New York: Basic Books.

Harvey, D. (1990), *The Condition of Postmodernity: An Enquiry into the Origins of Cultural Change*, Oxford: Blackwell.

Hawkes, T. (2003), *Structuralism and Semiotics*, London: Routledge.

Hayek, F.A. (1948), *Individualism and Economic Order*, London: Routledge and Kegan Paul.

Hayek, F.A. (1952), *The Counter-revolution of Science: Studies on the Abuse of Reason*, Glencoe, IL: Free Press.

Hayek, F.A. (1982), *Law, Legislation and Liberty*, London: Routledge and Kegan Paul.

Hayek, F.A. (1988), *The Fatal Conceit: The Errors of Socialism*, London: Routledge.

Hays, S. (1994), 'Structure and agency and the sticky problem of culture', *Sociological Theory*, **12**(1), 57–72.

Hazlitt, W. (1807), 'A reply to the Essay on Population by the Rev. T.R. Malthus', in P.P. Howe (ed.) (1930), *The Complete Works of William Hazlitt, Volume 1*, London: Dent, pp. 177–364.

Hazlitt, W. (1825), 'Mr. Malthus', in W. Hazlitt, *The Spirit of the Age*, reprinted 1991, Plymouth: Northcote House, pp. 164–79.

Heidegger, M. (1927), *Being and Time*, translated by J. Macquarrie and E. Robinson (1962), Oxford: Blackwell.

Heilbrun, J. and C.M. Gray (2001), *The Economics of Art and Culture*, 2nd edn, Cambridge: Cambridge University Press.

Held, D. (1980), *Introduction to Critical Theory: Horkheimer to Habermas*, London: Hutchinson.

Henderson, W. (1994), 'Metaphor and economics', in R.E. Backhouse (ed.), *New Directions in Economic Methodology*, London: Routledge, pp. 343–67.

Henderson, W. (2000), *John Ruskin's Political Economy*, London: Routledge.

Henwood, D. (2003), *After the New Economy*, New York: Free Press.

Herbert, S. (1971), 'Darwin, Malthus, and selection', *Journal of the History of Biology*, **4**(1), 209–17.

Herder, J.G. (1784–91), *Reflections on the Philosophy of the History of Mankind*, edited by F.E. Manuel (1968), Chicago, IL: University of Chicago Press.

Herskovits, M.J. (1952), *Economic Anthropology*, New York: Knopf.

Hesse, M. (1974), *The Structure of Scientific Inference*, London: Macmillan.

Hicks, J.R. (1939), *Value and Capital: An Inquiry into Some Fundamental Principles of Economic Theory*, Oxford: Oxford University Press.

Hicks, J.R. (1956), *A Revision of Demand Theory*, Oxford: Clarendon Press.

Hicks, J.R. (1979), *Causality in Economics*, Oxford: Blackwell.

Himmelweit, S. (2002), 'Making visible the hidden economy: the case for gender-impact analysis of economic policy', *Feminist Economics*, **8**(1), 49–70.

Himmelweit, S. (2007), 'The prospects for caring: economic theory and policy analysis', *Cambridge Journal of Economics*, **31**(4), 581–99.

Hirsch, F. (1977), *The Social Limits to Growth*, London: Routledge and Kegan Paul.

Hirshleifer, J. (1977), 'Economics from a biological viewpoint', *Journal of Law and Economics*, **20**(1), 1–52.

Hirshleifer, J. (1985), 'The expanding domain of economics', *American Economic Review*, **75**(6), 53–68.

Hobson, J.A. (1898), *John Ruskin: Social Reformer*, London: James Nisbet.

Hobson, J.A. (1902), *The Social Problem: Life and Work*, London: James Nisbet.

Hobson, J.A. (1938), *Confessions of an Economic Heretic*, London: Allen.

Hodge, R. and G. Kress (1993), *Language as Ideology*, 2nd edn, London: Routledge.

Hodgson, G.M. (1988), *Economics and Institutions: A Manifesto for a Modern Institutional Economics*, Cambridge: Polity Press.

Hodgson, G.M. (1989), 'Institutional economic theory: the old versus the new', *Review of Political Economy*, **1**(3), 249–69.

Hodgson, G.M. (1991), 'Hayek's theory of cultural evolution: an evaluation in the light of Vanberg's critique', *Economics and Philosophy*, **7**(1), 67–82.

Hodgson, G.M. (1993a), *Economics and Evolution: Bringing Life Back into Economics*, Cambridge: Polity Press.

Hodgson, G.M. (1993b), 'Institutional economics: surveying the "old" and the "new"', *Metroeconomica*, **44**(1), 1–28.

Hodgson, G.M. (1997), 'The evolutionary and non-Darwinian economics of Joseph Schumpeter', *Journal of Evolutionary Economics*, **7**(2), 131–45.

Hodgson, G.M. (1999a), *Economics and Institutions: On Evolutionary Economics and the Evolution of Economics*, Cheltenham, UK and Northampton, MA, USA: Edward Elgar.

Hodgson, G.M. (1999b), *Economics and Utopia: Why the Learning Economy is not the End of History*, London: Routledge.

Hodgson, G.M. (2001a), *How Economics Forgot History: The Problem of Historical Specificity in Social Science*, London: Routledge.

Hodgson G.M. (2001b), 'Is social evolution Lamarckian or Darwinian?', in J. Laurent and J. Nightingale (eds), *Darwinism and Evolutionary Economics*, Cheltenham, UK and Northampton, MA, USA: Edward Elgar, pp. 87–120.

Hodgson, G.M. (2002), 'Reconstitutive downward causation: social structure and the development of individual agency', in E. Fullbrook (ed.), *Intersubjectivity in Economics: Agents and Structures*, London: Routledge, pp. 159–80.

Hodgson, G.M. (2003), 'The hidden persuaders: institutions and individuals in economic theory', *Cambridge Journal of Economics*, **27**(2), 159–75.

Hodgson, G.M. (2004), *The Evolution of Institutional Economics: Agency, Structure and Darwinism in American Institutionalism*, London: Routledge.

Hodgson, G.M. (2006a), 'The uncritical political affinities of critical realism', in G.M. Hodgson, *Economics in the Shadows of Darwin and Marx*, Cheltenham, UK and Northampton, MA, USA: Edward Elgar, pp. 83–98.

Hodgson, G.M. (2006b), 'What are institutions?', *Journal of Economic Issues*, **40**(1), 1–25.

Hodgson, G.M. (2007), 'Evolutionary and institutional economics as the new mainstream?', *Evolutionary and Institutional Economics Review*, **4**(1), 7–25.

Hodgson, G.M. and T. Knudsen (2006a), 'Dismantling Lamarckism: why description of socio-economic evolution as Lamarckian is misleading', *Journal of Evolutionary Economics*, **16**(4), 343–66.

Hodgson, G.M. and T. Knudsen (2006b), 'Why we need a generalized Darwinism, and why generalized Darwinism is not enough', *Journal of Economic Behavior and Organization*, **61**(1), 1–19.

Hoksbergen, R. (1994), 'Postmodernism and institutionalism: toward a resolution of the debate on relativism', *Journal of Economic Issues*, **28**(3), 679–713.

Holland, J.H. (1998), *Emergence: From Chaos to Order*, Oxford: Oxford University Press.

Holmes, R. (1982), *Coleridge*, Oxford: Oxford University Press.

Holstein, J.A. and J.F. Gubrium (eds) (2007), *Handbook of Constructionist Research*, New York: Guilford Press.

Homans, G.C. (1964), 'Bringing men back in', *American Sociological Review*, **29**(6), 809–18.

Hoover, K.D. (1994), 'Pragmatism, pragmaticism and economic method', in R.E. Backhouse (ed.), *New Directions in Economic Methodology*, London: Routledge, pp. 286–315.

Horkheimer, M. and T.W. Adorno (1944), *Dialectic of Enlightenment*, reprinted 1973, London: Allen Lane.

Horwitz, S. (1992), 'Monetary exchange as an extra-linguistic social communication process', *Review of Social Economy*, **50**(2), 193–214.

Hudson, M. (2000), 'The use and abuse of mathematical economics', *Journal of Economic Studies*, **27**(4), 292–315.

Hudson, R. (2005), *Economic Geographies: Circuits, Flows and Spaces*, London: Sage.

Hughes, J. (2000), *Ecology and Historical Materialism*, Cambridge: Cambridge University Press.

Husserl, E. (1913), *Ideas: General Introduction to Pure Phenomenology*, translated by W.R. Boyce Gibson (1931), London: George Allen and Unwin.

Hutter, M. (1996), 'The impact of cultural economics on economic theory', *Journal of Cultural Economics*, **20**, 263–8.

Ingham, G.K. (1996), 'Some recent changes in the relationship between economics and sociology', *Cambridge Journal of Economics*, **20**(1), 243–75.

Ingham, G.K. (1999), 'Money is a social relation', in S. Fleetwood (ed.), *Critical Realism in Economics: Development and Debate*, London: Routledge, pp. 103–24.

Ingham, G.K. (2004), *The Nature of Money*, Cambridge: Polity Press.

Inglis, F. (1993), *Cultural Studies*, Oxford: Blackwell.

Ingrao, B. and G. Israel (1990), *The Invisible Hand: Economic Equilibrium in the History of Science*, Cambridge, MA: MIT Press.

Jackson, W.A. (1993), 'Culture, society and economic theory', *Review of Political Economy*, **5**(4), 453–69.

Jackson, W.A. (1994), 'The economics of ageing and the political economy of old age', *International Review of Applied Economics*, **8**(1), 31–45.

Jackson, W.A. (1995), 'Naturalism in economics', *Journal of Economic Issues*, **29**(3), 761–80.

Jackson, W.A. (1996), 'Cultural materialism and institutional economics', *Review of Social Economy*, **54**(2), 221–44.

Jackson, W.A. (1998), *The Political Economy of Population Ageing*, Cheltenham, UK and Lyme, USA: Edward Elgar.

Jackson, W.A. (1999), 'Dualism, duality and the complexity of economic institutions', *International Journal of Social Economics*, **26**(4), 545–58.

Jackson, W.A. (2002), 'Functional explanation in economics: a qualified defence', *Journal of Economic Methodology*, **9**(2), 169–89.

Jackson, W.A. (2003), 'Social structure in economic theory', *Journal of Economic Issues*, **37**(3), 727–46.

Jackson, W.A. (2005), 'Capabilities, culture and social structure', *Review of Social Economy*, **63**(1), 101–24.

Jackson, W.A. (2007a), 'Economic flexibility: a structural analysis', in S. Ioannides and K. Nielsen (eds), *Economics and the Social Sciences: Boundaries, Interaction and Integration*, Cheltenham, UK and Northampton, MA, USA: Edward Elgar, pp. 215–32.

Jackson, W.A. (2007b), 'On the social structure of markets', *Cambridge Journal of Economics*, **31**(2), 235–53.

Jaffé, W. (1975), 'Léon Walras, an economic adviser manqué', *Economic Journal*, **85**(4), 810–23.

James, P. (1979), *Population Malthus: His Life and Times*, London: Routledge and Kegan Paul.

James, W. (1890), *The Principles of Psychology*, New York: Holt.

Jameson, F. (1991), *Postmodernism, or The Cultural Logic of Late Capitalism*, London: Verso.

Jenks, C. (1993), *Culture*, London: Routledge.

Jennings, A.L. and W.J. Waller (1994), 'Evolutionary economics and cultural hermeneutics: Veblen, cultural relativism, and blind drift', *Journal of Economic Issues*, **28**(4), 997–1030.

Jennings, A.L. and W.J. Waller (1995), 'Culture: core concept reaffirmed', *Journal of Economic Issues*, **29**(2), 407–18.

Jennings, A.L. and W.J. Waller (1998), 'The place of biological science in Veblen's economics', *History of Political Economy*, **30**(2), 189–217.

Jessop, B. (2004), 'Critical semiotic analysis and cultural political economy', *Critical Discourse Studies*, **1**(2), 159–74.

Jessop, B. (2005), 'Cultural political economy, the knowledge-based economy and the state', in A. Barry and D. Slater (eds), *The Technological Economy*, London: Routledge, pp. 142–64.

Jessop, B. and S. Oosterlynck (2008), 'Cultural political economy: on making the cultural turn without falling into soft economic sociology', *Geoforum*, **39**(3), 1155–69.

Jessop, B. and N.-L. Sum (2001), 'Pre-disciplinary and post-disciplinary perspectives in political economy', *New Political Economy*, **6**(1), 89–101.

Jessop, B. and N.-L. Sum (2006), *Beyond the Regulation Approach: Putting Capitalist Economies in their Place*, Cheltenham, UK and Northampton, MA, USA: Edward Elgar.

Johansen, J.D. and S.E. Larsen (2002), *Signs in Use: An Introduction to Semiotics*, London: Routledge.

Johnson, M.L. (2005), 'The social construction of old age as a problem', in M.L. Johnson (ed.), *The Cambridge Handbook of Age and Ageing*, Cambridge: Cambridge University Press, pp. 563–71.

Jolink, A. (1996), *The Evolutionist Economics of Léon Walras*, London: Routledge.

Jones, E.L. (2006), *Cultures Merging: A Historical and Economic Critique of Culture*, Princeton, NJ: Princeton University Press.

Jones, G. (1980), *Social Darwinism and English Thought: The Interaction between Biological and Social Theory*, Brighton: Harvester Press.

Kalecki, M. (1943), 'Political aspects of full employment', *Political Quarterly*, **14**(4), 322–31.

Kane, R.H. (ed.) (2002), *The Oxford Handbook of Free Will*, Oxford: Oxford University Press.

Katona, G. (1951), *Psychological Analysis of Economic Behavior*, New York: McGraw-Hill.

Katona, G. (1975), *Psychological Economics*, New York: Elsevier.

Katzner, D.W. (2001), 'The significance, success, and failure of microeconomic theory', *Journal of Post Keynesian Economics*, **24**(1), 41–58.

Katzner, D.W. (2002), 'What are the questions?', *Journal of Post Keynesian Economics*, **25**(1), 51–68.

Katzner, D.W. (2003), 'Why mathematics in economics?', *Journal of Post Keynesian Economics*, **25**(4), 561–74.

Kauffman, S.A. (1995), *At Home in the Universe: The Search for the Laws of Self-organization and Complexity*, Oxford: Oxford University Press.

Kautsky, K. (1887), *The Economic Doctrines of Karl Marx*, translated by H.J. Stenning (1925), London: A & C. Black.

Keat, R. (1971), 'Positivism, naturalism, and anti-naturalism in the social sciences', *Journal for the Theory of Social Behaviour*, **1**(1), 3–17.

Kellner, D.M. (1989), *Critical Theory, Marxism and Modernity*, Cambridge: Polity Press.

Kellner, D.M. (1997), 'Overcoming the divide: cultural studies and political economy', in M. Ferguson and P. Golding (eds), *Cultural Studies in Question*, London: Sage, pp. 102–120.

Keynes, J.M. (1931), 'The end of laissez-faire', in J.M. Keynes, *Essays in Persuasion*, reprinted 1972, London: Macmillan, pp. 272–94.

Keynes, J.M. (1936), *The General Theory of Employment, Interest and Money*, London: Macmillan.

Keynes, J.M. (1937), 'The general theory of employment', *Quarterly Journal of Economics*, **51**(2), 209–23.

Keynes, J.M. (1939), 'Professor Tinbergen's method', *Economic Journal*, **49**(3), 558–68.

Khalil, E.L. (1997), 'Is the firm an individual?', *Cambridge Journal of Economics*, **21**, 519–44.

Kilpinen, E. (2003), 'Does pragmatism imply institutionalism?', *Journal of Economic Issues*, **37**(2), 291–304.

King, J.E. (1983), 'Utopian or scientific? A reconsideration of the Ricardian socialists', *History of Political Economy*, **15**(3), 345–73.

King, J.E. (2003), 'Non-Marxian socialism', in W.J. Samuels, J.E. Biddle and J.B. Davis (eds), *A Companion to the History of Economic Thought*, Oxford: Blackwell, pp. 184–200.

Kirman, A.P. (1989), 'The intrinsic limits of modern economic theory: the emperor has no clothes', *Economic Journal*, **99** (conference papers), 126–39.

Kirman, A.P. (2006), 'Demand theory and general equilibrium: from explanation to introspection, a journey down the wrong road', *History of Political Economy*, **38** (annual supplement), 246–80.

Kirzner, I.M. (1973), *Competition and Entrepreneurship*, Chicago, IL: University of Chicago Press.

Kirzner, I.M. (1976), 'On the method of Austrian economics', in E.G. Dolan (ed.), *The Foundations of Modern Austrian Economics*, Kansas City, MO: Sheed and Ward, pp. 40–51.

Kirzner I.M. (1999), 'Creativity and/or alertness: a reconsideration of the Schumpeterian entrepreneur', *Review of Austrian Economics*, **11**(1), 5–17.

Kitcher, P. (1985), *Vaulting Ambition: Sociobiology and the Quest for Human Nature*, Cambridge, MA: MIT Press.

Klaes, M. (2006), 'Keynes between modernism and post-modernism', in R.E. Backhouse and B.W. Bateman (eds), *The Cambridge Companion to Keynes*, Cambridge: Cambridge University Press, pp. 257–70.

Klamer, A. (2001), 'Making sense of economics: from falsification to rhetoric and beyond', *Journal of Economic Methodology*, **8**, 69–76.

Klamer, A. (2007), *Speaking of Economics: How to Get in the Conversation*, London: Routledge.

Knudsen, T. (2001), 'Nesting Lamarckism within Darwinian explanation: necessity in economics and possibility in biology', in J. Laurent and J. Nightingale (eds), *Darwinism and Evolutionary Economics*, Cheltenham, UK and Northampton, MA, USA: Edward Elgar, pp. 121–59.

Kohli, M. and J.W. Meyer (1986), 'Social structures and social construction of life stages', *Human Development*, **29**(3), 145–49.

Korsch, K. (1923), *Marxism and Philosophy*, translated by F. Halliday (1970), London: New Left Books.

Kotz, D.M. (1990), 'A comparative analysis of the theory of regulation and the social structures of accumulation theory', *Science and Society*, **54**, 5–28.

Kroeber, A.L. and C. Kluckhohn (1952), 'Culture: a critical review of concepts and definitions', *Peabody Museum Papers*, **47**, 1–223.

Kuhn, T. (1962), *The Structure of Scientific Revolutions*, Chicago, IL: University of Chicago Press.

Kumar, K. (1991), *Utopianism*, Buckingham: Open University Press.

Kurz, H.D. and N. Salvadori (eds) (1998), *The Elgar Companion to Classical Economics*, Cheltenham, UK and Lyme, USA: Edward Elgar.

Labriola, A. (1896), *Essays on the Materialistic Conception of History*, translated by C.H. Kerr (1908), Chicago: Kerr.

Lachmann, L.M. (1986), *The Market as an Economic Process*, Oxford: Basil Blackwell.

Lachmann, L.M. (1990), 'Austrian economics: a hermeneutic approach', in D. Lavoie (ed.), *Economics and Hermeneutics*, London: Routledge, pp. 134–46.

Lakatos, I. (1970), 'Falsification and the methodology of scientific research programmes', in I. Lakatos and A. Musgrave (eds), *Criticism and the Growth of Knowledge*, Cambridge: Cambridge University Press, pp. 91–195.

Lane, D.A. (1993), 'Artificial worlds and economics, Parts I and II', *Journal of Evolutionary Economics*, **3**(2), 89–107 and **3**(3), 177–97.

Langlois, R.N. (ed.) (1986), *Economics as a Process: Essays in the New Institutional Economics*, Cambridge: Cambridge University Press.

Lash, S. and J. Urry (1994), *Economies of Signs and Space*, London: Sage.

Lavoie, D. (ed.) (1990), *Economics and Hermeneutics*, London: Routledge.

Lavoie, D. (1994), 'The interpretive turn', in P.J. Boettke (ed.), *The Elgar Companion to Austrian Economics*, Aldershot, UK and Brookfield, USA: Edward Elgar, pp. 54–62.

Lavoie, M. (2004), 'Post Keynesian consumer theory: potential synergies with consumer research and economic psychology', *Journal of Economic Psychology*, **25**(5), 639–49.

Lawlor, M.S. (2006), 'William James's psychological pragmatism: habit, belief and purposive human behaviour', *Cambridge Journal of Economics*, **30**(3), 321–45.

Lawson, T. (1985a), 'Keynes, prediction and econometrics', in T. Lawson and H. Pesaran (eds), *Keynes's Economics: Methodological Issues*, London: Croom Helm, pp. 116–33.

Lawson, T. (1985b), 'Uncertainty and economic analysis', *Economic Journal*, **95**(4), 909–27.

Lawson, T. (1988), 'Probability and uncertainty in economic analysis', *Journal of Post Keynesian Economics*, **11**(1), 38–65.

Lawson, T. (1989), 'Abstraction, tendencies and stylised facts: a realist approach to economic analysis', *Cambridge Journal of Economics*, **13**(1), 59–78.

Lawson, T. (1994), 'Economics and expectations', in S.C. Dow and J. Hillard (eds), *Keynes, Knowledge and Uncertainty*, Aldershot, UK and Brookfield, USA: Edward Elgar, pp. 77–106.

Lawson, T. (1995), 'A realist perspective on contemporary "economic theory"', *Journal of Economic Issues*, **29**(1), 1–32.

Lawson, T. (1997), *Economics and Reality*, London: Routledge.

Lawson, T. (2003), *Reorienting Economics*, London: Routledge.

Lawson, T. (2006), 'The nature of heterodox economics', *Cambridge Journal of Economics*, **30**(4), 483–505.

Layder, D. (1985), 'Beyond empiricism? The promise of realism', *Philosophy of the Social Sciences*, **15**(3), 255–74.

Layder, D. (1987), 'Key issues in structuration theory: some critical remarks', *Current Perspectives in Social Theory*, **8**, 25–46.

Layder, D. (1990), *The Realist Image in Social Science*, London: Macmillan.

Layder, D. (2006), *Understanding Social Theory*, 2nd edn, London: Sage.

Lazear, E.P. (2000), 'Economic imperialism', *Quarterly Journal of Economics*, **115**(1), 99–146.

Lazonick, W. (1990), 'Labour process', in J. Eatwell, M. Milgate and P. Newman (eds), *Marxian Economics*, London: Macmillan, pp. 225–32.

LeClair, E.E. (1962), 'Economic theory and economic anthropology', *American Anthropologist*, **64**(6), 1179–203.

Leonard, T.C. (2005), 'Eugenics and economics in the progressive era', *Journal of Economic Perspectives*, **19**(4), 207–24.

Leslie, D. (1997), 'Flexibly specialized agencies? Reflexivity, identity and the advertising industry', *Environment and Planning A*, **29**(6), 1017–38.

Levine, D.P. (1997), 'Knowing and acting: on uncertainty in economics', *Review of Political Economy*, **9**(1), 5–17.

Levitas, R. (1990), *The Concept of Utopia*, London: Philip Allan.

Lewes, G.H. (1879), *Problems of Life and Mind: Third Series*, London: Trubner.

Lewis, P. (2000), 'Realism, causality and the problem of social structure', *Journal for the Theory of Social Behaviour*, **30**(3), 249–68.

Lewis, P. (ed.) (2004), *Transforming Economics: Perspectives on the Critical Realist Project*, London: Routledge.

Liagouras, G. (2007), 'Economics and sociology in the transition from industrial to post-industrial capitalism', in S. Ioannides and K. Nielsen (eds), *Economics and the Social Sciences: Boundaries, Interaction and Integration*, Cheltenham, UK and Northampton, MA, USA: Edward Elgar, pp. 63–90.

Liebhafsky, E.E. (1993), 'The influence of Charles Sanders Peirce on institutional economics', *Journal of Economic Issues*, **27**(3), 741–54.

Lipietz, A. (1993), 'From Althusserianism to "Regulation Theory"', in E.A. Kaplan and M. Sprinker (eds), *The Althusserian Legacy*, London: Verso, pp. 99–138.

List, F. (1841), *The National System of Political Economy*, translated by S.S. Lloyd (1904), London: Longmans Green.

Littleboy, B. (1990), *On Interpreting Keynes: A Study in Reconciliation*, London: Routledge.

Litvan, G. (1991), 'Democratic and socialist values in Karl Polanyi's thought', in M. Mendell and D. Salée (eds), *The Legacy of Karl Polanyi*, London: Macmillan, pp. 251–71.

Loasby, B.J. (1976), *Choice, Complexity and Ignorance: An Enquiry into the Economic Theory and Practice of Decision Making*, Cambridge: Cambridge University Press.

Lodewijks, L. (1994), 'Anthropologists and economists: conflict or co-operation?', *Journal of Economic Methodology*, **1**(1), 81–104.

López, J. and J. Scott (2000), *Social Structure*, Buckingham: Open University Press.

Löwy, M. (1987), 'The Romantic and the Marxist critique of modern civilization', *Theory and Society*, **16**(6), 891–904.

Löwy, M. and R. Sayre (2001), *Romanticism against the Tide of Modernity*, translated by C. Porter, Durham, NC: Duke University Press.

Lukács, G. (1923), *History and Class Consciousness: Studies in Marxist Dialectics*, translated by R. Livingstone (1971), London: Merlin Press.

Lundvall, B.-Å. and B. Johnson (1994), 'The learning economy', *Journal of Industrial Studies*, **1**(2), 23–42.

Lutz, M.A. (1999), *Economics for the Common Good: Two Centuries of Social Economic Thought in the Humanistic Tradition*, London: Routledge.

Lutz, M.A. (2002), 'Social economics, justice and the common good', *International Journal of Social Economics*, **29**(1), 26–44.

Lyon, D. (1988), *The Information Society: Issues and Illusions*, Cambridge: Polity Press.

Lyotard, J.-F. (1984), *The Postmodern Condition: A Report on Knowledge*, translated by G. Bennington and B. Massumi, Manchester: Manchester University Press.

Macneil, I.R. (1981), 'Economic analysis of contractual relations', in P. Burrows and C.G. Veljanovski (eds), *The Economic Approach to Law*, London: Butterworths, pp. 61–92.

Mäki, U. (1988), 'How to combine rhetoric and realism in the methodology of economics', *Economics and Philosophy*, **4**(1), 89–109.

Mäki, U. (1989), 'On the problem of realism in economics', *Ricerche Economiche*, **43**(1–2), 176–98.

Mäki, U. (1993), 'Two philosophies of the rhetoric of economics', in W. Henderson, T. Dudley-Evans and R. Backhouse (eds), *Economics and Language*, London: Routledge, pp. 23–50.

Mandler, G. (2007), *A History of Modern Experimental Psychology: From James and Wundt to Cognitive Science*, Cambridge, MA: MIT Press.

Manicas, P.T. (1987), *A History and Philosophy of the Social Sciences*, Oxford: Basil Blackwell.

Mannheim, K. (1936), *Ideology and Utopia: An Introduction to the Sociology of Knowledge*, London: Routledge and Kegan Paul.

Mannheim, K. (1953), 'Conservative thought', in K. Mannheim, *Essays in Sociology and Social Psychology*, Oxford: Oxford University Press, pp. 74–164.

Marcuse, H. (1964), *One-dimensional Man: Studies in the Ideology of Advanced Industrial Societies*, Boston, MA: Beacon Press.

Marshall, A. (1890–1920), *Principles of Economics*, 9th (variorum) edn (1961), London: Macmillan.

Martinez-Alier, J. (1987), *Ecological Economics: Energy, Environment and Society*, Oxford: Basil Blackwell.

Marx, K. (1844), *Economic and Philosophic Manuscripts of 1844*, translated by M. Milligan (1964), New York: International Publishers.

Marx, K. (1858), *Grundrisse*, translated by M. Nicolaus (1973), Harmondsworth: Penguin.

Marx, K. (1859), *A Contribution to the Critique of Political Economy*, translated by S.W. Ryazanskaya (1971), London: Lawrence and Wishart.

Marx, K. (1867), *Capital: A Critique of Political Economy, Volume I*, translated by B. Fowkes (1976), Harmondsworth: Penguin.

Marx, K. and F. Engels (1846), *The German Ideology*, edited by C.J. Arthur (1970), London: Lawrence and Wishart.

Marx, K. and F. Engels (1848), *The Communist Manifesto*, translated by S. Moore (1967), Harmondsworth: Penguin.

Mason, R. (2002), 'Conspicuous consumption in economic theory and thought', in E. Fullbrook (ed.), *Intersubjectivity in Economics: Agents and Structures*, London: Routledge, pp. 85–104.

Mavroudeas, S.D. (2006), 'A history of contemporary political economy and postmodernism', *Review of Radical Political Economics*, **38**(4), 499–518.

Maxwell, R. (ed.) (2001), *Culture Works: The Political Economy of Culture*, Minneapolis, MN: University of Minnesota Press.

May, C. (2002), *The Information Society: A Sceptical View*, Cambridge: Polity Press.

Mayer, K.U. (2004), 'Whose lives? How history, societies, and institutions define and shape life courses', *Research in Human Development*, **1**(3), 161–87.

Mayhew, A. (1987), 'Culture: core concept under attack', *Journal of Economic Issues*, **21**(2), 587–603.

Mayhew, A. (1989), 'Contrasting origins of the two institutionalisms: the social science context', *Review of Political Economy*, **1**(3), 319–33.

Mayhew, A. (1994), 'Culture', in G.M. Hodgson, W.J. Samuels and M.R. Tool (eds), *The Elgar Companion to Institutional and Evolutionary Economics*, Aldershot, UK and Brookfield, USA: Edward Elgar, pp. 115–19.

Mayhew, A. (1998), 'On the difficulty of evolutionary analysis', *Cambridge Journal of Economics*, **22**(4), 449–61.

Mayhew, A. (2002), 'All consumption is conspicuous', in E. Fullbrook (ed.), *Intersubjectivity in Economics: Agents and Structures*, London: Routledge, pp. 43–55.

Maynard Smith, J. (1976), 'Group selection', *Quarterly Review of Biology*, **51**, 277–83.

Mayr, E. (1976), 'Typological versus population thinking', in E. Mayr, *Evolution and the Diversity of Life: Selected Essays*, Cambridge, MA: Harvard University Press, pp. 26–9.

Mayr, E. (1985), 'How biology differs from the physical sciences', in D.J. Depew and B.H. Weber (eds), *Evolution at a Crossroads: The New Biology and the New Philosophy of Science*, Cambridge, MA: MIT Press, pp. 43–63.

McCarney, J. (2000), *Hegel on History*, London: Routledge.

McCarthy, F. (1994), *William Morris: A Life for Our Time*, London: Faber and Faber.

McCloskey, D.N. (1983), 'The rhetoric of economics', *Journal of Economic Literature*, **21**, 481–517.

McCloskey, D.N. (1985), *The Rhetoric of Economics*, Brighton: Wheatsheaf.

McCloskey, D.N. (1994), *Knowledge and Persuasion in Economics*, Cambridge: Cambridge University Press.

McDonough, T. (2008), 'Social structures of accumulation theory: the state of the art', *Review of Radical Political Economics*, **40**(2), 153–73.

McFall, L. (2004), *Advertising: A Cultural Economy*, London: Sage.

McLellan, D. (1995), *Ideology*, 2nd edn, Buckingham: Open University Press.

McMaster, R. (2001), 'The National Health Service, the "internal market" and trust', in J.B. Davis (ed.), *The Social Economics of Health Care*, London: Routledge, pp. 113–40.

Ménard, C. and M.M. Shirley (eds) (2005), *Handbook of New Institutional Economics*, New York: Springer.

Menger, C. (1871), *Principles of Economics*, translated by J. Dingwall and B.F. Hoselitz (1981), New York: New York University Press.

Metcalfe, J.S. (2005), 'Evolutionary concepts in relation to evolutionary economics', in K. Dopfer (ed.), *The Evolutionary Foundations of Economics*, Cambridge: Cambridge University Press, pp. 391–430.

Mick, D.G. (1986), 'Consumer research and semiotics: exploring the morphology of signs, symbols, and significance', *Journal of Consumer Research*, **13**(2), 196–213.

Migone, A. (2007), 'Hedonistic consumerism: patterns of consumption in contemporary capitalism', *Review of Radical Political Economics*, **39**(2), 173–200.

Milberg, W.S. (1991), 'Marxism, post-structuralism and the discourse of economics', *Rethinking Marxism*, **4**(2), 93–104.

Milberg, W.S. and B. Pietrykowski (1994), 'Objectivism, relativism and the importance of rhetoric for Marxist economics', *Review of Radical Political Economics*, **26**(1), 84–108.

Milgate, M. and J. Eatwell (1983), 'Unemployment and the market mechanism', in J. Eatwell and M. Milgate (eds), *Keynes's Economics and the Theory of Value and Distribution*, London: Duckworth, pp. 260–80.

Mill, J.S. (1838), 'Bentham', in A. Ryan (ed.) (1987), *John Stuart Mill and Jeremy Bentham: Utilitarianism and Other Essays*, Harmondsworth: Penguin, pp. 131–75.

Mill, J.S. (1840), 'Coleridge', in A. Ryan (ed.) (1987), *John Stuart Mill and Jeremy Bentham: Utilitarianism and Other Essays*, Harmondsworth: Penguin, pp. 176–226.

Mill, J.S. (1848), *Principles of Political Economy*, reprinted 1994, Oxford: Oxford University Press.

Mill, J.S. (1873), *Autobiography*, reprinted 1989, Harmondsworth: Penguin.

Mills, C.W. (1959), *The Sociological Imagination*, Oxford: Oxford University Press.

Milner, A. and J. Browitt (2002), *Contemporary Cultural Theory: An Introduction*, 3rd edn, London: Routledge.

Milonakis, D. and B. Fine (2008), *From Political Economy to Economics: Method, the Social and the Historical in the Evolution of Economic Theory*, London: Routledge.

Mirowski, P. (1987), 'The philosophical bases of institutional economics', *Journal of Economic Issues*, **21**(3), 1001–38.

Mirowski, P. (1989), *More Heat than Light: Economics as Social Physics*, Cambridge: Cambridge University Press.

Mirowski, P. (2002), *Machine Dreams: Economics Becomes a Cyborg Science*, Cambridge: Cambridge University Press.

Mirowski, P. (2007), 'Markets come to bits: evolution, computation and markomata in economic science', *Journal of Economic Behavior and Organization*, **63**(2), 209–42.

Mises, L. von (1949), *Human Action: A Treatise on Economics*, London: William Hodge.

Mises, L. von (1957), *Theory and History: An Interpretation of Social and Economic Evolution*, New Haven, CT: Yale University Press.

Mises, L. von (1978), *The Ultimate Foundation of Economic Science: An Essay on Method*, 2nd edn, Kansas City, MO: Sheed, Andrews and McMeel.

Mongiovi, G. (2002), 'Classics and moderns: Sraffa's legacy in economics', *Metroeconomica*, **53**(3), 223–41.

Montes, L. (2003), '*Das Adam Smith Problem*: its origins, the stages of the current debate, and one implication for our understanding of sympathy', *Journal of the History of Economic Thought*, **25**(1), 63–90.

Moore, G.C.G. (2005), 'Evangelical aesthete: Ruskin and the public provision of art', *History of Political Economy*, **37**(3), 483–508.

Morgan, L.H. (1877), *Ancient Society*, reprinted 2000, London: Transaction Publishers.

Morgan, M.S. (1990), *The History of Econometric Ideas*, Cambridge: Cambridge University Press.

Morris, W. (1882), *Hopes and Fears for Art*, London: Ellis and White.

Morris, W. (1888), *Signs of Change*, London: Reeves and Turner.

Morris, W. (1883–94), 'Lectures on socialism', in M. Morris (ed.) (1915), *The Collected Works of William Morris, Volume XXIII*, London: Longmans, Green and Co., pp. 141–281.

Morrow, J. (2006), *Thomas Carlyle*, London: Hambledon Continuum.

Mosco, V. (1996), *The Political Economy of Communication: Rethinking and Renewal*, London: Sage.

Mount, K.R. and S. Reiter (2002), *Computation and Complexity in Economic Behavior and Organizations*, Cambridge: Cambridge University Press.

Mouzelis, N. (1989), 'Restructuring structuration theory', *Sociological Review*, **37**, 613–35.

Mouzelis, N. (1995), *Sociological Theory: What Went Wrong?*, London: Routledge.

Munch, R. and N. Smelser (1987), 'Relating the micro and macro', in J. Alexander, B. Giesen, R. Munch and N. Smelser (eds), *The Micro–Macro Link*, Berkeley, CA: University of California Press, pp. 356–87.

Neale, W.C. (1982), 'Language and economics', *Journal of Economic Issues*, **16**(2), 355–69.

Neale, W.C. (1987), 'Institutions', *Journal of Economic Issues*, **21**(3), 1177–206.

Nell, E.J. (1992), *Transformational Growth and Effective Demand: Economics after the Capital Critique*, London: Macmillan.

Nell, E.J. (1998), *The General Theory of Transformational Growth: Keynes after Sraffa*, Cambridge: Cambridge University Press.

Nellhaus, T. (1998), 'Signs, social ontology and critical realism', *Journal for the Theory of Social Behaviour*, **28**(1), 1–24.

Nelson, J.A. (1993), 'Gender and economic ideologies', *Review of Social Economy*, **51**(3), 287–301.

Nelson, J.A. (1996), *Feminism, Objectivity and Economics*, London: Routledge.

Nelson, R.R. and S.G. Winter (1982), *An Evolutionary Theory of Economic Change*, Cambridge, MA: Harvard University Press.

Nelson, R.R. and S.G. Winter (2002), 'Evolutionary theorizing in economics', *Journal of Economic Perspectives*, **16**, 23–46.

Nicolaides, P. (1988), 'Limits to the expansion of neoclassical economics', *Cambridge Journal of Economics*, **12**(3), 313–28.

Nielsen, K. (1994), 'Fordism and post-Fordism', in G.M. Hodgson, W.J. Samuels and M.R. Tool (eds), *The Elgar Companion to Institutional and Evolutionary Economics*, Aldershot, UK and Brookfield, USA: Edward Elgar, pp. 246–51.

Nielsen, K. (2001), 'Institutionalist approaches in the social sciences: typology, dialogue and future challenges', *Journal of Economic Issues*, **35**(2), 505–16.

Nielsen, K. (2007), 'The "institutional turn" in the social sciences: a review of approaches and a future research agenda', in S. Ioannides and K. Nielsen (eds), *Economics and the Social Sciences: Boundaries, Interaction and Integration*, Cheltenham, UK and Northampton, MA, USA: Edward Elgar, pp. 91–111.

Nielsen, P. (2002), 'Reflections on critical realism in political economy', *Cambridge Journal of Economics*, **26**(6), 727–38.

Norgaard, R.B. (1992), 'Coevolution of economy, society and environment', in P. Ekins and M. Max-Neef (eds), *Real-Life Economics: Understanding Wealth Creation*, London: Routledge, pp. 76–86.

North, D.C. (1981), *Structure and Change in Economic History*, New York: Norton.

North, D.C. (1990), *Institutions, Institutional Change and Economic Performance*, Cambridge: Cambridge University Press.

North, D.C. (1994), 'Economic performance through time', *American Economic Review*, **84**(3), 359–67.

Noth, W. (1995), *Handbook of Semiotics*, Bloomington, IN: Indiana University Press.

O'Brien, D.P. (1981), 'Ricardian economics and the economics of David Ricardo', *Oxford Economic Papers*, **33**(3), 352–86.

O'Connor, J. (1998), 'Culture, nature, and the materialist conception of history', in J. O'Connor, *Natural Causes: Essays in Ecological Marxism*, New York: Guilford Press, pp. 29–47.

O'Connor, T. (2000), *Persons and Causes: The Metaphysics of Free Will*, Oxford: Oxford University Press.

O'Donnell, R.M. (1989), *Keynes: Philosophy, Economics and Politics*, London: Macmillan.

O'Grady, P. (2002), *Relativism*, Chesham: Acumen.

O'Hara, P.A. (1997), 'Veblen's critique of Marx's philosophical preconceptions of political economy', *European Journal of the History of Economic Thought*, **4**(1), 65–91.

O'Hara, P.A. (2000), *Marx, Veblen and Contemporary Institutional Political Economy: Principles and Unstable Dynamics of Capitalism*, Cheltenham, UK and Northampton, MA, USA: Edward Elgar.

Outhwaite, W. (1986), *Understanding Social Life: The Method Called Verstehen*, 2nd edn, Lewes: Jean Stroud.

Outhwaite, W. (1987), *New Philosophies of Social Science: Realism, Hermeneutics and Critical Theory*, London: Macmillan.

Outhwaite, W. (1990), 'Agency and structure', in J. Clark, C. Modgil and S. Modgil (eds), *Anthony Giddens: Consensus and Controversy*, London: Falmer Press, pp. 63–72.

Outhwaite, W. (2005), 'Interpretivism and interactionism', in A. Harrington (ed.), *Modern Social Theory: An Introduction*, Oxford: Oxford University Press, pp. 110–31.

Outram, D. (1995), *The Enlightenment*, Cambridge: Cambridge University Press.

Owen, R. (1813–16), 'A new view of society', in G. Claeys (ed.) (1991), *Robert Owen: A New View of Society and Other Writings*, Harmondsworth: Penguin, pp. 1–92.

Parsons, S.D. (2003), *Money, Time and Rationality in Max Weber: Austrian Connections*, London: Routledge.

Parsons, T. (1937), *The Structure of Social Action*, New York: McGraw-Hill.

Parsons, T. (1951), *The Social System*, New York: Free Press.

Pasinetti, L.L. (1993), *Structural Economic Dynamics: A Theory of the Economic Consequences of Human Learning*, Cambridge: Cambridge University Press.

Paul, D.B. (1984), 'Eugenics and the Left', *Journal of the History of Ideas*, **45**(4), 567–90.

Paul, D.B. (2003), 'Darwin, Social Darwinism and eugenics', in J. Hodge and G. Radick (eds), *The Cambridge Companion to Darwin*, Cambridge: Cambridge University Press, pp. 214–39.

Peach, T. (1993), *Interpreting Ricardo*, Cambridge: Cambridge University Press.

Peck, J. (2006), 'Why we shouldn't be bored with the political economy versus cultural studies debate', *Cultural Critique*, **64**, 92–126.

Peirce, C.S. (1893–1910), 'Logic as semiotic: the theory of signs', in J. Buchler (ed.) (1955), *Philosophical Writings of Peirce*, New York: Dover, pp. 98–119.

Persky, J. (1995), 'The ethology of homo economicus', *Journal of Economic Perspectives*, **9**(2), 221–31.

Pesaran, H. and R. Smith (1985), 'Keynes on econometrics', in T. Lawson and H. Pesaran (eds), *Keynes's Economics: Methodological Issues*, London: Croom Helm, pp. 134–50.

Peter, F. (2001), 'Rhetoric versus realism in economic methodology: a critical assessment of recent contributions', *Cambridge Journal of Economics*, **25**(5), 571–89.

Peterson, V.S. (2003), *A Critical Rewriting of Global Political Economy: Integrating Reproductive, Productive and Virtual Economies*, London: Routledge.

Phillipson, C. (1982), *Capitalism and the Construction of Old Age*, London: Macmillan.

Phillipson, C. (2005), 'The political economy of old age', in M.L. Johnson (ed.), *The Cambridge Handbook of Age and Ageing*, Cambridge: Cambridge University Press, pp. 563–71.

Pietrykowski, B.A. (1996), 'Alfred Schutz and the economists', *History of Political Economy*, **28**(2), 219–44.

Pietrykowski, B.A. (2007), 'Exploring new directions in the radical political economy of consumption', *Review of Radical Political Economics*, **39**(2), 257–83.

Pietrykowski, B.A. (2009), *The Political Economy of Consumer Behavior: Contesting Consumption*, London: Routledge.

Pinkard, T.P. (1988), *Hegel's Dialectic: The Explanation of Possibility*, Philadelphia, PA: Temple University Press.

Pinkard, T.P. (2002), *German Philosophy 1760–1860: The Legacy of Idealism*, Cambridge: Cambridge University Press.

Pippin, R. (1999), *Modernism as a Philosophical Problem*, 2nd edn, Oxford: Blackwell.

Plekhanov, G.V. (1895), 'The development of the monist theory of history', in G.V. Plekhanov, *Selected Philosophical Works, Volume 1*, reprinted 1961, London: Lawrence and Wishart, pp. 542–782.

Plekhanov, G.V. (1897), *The Materialist Conception of History*, reprinted 1976, London: Lawrence and Wishart.

Polanyi, K. (1944), *The Great Transformation: The Political and Economic Origins of Our Time*, New York: Rinehart.

Polanyi, K. (1957), 'The economy as instituted process', in K. Polanyi, C.M. Arensberg and H.W. Pearson (eds), *Trade and Markets in the Early Empires*, Chicago, IL: Henry Regnery, pp. 175–93.

Polanyi, M. (1967), *The Tacit Dimension*, London: Routledge and Kegan Paul.

Popper, K.R. (1959), *The Logic of Scientific Discovery*, London: Hutchinson.

Popper, K.R. (1965), *Conjectures and Refutations: The Growth of Scientific Knowledge*, 2nd edn, London: Routledge and Kegan Paul.

Popper, K.R. (1972), *Objective Knowledge: An Evolutionary Approach*, Oxford: Oxford University Press.

Porpora, D.V. (1989), 'Four concepts of social structure', *Journal for the Theory of Social Behaviour*, **19**(2), 195–211.

Potter, J. (1996), *Representing Reality: Discourse, Rhetoric and Social Construction*, London: Sage.

Potts, J. (2000), *The New Evolutionary Microeconomics: Complexity, Competence and Adaptive Behaviour*, Cheltenham, UK and Northampton, MA, USA: Edward Elgar.

Prendergast, C. (1986), 'Alfred Schutz and the Austrian school of economics', *American Journal of Sociology*, **92**(1), 1–26.

Prendergast, R. (2006), 'Schumpeter, Hegel and the vision of development', *Cambridge Journal of Economics*, **30**(2), 253–75.

Prychitko, D.L. (ed.) (1995), *Individuals, Institutions, Interpretations: Hermeneutics Applied to Economics*, Aldershot, UK: Avebury.

Prychitko, D.L. and V.H. Storr (2007), 'Communicative action and the radical constitution: the Habermasian challenge to Hayek, Mises and their descendants', *Cambridge Journal of Economics*, **31**(2), 255–74.

Psillos, S. (2003), 'The present state of the scientific realism debate', in P. Clark and K. Hawley (eds), *Philosophy of Science Today*, Oxford: Oxford University Press, pp. 59–82.

Putnam, H. (1981), *Reason, Truth and History*, Cambridge: Cambridge University Press.

Quine, W.V. (1969), *Ontological Relativity*, Cambridge, MA: Harvard University Press.

Quinn, K. and T.R. Green (1998), 'Hermeneutics and libertarianism: an odd couple', *Critical Review*, **12**(3), 207–23.

Radnitzky, G. and P. Bernholz (eds) (1987), *Economic Imperialism: The Economic Approach Applied Outside the Field of Economics*, New York: Paragon House.

Ramstad, Y. (1990), 'The institutionalism of John R. Commons: theoretical foundations of a volitional economics', *Research in the History of Economic Thought and Methodology*, **8**, 53–104.

Ramstad, Y. (1994), 'On the nature of economic evolution: John R. Commons and the metaphor of artificial selection', in L. Magnusson (ed.), *Evolutionary and Neo-Schumpeterian Approaches to Economics*, Boston, MA: Kluwer, pp. 65–121.

Ray, L. and A. Sayer (eds) (1999), *Culture and Economy after the Cultural Turn*, London: Sage.

Reinert, E.S. and Daastøl, A.M. (2004), 'The Other Canon: the history of Renaissance economics', in E.S. Reinert (ed.), *Globalization, Economic Development and Inequality: An Alternative Perspective*, Cheltenham, UK and Northampton, MA, USA: Edward Elgar, pp. 21–70.

Reisman, D.A. (2007), 'Economic sociology and institutional economics', *Journal of Institutional Economics*, 3(1), 91–112.

Reiss, M.J. and R. Straughan (1996), *Improving Nature? The Science and Ethics of Genetic Engineering*, Cambridge: Cambridge University Press.

Resnick, S. and R. Wolff (2006), *New Departures in Marxian Theory*, London: Routledge.

Reuten, G. (2003), 'Karl Marx: his work and the major changes in its inter- pretation', in W.J. Samuels, J.E. Biddle and J.B. Davis (eds), *A Companion to the History of Economic Thought*, Oxford: Blackwell, pp. 523–37.

Ricardo, D. (1817), *On the Principles of Political Economy and Taxation*, reprinted 1951, Cambridge: Cambridge University Press.

Richerson, P.J. and R. Boyd (2005), *Not by Genes Alone: How Culture Transformed Human Evolution*, Chicago: University of Chicago Press.

Rickman, H.P. (1961), *Meaning in History: W. Dilthey's Thoughts on History and Society*, London: George Allen and Unwin.

Ricoeur, P. (1976), *Interpretation Theory: Discourse and the Surplus of Meaning*, Fort Worth, TX: Texas Christian University Press.

Ricoeur, P. (1981), *Hermeneutics and the Human Sciences*, Cambridge: Cambridge University Press.

Rigby, S.H. (1998), *Marxism and History: A Critical Introduction*, 2nd edn, Manchester: Manchester University Press.

Riley, J.G. (2001), 'Silver signals: twenty-five years of screening and sig- nalling', *Journal of Economic Literature*, 39(2), 432–78.

Rizvi, S.A.T. (1994), 'The microfoundations project in general equilibrium theory', *Cambridge Journal of Economics*, 18(4), 357–77.

Robbins, L. (1937), *An Essay on the Nature and Significance of Economic Science*, London: Macmillan.

Robinson, J. (1977), 'What are the questions?', *Journal of Economic Literature*, 15(4), 1318–39.

Robotham, D. (2005), *Culture, Society, and Economy: Bringing Production Back In*, London: Sage.

Robson, A.J. (2002), 'Evolution and human nature', *Journal of Economic Perspectives*, 16(2), 89–106.

Rogers, J.A. (1972), 'Darwinism and Social Darwinism', *Journal of the History of Ideas*, 33(2), 265–80.

Rorty, R. (1980), *Philosophy and the Mirror of Nature*, Oxford: Basil Blackwell.

Rorty, R. (1991), *Objectivity, Relativism and Truth*, Cambridge: Cambridge University Press.

Rose, S.P.R., R.C. Lewontin and L.J. Kamin (1984), *Not in Our Genes: Biology, Ideology and Human Nature*, Harmondsworth: Penguin.

Rosenbaum, E.F. (1999), 'Culture, consumption and the causes of inequality', *Cambridge Journal of Economics*, **23**(3), 317–36.

Rosenbaum, E.F. (2000), 'What is a market? On the methodology of a contested concept', *Review of Social Economy*, **58**(4), 455–82.

Rosenberg, M. (1979), *Conceiving the Self*, New York: Basic Books.

Rosenberg, N. (1994), 'Joseph Schumpeter: radical economist', in N. Rosenberg, *Exploring the Black Box: Technology, Economics, and History*, Cambridge: Cambridge University Press, pp. 47–61.

Ross, I.S. (1995), *The Life of Adam Smith*, Oxford: Oxford University Press.

Rosser, J.B. (1999), 'On the complexities of complex economic dynamics', *Journal of Economic Perspectives*, **13**(4), 169–92.

Ruccio, D.F. (1991), 'Postmodernism and economics', *Journal of Post Keynesian Economics*, **13**(4), 495–510.

Ruccio, D.F. (2005), '(Un)real criticism', *Post-Autistic Economics Review*, **35**, article 5.

Ruccio, D.F. and J.L. Amariglio (2003), *Postmodern Moments in Modern Economics*, Princeton, NJ: Princeton University Press.

Runde, J.H. (1990), 'Keynesian uncertainty and the weight of arguments', *Economics and Philosophy*, **6**(2), 275–92.

Runde, J.H. (1991), 'Keynesian uncertainty and the instability of beliefs', *Review of Political Economy*, **3**(2), 125–45.

Ruse, M. (1979), *The Darwinian Revolution: Science Red in Tooth and Claw*, Chicago, IL: University of Chicago Press.

Ruse, M. (1989), 'Charles Darwin and group selection', in M. Ruse, *The Darwinian Paradigm*, London: Routledge, pp. 34–54.

Ruskin, J. (1857), 'The political economy of art', in E.T. Cook and A. Wedderburn (eds) (1905), *The Works of John Ruskin, Vol. XVI*, London: George Allen, pp. 15–103.

Ruskin, J. (1862), 'Unto this last: four essays on the first principles of political economy', in C. Wilmer (ed.) (1985), *John Ruskin: Unto this Last and Other Writings*, Harmondsworth: Penguin, pp. 155–228.

Ruskin, J. (1863), 'Munera Pulveris: six essays on the elements of political economy', in E.T. Cook and A. Wedderburn (eds) (1905), *The Works of John Ruskin, Vol. XVII*, London: George Allen, pp. 115–293.

Rutherford, M.H. (1983), 'John R. Commons's institutional economics', *Journal of Economic Issues*, **17**(3), 721–44.

Rutherford, M.H. (1989), 'What is wrong with the new institutional economics (and what is still wrong with the old)?', *Review of Political Economy*, **1**(3), 299–318.

Rutherford, M.H. (1994), *Institutions in Economics: The Old and the New Institutionalism*, Cambridge: Cambridge University Press.

Rutherford, M.H. (1998), 'Veblen's evolutionary programme: a promise unfulfilled', *Cambridge Journal of Economics*, **22**(4), 463–77.

Rutherford, M.H. (2001), 'Institutional economics: then and now', *Journal of Economic Perspectives*, **15**(3), 173–94.

Ryan, C.C. (1981), 'The fiends of commerce: Romantic and Marxist criticisms of classical political economy', *History of Political Economy*, **13**(1), 80–94.

Sahlins, M.D. (1974), *Stone Age Economics*, London: Tavistock.

Sahlins, M.D. (1976), *Culture and Practical Reason*, Chicago, IL: University of Chicago Press.

Sahlins, M.D. (1977), *The Use and Abuse of Biology: An Anthropological Critique of Sociobiology*, London: Tavistock.

Salanti, A. and E. Screpanti (eds) (1997), *Pluralism in Economics*, Cheltenham, UK and Lyme, USA: Edward Elgar.

Samuels, W.J. (ed.) (1990), *Economics as Discourse: An Analysis of the Language of Economists*, London: Kluwer.

Samuels, W.J. (1991), '"Truth" and "discourse" in the social construction of economic reality: an essay on the relation of knowledge to socio-economic policy', *Journal of Post Keynesian Economics*, **13**(4), 511–24.

Samuels, W.J. (1993), 'In (limited but affirmative) defence of nihilism', *Review of Political Economy*, **5**(2), 236–44.

Samuels, W.J. (2001), 'Some problems in the use of language in economics', *Review of Political Economy*, **13**(1), 91–100.

Samuels, W.J. (2003), 'Utopian economics', in W.J. Samuels, J.E. Biddle and J.B. Davis (eds), *A Companion to the History of Economic Thought*, Oxford: Blackwell, pp. 201–14.

Samuelson, P.A. (1947), *Foundations of Economic Analysis*, Cambridge, MA: Harvard University Press.

Sandel, M.J. (2007), *The Case against Perfection: Ethics in the Age of Genetic Engineering*, Cambridge, MA: Harvard University Press.

Sanderson, S.K. (1990), *Social Evolutionism: A Critical History*, Oxford: Blackwell.

Saussure, F. de (1916), *Course in General Linguistics*, reprinted 1983, London: Duckworth.

Sawyer, M.C. (1985), *The Economics of Michał Kalecki*, London: Macmillan.

Sayer, A. (1992), *Method in Social Science: A Realist Approach*, 2nd edn, London: Routledge.

Sayer, A. (1995), *Radical Political Economy: A Critique*, Oxford: Blackwell.

Sayer, A. (1997a), 'Critical realism and the limits to critical social science', *Journal for the Theory of Social Behaviour*, **27**(4), 473–88.

Sayer, A. (1997b), 'The dialectic of culture and economy', in R. Lee and J. Wills (eds), *Geographies of Economies*, London: Arnold, pp. 16–26.

Sayer, A. (2000), *Realism and Social Science*, London: Sage.

Sayer, A. (2001), 'For a critical cultural political economy', *Antipode*, **33**(4), 687–708.

Sayer, A. (2003), 'Markets, embeddedness and trust: problems of polysemy and idealism', in J.S. Metcalfe and A. Warde (eds), *Market Relations and the Competitive Process*, Manchester: Manchester University Press, pp. 41–57.

Schaffer, S. (1999), 'Enlightened automata', in W. Clark, J. Golinski and S. Schaffer (eds), *The Sciences in Enlightened Europe*, Chicago, IL: University of Chicago Press, pp. 126–65.

Schenk, H.G. (1966), *The Mind of the European Romantics: An Essay in Cultural History*, London: Constable.

Schiller, H.I. (1973), *The Mind Managers*, Boston, MA: Beacon Press.

Schiller, H.I. (1989), *Culture Inc.: The Corporate Takeover of Public Expression*, New York: Oxford University Press.

Schleiermacher, F. (1838), 'Hermeneutics and criticism', in A. Bowie (ed.) (1998), *Friedrich Schleiermacher: Hermeneutics and Criticism and Other Writings*, Cambridge: Cambridge University Press, pp. 3–224.

Schotter, A.R. (1981), *The Economic Theory of Social Institutions*, Cambridge: Cambridge University Press.

Schultz, D.P. and S.E. Schultz (2007), *A History of Modern Psychology*, 9th edn, Belmont, CA: Wadsworth.

Schumpeter, J.A. (1934), *The Theory of Economic Development: An Inquiry into Profits, Capital, Credit, Interest and the Business Cycle*, Cambridge, MA: Harvard University Press.

Schumpeter, J.A. (1939), *Business Cycles: A Theoretical, Historical and Statistical Analysis of the Capitalist Process*, 2 vols, New York: McGraw-Hill.

Schumpeter, J.A. (1942), *Capitalism, Socialism and Democracy*, New York: Harper.

Schumpeter, J.A. (1954), *History of Economic Analysis*, Oxford: Oxford University Press.

Screpanti, E. (2000), 'The postmodern crisis in economics and the revolution against modernism', *Rethinking Marxism*, **12**(1), 87–111.

Screpanti, E. and S. Zamagni (2005), *An Outline of the History of Economic Thought*, 2nd edn, Oxford: Oxford University Press.

Searle, J.R. (1990), 'Collective intentions and actions', in P. Cohen, J. Morgan and M.E. Pollack (eds), *Intentions in Communication*, Cambridge, MA: MIT Press.

Searle, J.R. (1995), *The Construction of Social Reality*, London: Allen Lane.

Searle, J.R. (2005), 'What is an institution?', *Journal of Institutional Economics*, **1**(1), 1–22.

Sebeok, T.A. (2001), *Signs: An Introduction to Semiotics*, Toronto, ON: University of Toronto Press.

Sent, E.-M. (2003), 'Pleas for pluralism', *Post-Autistic Economics Review*, **18**, article 1.

Shackle, G.L.S. (1955), *Uncertainty in Economics*, Cambridge: Cambridge University Press.

Shackle, G.L.S. (1967), *The Years of High Theory: Invention and Tradition in Economic Thought 1926–1939*, Cambridge: Cambridge University Press.

Shackle, G.L.S. (1969), *Decision, Order and Time*, 2nd edn, Cambridge: Cambridge University Press.

Shackle, G.L.S. (1972), *Epistemics and Economics*, Cambridge: Cambridge University Press.

Shackle, G.L.S. (1974), *Keynesian Kaleidics: The Evolution of a General Political Economy*, Edinburgh: Edinburgh University Press.

Sherman, H.J. (1995), *Reinventing Marxism*, Baltimore, MD: Johns Hopkins University Press.

Sherman, H.J. (2005), *How Society Makes Itself: The Evolution of Political and Economic Institutions*, Armonk, NY: M.E. Sharpe.

Simmel, G. (1907), *The Philosophy of Money*, 2nd edn, translated by T. Bottomore and D. Frisby (1990), London: Routledge.

Simon, H.A. (1957), *Models of Man: Social and Rational*, New York: Wiley.

Simon, H.A. (1981), *The Sciences of the Artificial*, 2nd edn, Cambridge, MA: MIT Press.

Simon, H.A. (1983), *Reason in Human Affairs*, Oxford: Basil Blackwell.

Sirgy, M.J. (1982), 'Self-concept in consumer behavior: a critical review', *Journal of Consumer Research*, **9**(3), 287–300.

Sismondi, J.C.L Simonde de (1827), *New Principles of Political Economy*, translated by R. Hyse (1991), London: Transaction Publishers.

Skidelsky, R. (1983), *John Maynard Keynes, Volume I: Hopes Betrayed 1883–1920*, London: Macmillan.

Slater, D.R. (1997), *Consumer Culture and Modernity*, Cambridge: Polity Press.

Slater, D.R. (2003), 'Cultures of consumption', in K. Anderson, M. Domosh, S. Pile and N.J. Thrift (eds), *Handbook of Cultural Geography*, London: Sage, pp. 147–63.

Smircich, L. (1983), 'Concepts of culture and organizational analysis', *Administrative Science Quarterly*, **28**(3), 339–58.

Smith, A. (1759), *The Theory of Moral Sentiments*, reprinted 1976, Oxford: Oxford University Press.

Smith, A. (1776), *An Inquiry into the Nature and Causes of the Wealth of Nations*, reprinted 1976, Oxford: Oxford University Press.

Smith, R. (2007), *Being Human: Historical Knowledge and the Creation of Human Nature*, Manchester: Manchester University Press.

Sober, E. (1981), 'Holism, individualism, and the units of selection', in P.D. Asquith and R.N. Giere (eds), *Philosophy of Science Association 1980*, Vol. 2, East Lancing, MI: Philosophy of Science Association, pp. 93–121.

Sober, E. and D.S. Wilson (1994), 'A critical review of philosophical work on the units of selection problem', *Philosophy of Science*, **61**, 534–55.

Stanfield, J.R. (1995), *Economics, Power and Culture: Essays in the Development of Radical Institutionalism*, London: Macmillan.

Stark, A. (2005), 'Warm hands in cold age – on the need of a new world order of care', *Feminist Economics*, **11**(2), 7–36.

Starr, M.A. (2007), 'Spending, saving, and self-control: cognition versus consumer culture', *Review of Radical Political Economics*, **39**(2), 214–29.

Staveren, I. van (2008), 'Capabilities and well-being', in J.B. Davis and W. Dolfsma (eds), *The Elgar Companion to Social Economics*, Cheltenham, UK and Northampton, MA, USA: Edward Elgar, pp. 139–52.

Steele, G.R. (2007), *The Economics of Friedrich Hayek*, 2nd edn, London: Palgrave Macmillan.

Sugden, R. (1986), *The Economics of Rights, Cooperation and Welfare*, Oxford: Basil Blackwell.

Sugden, R. (1989), 'Spontaneous order', *Journal of Economic Perspectives*, **3**(4), 85–97.

Swedberg, R. (1997), 'New economic sociology: what has been accomplished, what is ahead?', *Acta Sociologica*, **40**, 161–82.

Swedberg, R. (1998), *Max Weber and the Idea of Economic Sociology*, Princeton, NJ: Princeton University Press.

Swedberg, R. (2003), *Principles of Economic Sociology*, Princeton, NJ: Princeton University Press.

Swingewood, A. (1998), *Cultural Theory and the Problem of Modernity*, London: Macmillan.

Sztompka, P. (1993), *The Sociology of Social Change*, Oxford: Blackwell.

Tawney, R.H. (1926), *Religion and the Rise of Capitalism*, London: Murray.

Taylor, C. (1979a), *Hegel and Modern Society*, Cambridge: Cambridge University Press.

Taylor, C. (1979b), 'Interpretation and the sciences of man', in P. Rabinow and W.M. Sullivan (eds), *Interpretive Social Science: A Reader*, Berkeley, CA: University of California Press, pp. 25–71.

Thomas, B. (1991), 'Alfred Marshall on economic biology', *Review of Political Economy*, **3**(1), 1–14.

Thompson, E.P. (1955), *William Morris: Romantic to Revolutionary*, London: Lawrence and Wishart.

Thompson, E.P. (1960), *Out of Apathy*, London: Stevens.

Thompson, E.P. (1963), *The Making of the English Working Class*, London: Victor Gollancz.

Thompson, E.P. (1978), 'The poverty of theory or an orrery of errors', in E.P. Thompson, *The Poverty of Theory and Other Essays*, London: Merlin, pp. 1–210.

Thompson, G. (1982), 'The firm as a "dispersed" social agency', *Economy and Society*, **11**(3), 233–50.

Thompson, K. (1976), *Auguste Comte: The Foundation of Sociology*, London: Nelson.

Thompson, K. (1982), *Émile Durkheim*, London: Ellis Horwood.

Throsby, D. (1994), 'The production and consumption of the arts: a view of cultural economics', *Journal of Economic Literature*, **32**, 1–29.

Throsby, D. (1999), 'Cultural capital', *Journal of Cultural Economics*, **23**(1), 3–12.

Throsby, D. (2001), *Economics and Culture*, Cambridge: Cambridge University Press.

Tönnies, F. (1887), *Community and Civil Society*, reprinted 2001, Cambridge: Cambridge University Press.

Tönnies, F. (1925), 'The concept of *Gemeinschaft*', in W.J. Cahnman and R. Heberle (eds) (1971), *Ferdinand Tönnies on Sociology: Pure, Applied, and Empirical*, Chicago, IL: University of Chicago Press, pp. 62–72.

Touraine, A. (1995), *Critique of Modernity*, translated by D. Macey, Oxford: Blackwell.

Towse, R. (ed.) (1997), *Cultural Economics: The Arts, the Heritage and the Media Industries*, 2 volumes, Cheltenham, UK and Lyme, USA: Edward Elgar.

Towse, R. (ed.) (2003), *A Handbook of Cultural Economics*, Cheltenham, UK and Northampton, MA, USA: Edward Elgar.

Toye, J. (2000), *Keynes on Population*, Oxford: Oxford University Press.

Tribe, K. (1999), 'Adam Smith: critical theorist?', *Journal of Economic Literature*, **37**(2), 609–32.

Tribe, K. (2003), 'Historical schools of economics: German and English', in W.J. Samuels, J.E. Biddle and J.B. Davis (eds), *A Companion to the History of Economic Thought*, Oxford: Blackwell, pp. 215–30.

Trigg, A.B. (2001), 'Veblen, Bourdieu, and conspicuous consumption', *Journal of Economic Issues*, **35**(1), 99–115.

Trigger, B.G. (1998), *Sociocultural Evolution*, Oxford: Blackwell.

Trigilia, C. (2002), *Economic Sociology: State, Market and Society in Modern Capitalism*, Oxford: Blackwell.

Tullock, G. (1972), 'Economic imperialism', in J.M. Buchanan and R.D. Tollison (eds), *Theory of Public Choice: Political Applications of Economics*, Ann Arbor, MI: University of Michigan Press, pp. 317–29.

Tullock, G. (1979), 'Sociobiology and economics', *Atlantic Economic Journal*, **7**(3), 1–10.

Tuomela, R. (1995), *The Importance of Us: A Philosophical Study of Basic Social Notions*, Stanford, CA: Stanford University Press.

Turner, G. (2003), *British Cultural Studies: An Introduction*, 3rd edn, London: Routledge.

Turner, J.H. (1988), *A Theory of Social Interaction*, Cambridge: Polity Press.

Tylecote, A. (1991), *The Long Wave in the World Economy: The Present Crisis in Historical Perspective*, London: Routledge.

Tylor, E.B. (1871), *Primitive Culture*, New York: Harper.

Udehn, L. (1992), 'The limits of economic imperialism', in U. Himmelstrand (ed.), *Interfaces in Economic and Social Analysis*, London: Routledge, pp. 239–80.

Upchurch, A. (2005), 'William Morris and the case for public support of the arts', *History of Political Economy*, **37**(3), 509–34.

Van Bouwel, J. (2005), 'Towards a framework for pluralism in economics', *Post-Autistic Economics Review*, **30**, article 3.

Vanberg, V.J. (1986), 'Spontaneous market order and social rules: a critical examination of F.A. Hayek's theory of cultural evolution', *Economics and Philosophy*, **2**(1), 75–100.

Vanberg, V.J. (1994), 'Hayekian evolutionism – a reconstruction', in V.J. Vanberg, *Rules and Choice in Economics*, London: Routledge, pp. 95–106.

Vandewalle, G. (1986), 'Romanticism and neo-romanticism in political economy', *History of Political Economy*, **18**(1), 33–47.

Vaughan, W. (1994), *Romanticism and Art*, London: Thames and Hudson.

Veblen, T.B. (1898), 'Why is economics not an evolutionary science?', *Quarterly Journal of Economics*, **12**(3), 373–97.

Veblen, T.B. (1899), *The Theory of the Leisure Class: An Economic Study in the Evolution of Institutions*, New York: Macmillan.

Veblen, T.B. (1906), 'The socialist economics of Karl Marx and his followers I: the theories of Karl Marx', *Quarterly Journal of Economics*, **20**(3), 578–95.

Veblen, T.B. (1907), 'The socialist economics of Karl Marx and his followers II: the later Marxism', *Quarterly Journal of Economics*, **21**(1), 299–322.

Vico, G. (1744), *Principles of the New Science Concerning the Common Nature of Nations*, 3rd edn, translated by D. Marsh (1999), London: Penguin.

Vorzimmer, P.J. (1969), 'Darwin, Malthus, and the theory of natural selection', *Journal of the History of Ideas*, **30**(4), 527–42.

Vromen, J.J. (1995), *Economic Evolution: An Enquiry into the Foundations of New Institutional Economics*, London: Routledge.

Vromen, J.J. (2001), 'The human agent in evolutionary economics', in J. Laurent and J. Nightingale (eds), *Darwinism and Evolutionary Economics*, Cheltenham, UK and Northampton, MA, USA: Edward Elgar, pp. 184–208.

Vromen, J.J. (2004), 'Conjectural revisionary ontology', *Post-Autistic Economics Review*, **29**, article 4.

Waldrop, M.M. (1992), *Complexity: The Emerging Science at the Edge of Order and Chaos*, New York: Simon and Schuster.

Walker, A. (1981), 'Towards a political economy of old age', *Ageing and Society*, **1**(1), 73–94.

Waller, W.J. (1982), 'The evolution of the Veblenian dichotomy', *Journal of Economic Issues*, **16**(3), 757–71.

Waller, W.J. (1988), 'The concept of habit in economic analysis', *Journal of Economic Issues*, **22**(1), 113–26.

Waller, W.J. (1994), 'Veblenian dichotomy and its critics', in G.M. Hodgson, W.J. Samuels and M.R. Tool (eds), *The Elgar Companion to Institutional and Evolutionary Economics L-Z*, Aldershot, UK and Brookfield, USA: Edward Elgar, pp. 368–72.

Walters, B. and D. Young (2001), 'Critical realism as a basis for economic methodology: a critique', *Review of Political Economy*, **13**(4), 483–501.

Watson, G. (ed.) (2003), *Free Will*, 2nd edn, Oxford: Oxford University Press.

Webb, J.L. (2002), 'Dewey: back to the future', *Journal of Economic Issues*, **36**(4), 981–1003.

Weber, M. (1904–05), *The Protestant Ethic and the Spirit of Capitalism*, translated by S. Kalberg (2002), Oxford: Blackwell.

Weber, M. (1921–22), *Economy and Society: An Outline of Interpretive Sociology*, edited by G. Roth and C. Wittich (1968), New York: Bedminster Press.

Webster, F. (2002), *Theories of the Information Society*, 2nd edn, London: Routledge.

Weintraub, E.R. (2002), *How Economics Became a Mathematical Science*, Durham, NC: Duke University Press.

Welch, P.J. (2006), 'Thomas Carlyle on utilitarianism', *History of Political Economy*, **38**(2), 377–89.

Wheelock, J. (1992), 'The household in the total economy', in P. Ekins and M. Max-Neef (eds), *Real-Life Economics: Understanding Wealth Creation*, London: Routledge, pp. 124–35.

Wheelock, J. and E. Oughton (1996), 'The household as a focus for research', *Journal of Economic Issues*, **30**, 143–59.

Wible, J.R. (1985), 'An epistemic critique of rational expectations and the neoclassical macroeconomics research program', *Journal of Post Keynesian Economics*, **7**(2), 269–81.

Wilk, R.R. (1996), *Economies and Cultures: Foundations of Economic Anthropology*, Boulder, CO: Westview Press.

Williams, G.C. (1986), 'A defence of reductionism in evolutionary biology', *Oxford Surveys in Evolutionary Biology*, **2**, 1–27.

Williams, R. (1958a), *Culture and Society: Coleridge to Orwell*, London: Chatto and Windus.

Williams, R. (1958b), 'Culture is ordinary', in N. Mackenzie (ed.), *Conviction*, London: MacGibbon and Kee, pp. 74–92.

Williams, R. (1961), *The Long Revolution*, London: Chatto and Windus.

Williams, R. (1977), *Marxism and Literature*, Oxford: Oxford University Press.

Williams, R. (1980), 'Base and superstructure in Marxist cultural theory', in R. Williams, *Problems in Materialism and Culture: Selected Essays*, London: Verso, pp. 31–49.

Williams, R. (1981a), 'Communications, technologies and social institutions', in R. Williams (ed.), *Contact: Human Communication and its History*, London: Thames and Hudson, pp. 226–38.

Williams, R. (1981b), *Culture*, London: Fontana Press.

Williams, R. (1988), *Keywords: A Vocabulary of Culture and Society*, 2nd edn, London: Fontana Press.

Williams, R. (1989a), 'Communications and community', in R. Williams, *Resources of Hope: Culture, Democracy, Socialism*, London: Verso, pp. 19–31.

Williams, R. (1989b), 'When was modernism?', in R. Williams, *The Politics of Modernism: Against the New Conformists*, London: Verso, pp. 31–5.

Williamson, J. (1978), *Decoding Advertisements: Ideology and Meaning in Advertising*, London: Marion Boyars.

Williamson, O.E. (1975), *Markets and Hierarchies: Analysis and Anti-trust Implications: A Study in the Economics of Internal Organization*, New York: Free Press.

Williamson, O.E. (1985), *The Economic Institutions of Capitalism: Firms, Markets, Relational Contracting*, London: Routledge.

Williamson, O.E. (2000), 'The new institutional economics: taking stock, looking ahead', *Journal of Economic Literature*, **38**(3), 595–613.

Wilmer, C. (1996), 'Was Ruskin a materialist?', in M. Wheeler (ed.), *Time and Tide: Ruskin and Science*, London: Pilkington Press, pp. 85–97.

Wilson, D.S. (1983), 'The group selection controversy: history and current status', *Annual Review of Ecology and Systematics*, **14**, 159–88.

Wilson, E.O. (1975), *Sociobiology*, Cambridge, MA: Harvard University Press.

Wilson, E.O. (1978), *On Human Nature*, Cambridge, MA: Harvard University Press.

Wilson, M.C. (2005), 'Institutionalism, critical realism, and the critique of mainstream economics', *Journal of Institutional Economics*, **1**(2), 217–31.

Wilson, M.C. (2007), 'Uncertainty and probability in institutional economics', *Journal of Economic Issues*, **41**(4), 1087–107.

Winch, D. (1996), *Riches and Poverty: An Intellectual History of Political Economy in Britain, 1750–1834*, Cambridge: Cambridge University Press.

Winch, P. (1958), *The Idea of a Social Science*, London: Routledge and Kegan Paul.

Witt, U. (ed.) (1993), *Evolutionary Economics*, Aldershot, UK and Brookfield, USA: Edward Elgar.

Witt, U. (2003), *The Evolving Economy: Essays on the Evolutionary Approach to Economics*, Cheltenham, UK and Northampton, MA, USA: Edward Elgar.

Witt, U. (2004), 'On the proper interpretation of "evolution" in economics and its implications for production theory', *Journal of Economic Methodology*, **11**(2), 125–46.

Wrong, D.H. (1961), 'The oversocialized conception of man in modern sociology', *American Sociological Review*, **26**(2), 183–93.

Zafirovski, M. and B.B. Levine (1997), 'Economic sociology reformulated: the interface between economics and sociology', *American Journal of Economics and Sociology*, **56**(3), 265–85.

Zakia, R.D. and M. Nadin (1987), 'Semiotics, advertising and marketing', *Journal of Consumer Marketing*, **4**(2), 5–12.

Zelizer, V.A. (1988), 'Beyond the polemics on the market: establishing a theoretical and empirical agenda', *Sociological Forum*, **3**(4), 614–34.

Zelizer, V.A. (2001), 'Economic sociology', in N. Smelser and P. Baltes (eds), *International Encyclopedia of the Social and Behavioral Sciences*, vol. 6, Amsterdam: Elsevier, pp. 4128–32.

Zelizer, V.A. (2002), 'Enter culture', in M.F. Guillén, R. Collins, P. England and M. Meyer (eds), *The New Economic Sociology: Developments in an Emerging Field*, New York: Russell Sage Foundation, pp. 101–25.

# Index